DEMOSTHENES, SPEECHES 23–26

# THE ORATORY OF CLASSICAL GREECE

*Translated with Notes* • *Michael Gagarin, Series Editor*
VOLUME 15

# DEMOSTHENES, SPEECHES 23–26

*Translated with introduction and notes by*

*Edward Harris*

 UNIVERSITY OF TEXAS PRESS, AUSTIN

This book has been supported by an endowment dedicated to classics and the ancient world and funded by the Areté Foundation; the Gladys Krieble Delmas Foundation; the Dougherty Foundation; the James R. Dougherty, Jr. Foundation; the Rachael and Ben Vaughan Foundation; and the National Endowment for the Humanities.

Requests for permission to reproduce material from this work should be sent to:
    Permissions
    University of Texas Press
    P.O. Box 7819
    Austin, TX 78713-7819
    utpress.utexas.edu/rp-form

∞ The paper used in this book meets the minimum requirements of ANSI/NISO Z39.48-1992 (R1997) (Permanence of Paper).

Library of Congress Cataloging-in-Publication Data

Names: Demosthenes, author. | Harris, Edward Monroe, translator, writer of supplementary textual content. | Demosthenes. Against Aristocrates. English. | Demosthenes. Against Timocrates. English. | Demosthenes. Against Aristogeiton. English.
Title: Demosthenes, speeches 23/26 / translated with introduction and notes by Edward Harris.
Other titles: Speeches 23–26 | Oratory of classical Greece ; v. 15.
Description: First edition. | Austin : University of Texas Press, 2018. | Series: The oratory of classical Greece ; volume 15 | Includes bibliographical references and index.
Identifiers: LCCN 2017015721
    ISBN 978-1-4773-1351-0 (cloth : alk. paper)
    ISBN 978-1-4773-1352-7 (pbk. : alk. paper)
    ISBN 978-1-4773-1353-4 (library e-book)
    ISBN 978-1-4773-1354-1 (nonlibrary e-book)
Subjects: LCSH: Demosthenes—Translations into English. | Speeches, addresses, etc., Greek—Translation into English. | Athens (Greece)—Politics and government—Early works to 1800.
Classification: LCC PA3951 .E5 2018 | DDC 885/.01—dc23
LC record available at https://lccn.loc.gov/2017015721

doi:10.7560/313510

For Selene

# CONTENTS

# SERIES EDITOR'S PREFACE

This is the fifteenth and final volume in the series of *The Oratory of Classical Greece*. The aim of the series is to make available primarily for those who do not read Greek up-to-date, accurate, and readable translations with introductions and explanatory notes of all the surviving works and major fragments of the Attic orators of the classical period (ca. 420–320 BCE): Aeschines, Andocides, Antiphon, Demosthenes, Dinarchus, Hyperides, Isaeus, Isocrates, Lycurgus, and Lysias. This volume contains two of Demosthenes' important public speeches that are not only of great interest in themselves but that also shed light on many aspects of Athenian law, especially homicide law (in Dem. 23). The two other speeches in the volume were both certainly written in the Hellenistic period and falsely attributed to Demosthenes; they shed light on the reception of Demosthenes in this later period.

This volume, like the others in the series, has benefited greatly from the careful attention of many at the University of Texas Press, including Director Dave Hamrick, Senior Editor Jim Burr, Senior Manuscript Editor Lynne Chapman, and copy editor Nancy Moore. As always, they have been a pleasure to work with.

—M. G.

# TRANSLATOR'S PREFACE

When writing a book, one incurs many debts. I would first like to thank the two conscientious readers for the press, James Sickinger and David Whitehead, for their thorough and helpful reports. They caught errors, noted omissions, and made several constructive suggestions for improvement. Mirko Canevaro read the entire manuscript and offered expert advice about the documents inserted into the texts of *Against Aristocrates* and *Against Timocrates* and about the stichometry of the speeches. I would also like to thank Mirko for sharing with me a forthcoming essay about the document at *Against Timocrates* 20–23, in which he shows that the flawed attempt of M. H. Hansen to defend its authenticity contains many errors and overlooks key evidence. I am also glad that all three agree that the two speeches *Against Aristogeiton* cannot have been written by Demosthenes but were composed by an anonymous author in the Hellenistic or Roman period. Michael Gagarin drew my attention to minor errors and omissions. Vasia Psilakakou proofread the entire manuscript at an early stage, verified references, and checked the translation. Jakub Filonik read a draft of the translation of the two speeches *Against Aristogeiton* and made several good suggestions. Janek Kucharski alerted me to an important piece of evidence about the authenticity of *Against Aristogeiton* II, and Peter Long gave me good advice about the verdict in the prosecution of Timocrates. Jim Burr was very helpful at the initial stages and made sure that the entire process from initial submission to final acceptance ran smoothly. Lynne Chapman did a terrific job moving the manuscript through all the stages of production, especially copyediting and proofreading. Lynne had a sharp eye for detail, always responded promptly to my requests, and did everything with consummate tact (which is very important when dealing with headstrong authors). Finally, Nancy Moore did splendid work copy-editing the entire manuscript. I am deeply grateful for her careful attention to detail and her sensible advice.

I dedicate this book to my wife Selene Psoma, who taught me to have doubts about Demosthenes' policies.

—E. H.

# SERIES INTRODUCTION
## Greek Oratory

〰〰〰〰〰〰〰〰〰〰〰〰〰〰〰〰〰〰〰〰〰〰〰〰〰〰〰〰〰〰〰〰〰〰〰〰〰〰〰〰〰

## By Michael Gagarin

### ORATORY IN CLASSICAL ATHENS

From as early as Homer (and undoubtedly much earlier) the Greeks placed a high value on effective speaking. Even Achilles, whose greatness was primarily established on the battlefield, was brought up to be "a speaker of words and a doer of deeds" (*Iliad* 9.443); and Athenian leaders of the sixth and fifth centuries,[1] such as Solon, Themistocles, and Pericles, were all accomplished orators. Most Greek literary genres—notably epic, tragedy, and history—underscore the importance of oratory by their inclusion of set speeches. The formal pleadings of the envoys to Achilles in the *Iliad*, the messenger speeches in tragedy reporting events like the battle of Salamis in Aeschylus' *Persians* or the gruesome death of Pentheus in Euripides' *Bacchae*, and the powerful political oratory of Pericles' funeral oration in Thucydides are but a few of the most notable examples of the Greeks' never-ending fascination with formal public speaking, which was to reach its height in the public oratory of the fourth century.

In early times, oratory was not a specialized subject of study but was learned by practice and example. The formal study of rhetoric as an "art" (*technē*) began, we are told, in the middle of the fifth century in Sicily with the work of Corax and his pupil Tisias.[2] These two are scarcely more than names to us, but

---

[1] All dates in this volume are BC unless the contrary is either indicated or obvious.

[2] See Kennedy 1963: 26–51. Cole 1991 has challenged this traditional picture, arguing that the term "rhetoric" was coined by Plato to designate and denigrate an activity he strongly opposed. Cole's own reconstruction is not

another famous Sicilian, Gorgias of Leontini (ca. 490–390), developed a new style of argument and is reported to have dazzled the Athenians with a speech delivered when he visited Athens in 427. Gorgias initiated the practice, which continued into the early fourth century, of composing speeches for mythical or imaginary occasions. The surviving examples reveal a lively intellectual climate in the late fifth and early fourth centuries, in which oratory served to display new ideas, new forms of expression, and new methods of argument.[3] This tradition of "intellectual" oratory was continued by the fourth-century educator Isocrates and played a large role in later Greek and Roman education.

In addition to this intellectual oratory, at about the same time the practice also began of writing speeches for real occasions in public life, which we may designate "practical" oratory. For centuries Athenians had been delivering speeches in public settings (primarily the courts and the Assembly), but these had always been composed and delivered impromptu, without being written down and thus without being preserved. The practice of writing speeches began in the courts and then expanded to include the Assembly and other settings. Athens was one of the leading cities of Greece in the fifth and fourth centuries, and its political and legal systems depended on direct participation by a large number of citizens; all important decisions were made by these large bodies, and the primary means of influencing these decisions was oratory.[4] Thus, it is not surprising that oratory flourished in Athens,[5] but it may not be immediately obvious why it should be written down.

---

without problems, but he does well to remind us how thoroughly the traditional view of rhetoric depends on one of its most ardent opponents.

[3] Of these only Antiphon's Tetralogies are included in this series. Gorgias' *Helen* and *Palamedes*, Alcidamas' *Odysseus*, and Antisthenes' *Ajax* and *Odysseus* are translated in Gagarin and Woodruff 1995.

[4] Yunis 1996 has a good treatment of political oratory from Pericles to Demosthenes.

[5] All our evidence for practical oratory comes from Athens, with the exception of Isocrates 19, written for a trial in Aegina. Many speeches were undoubtedly delivered in courts and political forums in other Greek cities, but it may be that such speeches were written down only in Athens.

The pivotal figure in this development was Antiphon, one of the fifth-century intellectuals who are often grouped together under the name "Sophists."[6] Like some of the other sophists he contributed to the intellectual oratory of the period, but he also had a strong practical interest in law. At the same time, Antiphon had an aversion to public speaking and did not directly involve himself in legal or political affairs (Thucydides 8.68). However, he began giving general advice to other citizens who were engaged in litigation and were thus expected to address the court themselves. As this practice grew, Antiphon went further, and around 430 he began writing out whole speeches for others to memorize and deliver. Thus began the practice of "logography," which continued through the next century and beyond.[7] Logography particularly appealed to men like Lysias, who were metics, or noncitizen residents of Athens. Since they were not Athenian citizens, they were barred from direct participation in public life, but they could contribute by writing speeches for others.

Antiphon was also the first (to our knowledge) to write down a speech he would himself deliver, writing the speech for his own defense at his trial for treason in 411. His motive was probably to publicize and preserve his views, and others continued this practice of writing down speeches they would themselves deliver in the courts and (more rarely) the Assembly.[8] Finally, one other type of practical oratory was the special tribute delivered on certain important public occasions, the best known of which is the funeral oration. It is convenient to designate these three types of

---

[6] The term "sophist" was loosely used through the fifth and fourth centuries to designate various intellectuals and orators, but under the influence of Plato, who attacked certain figures under this name, the term is now used of a specific group of thinkers; see Kerferd 1981.

[7] For Antiphon as the first to write speeches, see Photius, *Bibliotheca* 486a7–11 and [Plut.], *Moralia* 832c–d. The latest extant speech can be dated to 320, but we know that at least one orator, Dinarchus, continued the practice after that date.

[8] Unlike forensic speeches, speeches for delivery in the Assembly were usually not composed beforehand in writing, since the speaker could not know exactly when or in what context he would be speaking; see further Trevett 1996.

oratory by the terms Aristotle later uses: forensic (for the courts), deliberative (for the Assembly), and epideictic (for display).[9]

In the century from about 420 to 320, dozens—perhaps even hundreds—of now unknown orators and logographers must have composed speeches that are now lost, but only ten of these men were selected for preservation and study by ancient scholars, and only works collected under the names of these ten have been preserved. Some of these works are undoubtedly spurious, though in most cases they are fourth-century works by a different author rather than later "forgeries." Indeed, modern scholars suspect that as many as seven of the speeches attributed to Demosthenes may have been written by Apollodorus, son of Pasion, who is sometimes called "the eleventh orator."[10] Including these speeches among the works of Demosthenes may have been an honest mistake, or perhaps a bookseller felt he could sell more copies of these speeches if they were attributed to a more famous orator.

In alphabetical order the Ten Orators are as follows:[11]

• AESCHINES (ca. 390–ca. 322) rose from obscure origins to become an important Athenian political figure, first an ally, then a bitter enemy of Demosthenes. His three speeches all concern major public issues. The best known of these (Aes. 3) was delivered at the trial in 330, when Demosthenes responded with *On the Crown* (Dem. 18). Aeschines lost the case and was forced to leave Athens and live the rest of his life in exile.

---

[9] *Rhetoric* 1.3. Intellectual orations, like Gorgias' *Helen*, do not easily fit into Aristotle's classification. For a fuller (but still brief) introduction to Attic oratory and the orators, see Edwards 1994.

[10] See Trevett 1992.

[11] The Loeb volumes of *Minor Attic Orators* also include the prominent Athenian political figure Demades (ca. 385–319), who was not one of the Ten; but the only speech that has come down to us under his name is a later forgery. It is possible that Demades and other fourth-century politicians who had a high reputation for public speaking did not put any speeches in writing, especially if they rarely spoke in the courts (see above n. 8).

* ANDOCIDES (ca. 440–ca. 390) is best known for his role in the scandal of 415, when just before the departure of the fateful Athenian expedition to Sicily during the Peloponnesian War (431–404), a band of young men mutilated statues of Hermes, and at the same time information was revealed about the secret rites of Demeter. Andocides was exiled but later returned. Two of the four speeches in his name give us a contemporary view of the scandal: one pleads for his return, the other argues against a second period of exile.

* ANTIPHON (ca. 480–411), as already noted, wrote forensic speeches for others and only once spoke himself. In 411 he participated in an oligarchic coup by a group of 400, and when the democrats regained power he was tried for treason and executed. His six surviving speeches include three for delivery in court and the three Tetralogies—imaginary intellectual exercises for display or teaching that consist of four speeches each, two on each side. All six of Antiphon's speeches concern homicide, probably because these stood at the beginning of the collection of his works. Fragments of some thirty other speeches cover many different topics.

* DEMOSTHENES (384–322) is generally considered the best of the Attic orators. Although his nationalistic message is less highly regarded today, his powerful mastery of and ability to combine many different rhetorical styles continues to impress readers. Demosthenes was still a child when his wealthy father died. The trustees of the estate apparently misappropriated much of it, and when he came of age, he sued them in a series of cases (27–31), regaining some of his fortune and making a name as a powerful speaker. He then wrote speeches for others in a variety of cases, public and private, and for his own use in court (where many cases involved major public issues), and in the Assembly, where he opposed the growing power of Philip of Macedon. The triumph of Philip and his son Alexander the Great eventually put an end to Demosthenes' career. Some sixty speeches have come down under his name, about a third of them of questionable authenticity.

* DINARCHUS (ca. 360–ca. 290) was born in Corinth but spent much of his life in Athens as a metic (a noncitizen resident).

His public fame came primarily from writing speeches for the prosecutions surrounding the Harpalus affair in 324, when several prominent figures (including Demosthenes) were accused of bribery. After 322 he had a profitable career as a logographer.

- HYPERIDES (389/8–322) was a political leader and logographer of so many different talents that he was called the pentathlete of orators. He was a leader of the Athenian resistance to Philip and Alexander and (like Demosthenes) was condemned to death after Athens' final surrender. One speech and substantial fragments of five others have been recovered from papyrus remains; otherwise, only fragments survive.

- ISAEUS (ca. 415–ca. 340) wrote speeches on a wide range of topics, but the eleven complete speeches that survive, dating from ca. 390 to ca. 344, all concern inheritance. As with Antiphon, the survival of these particular speeches may have been the result of the later ordering of his speeches by subject; we have part of a twelfth speech and fragments and titles of some forty other works. Isaeus is said to have been a pupil of Isocrates and the teacher of Demosthenes.

- ISOCRATES (436–338) considered himself a philosopher and educator, not an orator or rhetorician. He came from a wealthy Athenian family but lost most of his property in the Peloponnesian War, and in 403 he took up logography. About 390 he abandoned this practice and turned to writing and teaching, setting forth his educational, philosophical, and political views in essays that took the form of speeches but were not meant for oral delivery. He favored accommodation with the growing power of Philip of Macedon and panhellenic unity. His school was based on a broad concept of rhetoric and applied philosophy; it attracted pupils from the entire Greek world (including Isaeus, Lycurgus, and Hyperides) and became the main rival of Plato's Academy. Isocrates greatly influenced education and rhetoric in the Hellenistic, Roman, and modern periods until the eighteenth century.

- LYCURGUS (ca. 390–ca. 324) was a leading public official who restored the financial condition of Athens after 338 and played a large role in the city for the next dozen years. He brought charges of corruption or treason against many other officials, usually with success. Only one speech survives.

• LYSIAS (ca. 445–ca. 380) was a metic—an official resident of Athens but not a citizen. Much of his property was seized by the Thirty during their short-lived oligarchic coup in 404–403. Perhaps as a result he turned to logography. More than thirty speeches survive in whole or in part, though the authenticity of some is doubted. We also have fragments or know the titles of more than a hundred others. The speeches cover a wide range of cases, and he may have delivered one himself (Lys. 12), on the death of his brother at the hands of the Thirty. Lysias is particularly known for his vivid narratives, his *ēthopoiïa*, or "creation of character," and his prose style, which became a model of clarity and vividness.

## THE WORKS OF THE ORATORS

As soon as speeches began to be written down, they could be preserved. We know little about the conditions of book "publication" (i.e., making copies for distribution) in the fourth century, but there was an active market for books in Athens, and some of the speeches may have achieved wide circulation.[12] An orator (or his family) may have preserved his own speeches, perhaps to advertise his ability or demonstrate his success, or booksellers may have collected and copied them in order to make money.

We do not know how closely the preserved text of these speeches corresponded to the version actually delivered in court or in the Assembly. Speakers undoubtedly extemporized or varied from their text on occasion, but there is no good evidence that deliberative speeches were substantially revised for publication.[13] In forensic oratory a logographer's reputation would derive first and

---

[12]Dover's discussion (1968) of the preservation and transmission of the works of Lysias (and perhaps others under his name) is useful not just for Lysias but for the other orators too. His theory of shared authorship between logographer and litigant, however, is unconvincing (see Usher 1976).

[13]See further Trevett 1996: 437–439.

foremost from his success with jurors. If a forensic speech was victorious, there would be no reason to alter it for publication, and if it lost, alteration would probably not deceive potential clients. Thus, the published texts of forensic speeches were probably quite faithful to the texts that were provided to clients, and we have little reason to suspect substantial alteration in the century or so before they were collected by scholars in Alexandria (see below).

In addition to the speaker's text, most forensic speeches have breaks for the inclusion of documents. The logographer inserted a notation in his text—such as *nomos* ("law") or *martyria* ("testimony")—and the speaker would pause while the clerk read out the text of a law or the testimony of witnesses. Many speeches survive with only a notation that a *nomos* or *martyria* was read at that point, but in some cases the text of the document is included. It used to be thought that these documents were all creations of later scholars, but many (though not all) are now accepted as genuine.[14]

With the foundation of the famous library in Alexandria early in the third century, scholars began to collect and catalogue texts of the orators, along with many other classical authors. Only the best orators were preserved in the library, many of them represented by over 100 speeches each (some undoubtedly spurious). Only some of these works survived in manuscript form to the modern era; more recently a few others have been discovered on ancient sheets of papyrus, so that today the corpus of Attic Oratory consists of about 150 speeches, together with a few letters and other works. The subject matter ranges from important public issues and serious crimes to business affairs, lovers' quarrels, inheritance disputes, and other personal or family matters.

In the centuries after these works were collected, ancient scholars gathered biographical facts about their authors, produced grammatical and lexicographic notes, and used some of the speeches as evidence for Athenian political history. But the ancient scholars who were most interested in the orators were those who studied prose style, the most notable of these being Diony-

---

[14] See MacDowell 1990: 43–47; Todd 1993: 44–45.

sius of Halicarnassus (first century BC), who wrote treatises on several of the orators,[15] and Hermogenes of Tarsus (second century AD), who wrote several literary studies, including *On Types of Style*.[16] But relative to epic or tragedy, oratory was little studied; and even scholars of rhetoric whose interests were broader than style, like Cicero and Quintilian, paid little attention to the orators, except for the acknowledged master, Demosthenes.

Most modern scholars until the second half of the twentieth century continued to treat the orators primarily as prose stylists.[17] The reevaluation of Athenian democracy by George Grote and others in the nineteenth century stimulated renewed interest in Greek oratory among historians; and increasing interest in Athenian law during that century led a few legal scholars to read the orators. But in comparison with the interest shown in the other literary genres—epic, lyric, tragedy, comedy, and even history—Attic oratory has been relatively neglected until the last third of the twentieth century. More recently, however, scholars have discovered the value of the orators for the broader study of Athenian culture and society. Since Dover's ground-breaking works on popular morality and homosexuality,[18] interest in the orators has been increasing rapidly, and they are now seen as primary representatives of Athenian moral and social values, and as evidence for social and economic conditions, political and social ide-

---

[15] Dionysius' literary studies are collected and translated in Usher 1974–1985.

[16] Wooten 1987. Stylistic considerations probably also influenced the selection of the "canon" of ten orators; see Worthington 1994.

[17] For example, the most popular and influential book ever written on the orators, Jebb's *The Attic Orators* (1875), was presented as an "attempt to aid in giving Attic Oratory its due place in the history of Attic Prose" (I.xiii). This modern focus on prose style can plausibly be connected to the large role played by prose composition (the translation of English prose into Greek, usually in imitation of specific authors or styles) in the Classics curriculum, especially in Britain.

[18] Dover (1974, 1978). Dover recently commented (1994: 157), "When I began to mine the riches of Attic forensic oratory I was astonished to discover that the mine had never been exploited."

ology, and in general those aspects of Athenian culture that in the past were commonly ignored by historians of ancient Greece but are of increasing interest and importance today, including women and the family, slavery, and the economy.

## GOVERNMENT AND LAW IN CLASSICAL ATHENS

The hallmark of the Athenian political and legal systems was its amateurism. Most public officials, including those who supervised the courts, were selected by lot and held office for a limited period, typically a year. Thus a great many citizens held public office at some point in their lives, but almost none served for an extended period of time or developed the experience or expertise that would make them professionals. All significant policy decisions were debated and voted on in the Assembly, where the quorum was 6,000 citizens, and all significant legal cases were judged by bodies of 200 to 500 jurors or more. Public prominence was not achieved by election (or selection) to public office but depended rather on a man's ability to sway the majority of citizens in the Assembly or jurors in court to vote in favor of a proposed course of action or for one of the litigants in a trial. Success was never permanent, and a victory on one policy issue or a verdict in one case could be quickly reversed in another.[19] In such a system the value of public oratory is obvious, and in the fourth century, oratory became the most important cultural institution in Athens, replacing drama as the forum where major ideological concerns were displayed and debated.

Several recent books give good detailed accounts of Athenian government and law,[20] and so a brief sketch can suffice here. The

---

[19]In the Assembly this could be accomplished by a reconsideration of the question, as in the famous Mytilenean debate (Thuc. 3.36–50); in court a verdict was final, but its practical effects could be thwarted or reversed by later litigation on a related issue.

[20]For government, see Sinclair 1988, Hansen 1991; for law, MacDowell 1978, Todd 1993, and Boegehold 1995 (Bonner 1927 is still helpful). Much of our information about the legal and political systems comes from a work attributed to Aristotle but perhaps written by a pupil of his, *The Athenian*

main policy-making body was the Assembly, open to all adult male citizens; a small payment for attendance enabled at least some of the poor to attend along with the leisured rich. In addition, a Council of 500 citizens, selected each year by lot with no one allowed to serve more than two years, prepared material for and made recommendations to the Assembly; a rotating subgroup of this Council served as an executive committee, the Prytaneis. Finally, numerous officials, most of them selected by lot for one-year terms, supervised different areas of administration and finance. The most important of these were the nine Archons (lit. "rulers"): the eponymous Archon after whom the year was named, the Basileus ("king"),[21] the Polemarch, and the six Thesmothetae. Councilors and almost all these officials underwent a preliminary examination (*dokimasia*) before taking office, and officials submitted to a final accounting (*euthynai*) upon leaving; at these times any citizen who wished could challenge a person's fitness for his new position or his performance in his recent position.

There was no general taxation of Athenian citizens. Sources of public funding included the annual tax levied on metics, various fees and import duties, and (in the fifth century) tribute from allied cities; but the source that figures most prominently in the orators is the Athenian system of liturgies (*leitourgiai*), by which in a regular rotation the rich provided funding for certain special public needs. The main liturgies were the *chorēgia*, in which a sponsor (*chorēgos*) supervised and paid for the training and performance of a chorus which sang and danced at a public festival,[22] and the trierarchy, in which a sponsor (trierarch) paid to equip and usually commanded a trireme, or warship, for a year. Some of these liturgies required substantial expenditures, but even so, some men spent far more than required in order to promote themselves and

---

*Constitution* (*Ath. Pol.*—conveniently translated with notes by Rhodes 1984). The discovery of this work on a papyrus in Egypt in 1890 caused a major resurgence of interest in Athenian government.

[21] Modern scholars often use the term *archōn basileus* or "king archon," but Athenian sources (e.g., *Ath. Pol.* 57) simply call him the *basileus*.

[22] These included the productions of tragedy and comedy, for which the main expense was for the chorus.

their public careers, and litigants often tried to impress the jurors by referring to liturgies they had undertaken (see, e.g., Lys. 21.1–n5). A further twist on this system was that if a man thought he had been assigned a liturgy that should have gone to someone else who was richer than he, he could propose an exchange of property (*antidosis*), giving the other man a choice of either taking over the liturgy or exchanging property with him. Finally, the rich were also subject to special taxes (*eisphorai*) levied as a percentage of their property in times of need.

The Athenian legal system remained similarly resistant to professionalization. Trials and the procedures leading up to them were supervised by officials, primarily the nine Archons, but their role was purely administrative, and they were in no way equivalent to modern judges. All significant questions about what we would call points of law were presented to the jurors, who considered them together with all other issues when they delivered their verdict at the end of the trial.[23] Trials were "contests" (*agōnes*) between two litigants, each of whom presented his own case to the jurors in a speech, plaintiff first, then defendant; in some cases each party then spoke again, probably in rebuttal. Since a litigant had only one or two speeches in which to present his entire case, and no issue was decided separately by a judge, all the necessary factual information and every important argument on substance or procedure, fact or law, had to be presented together. A single speech might thus combine narrative, argument, emotional appeal, and various digressions, all with the goal of obtaining a favorable verdict. Even more than today, a litigant's primary task was to control the issue—to determine which issues the jurors would consider most important and which questions they would have in their minds as they cast their votes. We only

---

[23]Certain religious "interpreters" (*exēgētai*) were occasionally asked to give their opinion on a legal matter that had a religious dimension (such as the prosecution of a homicide), but although these opinions could be reported in court (e.g., Dem. 47.68–73), they had no official legal standing. The most significant administrative decision we hear of is the refusal of the Basileus to accept the case in Antiphon 6 (see 6.37–46).

rarely have both speeches from a trial,[24] and we usually have little or no external evidence for the facts of a case or the verdict. We must thus infer both the facts and the opponent's strategy from the speech we have, and any assessment of the overall effectiveness of a speech and of the logographer's strategy is to some extent speculative.

Before a trial there were usually several preliminary hearings for presenting evidence; arbitration, public and private, was available and sometimes required. These hearings and arbitration sessions allowed each side to become familiar with the other side's case, so that discussions of "what my opponent will say" could be included in one's speech. Normally a litigant presented his own case, but he was often assisted by family or friends. If he wished (and could afford it), he could enlist the services of a logographer, who presumably gave strategic advice in addition to writing a speech. The speeches were timed to ensure an equal hearing for both sides,[25] and all trials were completed within a day. Two hundred or more jurors decided each case in the popular courts, which met in the Agora.[26] Homicide cases and certain other religious trials (e.g., Lys. 7) were heard by the Council of the Areopagus or an associated group of fifty-one Ephetae. The Areopagus was composed of all former Archons—perhaps 150–200 members at most times. It met on a hill called the Areopagus ("rock of Ares") near the Acropolis.

Jurors for the regular courts were selected by lot from those citizens who registered each year and who appeared for duty that day; as with the Assembly, a small payment allowed the poor to serve. After the speakers had finished, the jurors voted immediately without any formal discussion. The side with the majority won; a tie vote decided the case for the defendant. In some cases where the penalty was not fixed, after a conviction the jurors

---

[24]The exceptions are Demosthenes 19 and Aeschines 2, Aeschines 3 and Demosthenes 18, and Lysias 6 (one of several prosecution speeches) and Andocides 1; all were written for major public cases.

[25]Timing was done by means of a water clock, which in most cases was stopped during the reading of documents.

[26]See Boegehold 1995.

voted again on the penalty, choosing between penalties proposed by each side. Even when we know the verdict, we cannot know which of the speaker's arguments contributed most to his success or failure. However, a logographer could probably learn from jurors which points had or had not been successful, so that arguments that are found repeatedly in speeches probably were known to be effective in most cases.

The first written laws in Athens were enacted by Draco (ca. 620) and Solon (ca. 590), and new laws were regularly added. At the end of the fifth century the existing laws were reorganized, and a new procedure for enacting laws was instituted; thereafter a group of Law-Givers (*nomothetai*) had to certify that a proposed law did not conflict with any existing laws. There was no attempt, however, to organize legislation systematically, and although Plato, Aristotle, and other philosophers wrote various works on law and law-giving, these were either theoretical or descriptive and had no apparent influence on legislation. Written statutes generally used ordinary language rather than precise legal definitions in designating offenses, and questions concerning precisely what constituted a specific offense or what was the correct interpretation of a written statute were decided (together with other issues) by the jurors in each case. A litigant might, of course, assert a certain definition or interpretation as "something you all know" or "what the lawgiver intended," but such remarks are evidently tendentious and cannot be taken as authoritative.

The result of these procedural and substantive features was that the verdict depended largely on each litigant's speech (or speeches). As one speaker puts it (Ant. 6.18), "When there are no witnesses, you (jurors) are forced to reach a verdict about the case on the basis of the prosecutor's and defendant's words alone; you must be suspicious and examine their accounts in detail, and your vote will necessarily be cast on the basis of likelihood rather than clear knowledge." Even the testimony of witnesses (usually on both sides) is rarely decisive. On the other hand, most speakers make a considerable effort to establish facts and provide legitimate arguments in conformity with established law. Plato's view of rhetoric as a clever technique for persuading an ignorant crowd that the false is true is not borne out by the speeches, and the legal system does not appear to have produced many arbitrary or clearly unjust results.

The main form of legal procedure was a *dikē* ("suit") in which the injured party (or his relatives in a case of homicide) brought suit against the offender. Suits for injuries to slaves would be brought by the slave's master, and injuries to women would be prosecuted by a male relative. Strictly speaking, a *dikē* was a private matter between individuals, though like all cases, *dikai* often had public dimensions. The other major form of procedure was a *graphē* ("writing" or "indictment") in which "anyone who wished" (i.e., any citizen) could bring a prosecution for wrongdoing. *Graphai* were instituted by Solon, probably in order to allow prosecution of offenses where the victim was unable or unlikely to bring suit himself, such as selling a dependent into slavery; but the number of areas covered by *graphai* increased to cover many types of public offenses as well as some apparently private crimes, such as *hybris*.

The system of prosecution by "anyone who wished" also extended to several other more specialized forms of prosecution, like *eisangelia* ("impeachment"), used in cases of treason. Another specialized prosecution was *apagōgē* ("summary arrest"), in which someone could arrest a common criminal (*kakourgos*, lit. "evildoer"), or have him arrested, on the spot. The reliance on private initiative meant that Athenians never developed a system of public prosecution; rather, they presumed that everyone would keep an eye on the behavior of his political enemies and bring suit as soon as he suspected a crime, both to harm his opponents and to advance his own career. In this way all public officials would be watched by someone. There was no disgrace in admitting that a prosecution was motivated by private enmity.

By the end of the fifth century the system of prosecution by "anyone who wished" was apparently being abused by so-called sykophants (*sykophantai*), who allegedly brought or threatened to bring false suits against rich men, either to gain part of the fine that would be levied or to induce an out-of-court settlement in which the accused would pay to have the matter dropped. We cannot gauge the true extent of this problem, since speakers usually provide little evidence to support their claims that their opponents are sykophants, but the Athenians did make sykophancy a crime. They also specified that in many public procedures a plaintiff who either dropped the case or failed to obtain one-fifth of the votes would have to pay a heavy fine of 1,000 drachmas. Despite this, it appears that litigation was common in Athens and was seen by some as excessive.

Over the course of time, the Athenian legal and political systems have more often been judged negatively than positively. Philosophers and political theorists have generally followed the lead of Plato (427–347), who lived and worked in Athens his entire life while severely criticizing its system of government as well as many other aspects of its culture. For Plato, democracy amounted to the tyranny of the masses over the educated elite and was destined to collapse from its own instability. The legal system was capricious and depended entirely on the rhetorical ability of litigants with no regard for truth or justice. These criticisms have often been echoed by modern scholars, who particularly complain that law was much too closely interwoven with politics and did not have the autonomous status it achieved in Roman law and continues to have, at least in theory, in modern legal systems.

Plato's judgments are valid if one accepts the underlying presuppositions, that the aim of law is absolute truth and abstract justice and that achieving the highest good of the state requires thorough and systematic organization. Most Athenians do not seem to have subscribed to either the criticisms or the presuppositions, and most scholars now accept the long-ignored fact that despite major external disruptions in the form of wars and two short-lived coups brought about by one of these wars, the Athenian legal and political systems remained remarkably stable for almost two hundred years (508–320). Moreover, like all other Greek cities at the time, whatever their form of government, Athenian democracy was brought to an end not by internal forces but by the external power of Philip of Macedon and his son Alexander. The legal system never became autonomous, and the rich sometimes complained that they were victims of unscrupulous litigants, but there is no indication that the people wanted to yield control of the legal process to a professional class, as Plato recommended. For most Athenians—Plato being an exception in this and many other matters—one purpose of the legal system was to give everyone the opportunity to have his case heard by other citizens and have it heard quickly and cheaply; and in this it clearly succeeded.

Indeed, the Athenian legal system also served the interests of the rich, even the very rich, as well as the common people, in that it provided a forum for the competition that since Homer had been an important part of aristocratic life. In this competition, the rich used the courts as battlegrounds, though their main weapon was the rhetoric of popular ideology, which hailed the rule of law and promoted the ideal of moderation and restraint.[27] But those who aspired to political leadership and the honor and status that accompanied it repeatedly entered the legal arena, bringing suit against their political enemies whenever possible and defending themselves against suits brought by others whenever necessary. The ultimate judges of these public competitions were the common people, who seem to have relished the dramatic clash of individuals and ideologies. In this respect fourth-century oratory was the cultural heir of fifth-century drama and was similarly appreciated by the citizens. Despite the disapproval of intellectuals like Plato, most Athenians legitimately considered their legal system a hallmark of their democracy and a vital presence in their culture.

## THE TRANSLATION OF GREEK ORATORY

The purpose of this series is to provide students and scholars in all fields with accurate, readable translations of all surviving classical Attic oratory, including speeches whose authenticity is disputed, as well as the substantial surviving fragments. In keeping with the originals, the language is for the most part nontechnical. Names of persons and places are given in the (generally more familiar) Latinized forms, and names of officials or legal procedures have been translated into English equivalents, where possible. Notes are intended to provide the necessary historical and cultural background; scholarly controversies are generally not dis-

---

[27] Ober 1989 is fundamental; see also Cohen 1995, Harris 2006, and Harris 2013.

cussed. The notes and introductions refer to scholarly treatments in addition to those listed below, which the reader may consult for further information.

Cross-references to other speeches follow the standard numbering system, which is now well established except in the case of Hyperides (for whom the numbering of the Oxford Classical Text is used).[28] References are by work and section (e.g., Dem. 24.73); spurious works are not specially marked; when no author is named (e.g., 24.73), the reference is to the same author as the annotated passage.

ABBREVIATIONS

Aes.       = Aeschines
And.       = Andocides
Ant.       = Antiphon
Arist.     = Aristotle
Aristoph. = Aristophanes
*Ath. Pol.* = *The Athenian Constitution*
Dem.       = Demosthenes
Din.       = Dinarchus
Herod.     = Herodotus
Hyp.       = Hyperides
Is.        = Isaeus
Isoc.      = Isocrates
Lyc.       = Lycurgus
Lys.       = Lysias
Plut.      = Plutarch
Thuc.      = Thucydides
Xen.       = Xenophon

NOTE ON CURRENCY: The main unit of Athenian currency was the drachma; this was divided into obols and larger amounts were designated minas and talents.

---

[28] For a listing of all the orators and their works, with classifications (forensic, deliberative, epideictic) and rough dates, see Edwards 1994: 74–79.

1 drachma = 6 obols
1 mina    = 100 drachmas
1 talent   = 60 minas (6,000 drachmas)

It is impossible to give an accurate equivalence in terms of modern currency, but it may be helpful to remember that the daily wage of some skilled workers was a drachma in the mid-fifth century and 2–2½ drachmas in the later fourth century. Thus it may not be too misleading to think of a drachma as worth about $50 or £33 and a talent as about $300,000 or £200,000 in 1997 currency.

BIBLIOGRAPHY OF WORKS CITED

Boegehold, Alan L., 1995: *The Lawcourts at Athens: Sites, Buildings, Equipment, Procedure, and Testimonia.* Princeton.
Bonner, Robert J., 1927: *Lawyers and Litigants in Ancient Athens.* Chicago.
Carey, Christopher, 1997: *Trials from Classical Athens.* London.
Cohen, David, 1995: *Law, Violence and Community in Classical Athens.* Cambridge.
Cole, Thomas, 1991: *The Origins of Rhetoric in Ancient Greece.* Baltimore.
Dover, Kenneth J., 1968: *Lysias and the Corpus Lysiacum.* Berkeley.
———, 1974: *Greek Popular Morality in the Time of Plato and Aristotle.* Oxford.
———, 1978: *Greek Homosexuality.* London.
———, 1994: *Marginal Comment.* London.
Edwards, Michael, 1994: *The Attic Orators.* London.
Gagarin, Michael, and Paul Woodruff, 1995: *Early Greek Political Thought from Homer to the Sophists.* Cambridge.
Hansen, Mogens Herman, 1991: *The Athenian Democracy in the Age of Demosthenes.* Oxford.
Harris, E. M., 2006: *Democracy and the Rule of Law in Classical Athens: Essays on Law, Society, and Politics.* Cambridge.
———, 2013: *The Rule of Law in Action in Democratic Athens.* Oxford.

Jebb, Richard, 1875: *The Attic Orators*, 2 vols. London.

Kennedy, George A., 1963: *The Art of Persuasion in Greece*. Princeton.

Kerferd, G. B., 1981: *The Sophistic Movement*. Cambridge.

MacDowell, Douglas M., 1978: *The Law in Classical Athens*. London.

———, ed. 1990: *Demosthenes, Against Meidias*. Oxford.

Ober, Josiah, 1989: *Mass and Elite in Democratic Athens*. Princeton.

Rhodes, P. J., trans., 1984: *Aristotle, The Athenian Constitution*. Penguin Books.

Sinclair, R. K., 1988: *Democracy and Participation in Athens*. Cambridge.

Todd, Stephen, 1993: *The Shape of Athenian Law*. Oxford.

Trevett, Jeremy, 1992: *Apollodoros the Son of Pasion*. Oxford.

———, 1996: "Did Demosthenes Publish His Deliberative Speeches?" *Hermes* 124: 425–441.

Usher, Stephen, 1976: "Lysias and His Clients," *Greek, Roman and Byzantine Studies* 17: 31–40.

———, trans., 1974–1985: *Dionysius of Halicarnassus, Critical Essays*. 2 vols. Loeb Classical Library. Cambridge, MA.

———, 1999: *Greek Oratory: Tradition and Originality*. Oxford.

Wooten, Cecil W., trans., 1987: *Hermogenes' On Types of Style*. Chapel Hill, NC.

Worthington, Ian, 1994: "The Canon of the Ten Attic Orators," in *Persuasion: Greek Rhetoric in Action*, ed. Ian Worthington. London: 244–263.

Yunis, Harvey, 1996: *Taming Democracy: Models of Political Rhetoric in Classical Athens*. Ithaca, NY.

DEMOSTHENES, SPEECHES 23–26

# INTRODUCTION TO DEMOSTHENES

*By Michael Gagarin*

Since antiquity Demosthenes (384–322 BC) has usually been judged the greatest of the Attic orators. Although the patriotic and nationalistic tenor of his message has been more highly regarded in some periods of history than in others, he is unique in his mastery of so many different rhetorical styles and his ability to blend them into a powerful ensemble.

## LIFE

Demosthenes was born into an old wealthy Athenian family. His father Demosthenes owned workshops that made swords and furniture. His maternal grandfather, Gylon, had been exiled from Athens and lived in the Crimea, where his mother Cleobule was born (perhaps to a Scythian mother). When Demosthenes was seven, his father died leaving his estate in the trust of several guardians. According to Demosthenes' own account, the guardians mismanaged and defrauded the estate to the point that when he turned eighteen, the age of majority, he received almost nothing. He devoted the next several years to recovering his property, first studying forensic pleading and then bringing a series of suits against the guardians to recover his patrimony (speeches 27–31). He won the first case (27, *Against Aphobus I*), but then had to bring several more suits in order to collect the amount awarded him by the court. In the course of these trials he gained a reputation as a successful speaker, became sought after by others, and began to write speeches for a wide range of private suits, including inheritance, shipping loans, assault, and trespass. His clients included one of the richest men in Athens, the banker Phormio;

the speech *For Phormio* (36) involves a dispute over twenty talents (equivalent to several million dollars today). Demosthenes' vivid characterization of the honest, hard-working Phormio and his malicious and extravagant opponent proved so convincing that the jurors reportedly refused to listen to the other side and took the highly unusual step of voting immediately for Phormio.

In 355 Demosthenes became involved in his first major public case (22, *Against Androtion*). By this time it was common for ambitious or influential citizens to bring legal charges against their political opponents on matters of public interest. Charges of proposing an illegal decree (the *graphē paranomōn*) were particularly common; these involved the indictment of the proposer of a decree on the ground that it conflicted with existing law.[1] Although these speeches addressed the specific issue of a conflict between laws, it was generally accepted that the merits of the decree, and of its proposer, were also relevant factors, and these cases formed a major arena for the ongoing political struggles between leading figures in the city.

About the same time Demosthenes also began to publish speeches on public issues which he delivered in the assembly, and after 350, although he continued from time to time to write speeches for private disputes, he turned his attention primarily to public policy, especially relations between Athens and the growing power of Macedon under King Philip. Demosthenes' strategy throughout was to increase Athens' military readiness, to oppose Philip's expansion and to support other Greek cities in their resistance to it. Most notable in support of these objectives were the three *Olynthiacs* (1–3) in 349 unsuccessfully urging support for the city of Olynthus (which soon afterwards fell to Philip) and the four *Philippics* (4, 6, 9, 10) in 351–341 urging greater opposition to Philip. But Philip continued to extend his power into Greece, and in 338 he defeated a combined Greek force (includ-

---

[1] One might compare the U.S. procedure of challenging the constitutionality of a law in court. Differences include the fact that today no charge is brought against the proposer of the law and that the case is heard by a small panel of professional judges, not the hundreds of untrained jurors who would have heard the case in Athens.

ing Athens) at the battle of Chaeronea in Boeotia, north of Attica. This battle is usually taken to mark the end of the Greek cities' struggle to remain independent.

After Chaeronea Demosthenes continued to urge resistance to Philip, but his efforts were largely ineffectual and his successes and failures are more a matter of internal Athenian politics. His most prominent opponent during this period was Aeschines, who had been acquitted earlier (343) when Demosthenes brought a suit against him in connection with a delegation to Philip on which both men had served (19, cf. Aeschines 2). After Chaeronea, when a minor ally of Demosthenes named Ctesiphon proposed a decree awarding a crown to Demosthenes in recognition of his service to the city, Aeschines brought a *graphē paranomōn* against Ctesiphon (Aeschines 3). The suit, which was not tried until 330, raised legal objections to the proposed decree but also attacked the person and career of Demosthenes at considerable length. Demosthenes responded with his most famous speech *On the Crown* (18), often known by its Latin name *De Corona*. The verdict was so one-sided that Aeschines was fined for not receiving one-fifth of the votes and went into exile. This was Demosthenes' greatest triumph. The last years of his life, however, resulted in notable defeats, first in the rather shadowy Harpalus affair (324–323), from which no speech of his survives (but see Dinarchus 1). Shortly afterwards he was condemned to death at the instigation of pro-Macedonian forces and committed suicide.

WORKS

Sixty-one speeches and some miscellaneous works, including a collection of letters, have come down to us under Demosthenes' name. The authenticity of many of these has been challenged, often because of the allegedly poor quality of the work; but this reason is less often accepted today, and most of the public speeches and many of the private speeches are now thought to be authentic. Among the main exceptions are a group of private speeches (45, 46, 49, 50, 52, 53, 59, and possibly 47 and 51) that were delivered by Apollodorus and are now commonly thought to have been composed by him (Trevett 1992).

Apart from a funeral oration (60) and collections of proems and letters, Demosthenes' works fall into two groups, the assembly speeches (1–17) and the court speeches (18–59); the latter can be further divided into public and private speeches, though these are not formal legal categories. Notable among the public forensic speeches are *Against Meidias* (21), which has recently drawn attention for its pronouncements on Athenian public values, and his last surviving speech, *On the Crown* (18), generally recognized as his masterpiece. In this speech he uses his entire repertory of rhetorical strategies to defend his life and political career. He treats the legal issues of the case briefly, as being of minor concern, and then defends his conduct during the past three decades of Athenian history, arguing that even when his policy did not succeed, on each occasion it was the best policy for the city, in contrast to Aeschines' policies, which, when he ventured to propose any, were disastrous. Demosthenes' extensive personal attack on Aeschines' life and family may be too harsh for modern taste, but the blending of facts, innuendoes, sarcasm, rhetorical questions, and other devices is undeniably effective.

Demosthenes' private speeches have recently begun to attract more interest from scholars, who draw from them insight into Athenian social, political, and economic life. Only the speeches concerned with recovering his inheritance (27–31) were delivered by Demosthenes himself; the rest were written for delivery by other litigants. We have already noted *For Phormio*, which is one of several having to do with banking. *Against Conon* (54) alleges an assault by several young rowdies spurred on by their father, and *Against Neaera* (59), delivered and probably written by Apollodorus, recounts the life of a former slave woman and her affairs with different Athenian men.

STYLE

Demosthenes is a master of Greek prose style; he paid careful attention to style, and to the oral delivery of his speeches. His Roman counterpart, Cicero, modeled his oratorical style (and some other features of his work) in part on Demosthenes' Greek. Although Demosthenes' style varied considerably over the course of time and among the different types of speeches, later assessments of his style are based primarily on the public forensic speeches, and especially the last of these, *On the Crown*. Long and sometimes elaborate sentences are one feature of his style, but Demosthenes' true greatness is his ability to write in many styles and to vary his style, mixing different features together both to suit the topic and to give variety and vigor to his speeches. The final product required great skill and practice to deliver effectively, and the stories about Demosthenes' rigorous training in delivery (see in general Plutarch, *Life of Demosthenes* 6–7), even if not literally true, accurately reflect his priorities. Indeed, only by reading aloud sections of *On the Crown* in Greek can one truly appreciate the power and authority of his prose.

SIGNIFICANCE

Demosthenes played a vital role in Athenian public affairs for some thirty years. His advocacy of the vigilant defense of Greece against foreign invaders, though ultimately unsuccessful in preserving Greek freedom, inspired his fellow Athenians with patriotic loyalty, and has similarly inspired many others in later times. In recent times political rhetoric has not been so widely admired as in the past, and Demosthenes is less read today than he used to be. But he still represents the greatest achievement of Greek oratory and stands as one of the greatest orators of any age.

# INTRODUCTION TO THIS VOLUME

## By Edward Harris

The speeches *Against Aristocrates* and *Against Timocrates* were delivered at trials during the decade following the Social War (357–355 BCE). This period marked an important transition in the history of Athenian democracy. Earlier in the fourth century the Athenians attempted to regain the hegemony that they had lost by their defeat in the Peloponnesian War.[1] In 378 the Athenians created a league of allies and portrayed themselves as the champions of Greek freedom against Spartan oppression.[2] The charter of the new league was an attempt to avoid all the mistakes the Athenians had made during the fifth century: the Athenians pledged to leave their allies free and autonomous, not to impose garrisons or governors, not to collect tribute, not to allow Athenian citizens to acquire land in the territory of their allies, and not to alter their constitutions.[3]

The new league got off to a promising start: in 376 Chabrias defeated the Spartan fleet off Naxos, freeing the Athenians from a Spartan blockade. Many Greek states in Ionia and Central Greece joined the new league, and in 375 Timotheus gained allies in Western Greece and defeated another Spartan fleet at Alyzia.[4]

---

[1] For the revival of Athenian ambitions to regain leadership, see Seager 1967.

[2] On the Second Athenian League, see Cargill 1981 and Dreher 1995.

[3] *Inscriptiones Graecae* (hereafter, *IG*) ii² 43. For a translation with brief commentary, see Rhodes and Osborne 2003 no. 22.

[4] For Chabrias' victory at Naxos, see Xen. *Hellenica* 5.4.61; Diodorus 15.34–35. For Timotheus' victory at Alyzia, see Xen. *Hellenica* 5.4.62–66.

But the alliance was weakened by the defection of Thebes in 371.[5] After the Thebans defeated the Spartans at Leuctra later that year and invaded the Peloponnese, the Athenians voted to conclude an alliance with Sparta and destroyed the main rationale for the new league. The Athenians further undermined their claim of protecting Greek liberty when they revived their territorial ambitions in Northern Greece.[6] Between 368 and 359, Iphicrates, then Timotheus commanded Athenian forces in the Chalcidice and the Chersonnese, but they failed to capture Amphipolis.[7]

By 357 the city of Byzantium and the powerful islands of Chios and Rhodes no longer saw any reason to accept Athenian leadership and started a revolt with the encouragement of Mausolus, the dynast of Caria.[8] The Athenians sent the general Chares with a fleet to blockade Chios, but they were defeated in late 356.[9] The Chians, Rhodians, and Byzantines then attacked the Athenian possessions at Imbros and Lemnos and laid siege to Samos. The Athenians responded by sending a fleet of sixty ships under Iphicrates and Menestheus to join Chares and attack Byzantium. The rebels struck a decisive blow against this force in 355 at the battle of Embata near Erythrae.[10] The Athenians were now short of funds, and Chares attempted to raise money by hiring out Athenian troops to the rebellious satrap Artabazus. But this strategy ran aground when the Persian King sent a protest to Athens and threatened to side with their enemies.[11] Isolated and without resources, the Athenians were forced to make peace and accept the withdrawal of their most powerful allies from the league.

---

[5] See Buckler 1980: 48–55.

[6] For an analysis of the reasons for the failure of the Second Athenian League, see Cawkwell 1981.

[7] For Iphicrates' attempt to capture Amphipolis, see *Against Aristocrates* 149, with notes. For Athenian campaigns in the Chersonnese during 365 to 358, see *Against Aristocrates* 160–186.

[8] For the role of Mausolus, see Dem. 15.3, with Hornblower 1982: 204–218.

[9] On the defeat at Chios, see Diodorus 16.7; Plut. *Phocion* 6; Dem. 20.81.

[10] For the battle of Embata, see Nepos *Timotheus* 4, *Iphicrates* 3.3; Polyaenus 3.9.29; Diodorus 16.21.3–4 (mistakenly placing the battle in the Hellespont); Isoc. 15.129; Din. 1.14.

[11] Diodorus 16.22.1–2; Dem. 15.26; Isoc. 8.16.

The defeat exposed the weaknesses of the Athenian military and sparked a vigorous debate about Athenian foreign policy and financial administration. According to Isocrates (8.61–81), the lesson to be learned from the debacle in the Social War was that the Athenians should abandon their ambitions to regain a naval empire. In his work *Ways and Means* Xenophon advised the Athenians to give up their dreams of conquest and acquire wealth by encouraging commerce and exploitation of the silver mines at Laurion.[12] Several politicians took practical steps to address the crisis. During the Social War Periander enacted a reform of the trierarchy.[13] Eubulus reorganized the Theoric Fund during this period and used its resources to embark on an ambitious building program (Aes. 3.25).[14] Demosthenes too joined the debate. In an early speech to the Assembly, Demosthenes (14.16–23) proposed to increase the number of contributors in the symmories (the groups organized to raise money for the fleet). In 356 Leptines passed a law to abolish exemptions from liturgies because he thought that these exemptions were responsible for the problems in the administration of the liturgical system. These exemptions had been granted as rewards for public service, but Leptines thought that they reduced the amount of public income.[15] In his *Olynthiacs* delivered in 349/8, Demosthenes (1.19–20, 3.10–13) attacks the habit of taking money from the Military Fund for festivals instead of using it for soldiers' pay and equipment.[16] Andro-

---

[12]For an excellent commentary on Xenophon's *Ways and Means*, see Gauthier 1976.

[13]See Dem. 21.155, with Gabrielsen 1994: 182–199.

[14]There is no reason to believe that the Theoric Fund was created in this period under Eubulus. See *Against Timocrates* 134n.

[15]On Demosthenes' speech *Against Leptines*, see E. M. Harris 2008: 15–74. For an introduction, text, Italian translation and detailed commentary, see Canevaro 2016. For a recent text and commentary in English, see Kremmydas 2012, with the remarks of Trevett 2013. There is no reason to think that Demosthenes was motivated by an elite bias in this speech (*pace* Burke 2002). See Canevaro 2009: 65–66.

[16]There is no evidence that Demosthenes was opposed to Eubulus' policies or hostile to the Theoric Fund. In the *Fourth Philippic*, Demosthenes

tion and Satyrus may have been assigned to collect arrears of the war tax at this time.[17]

Some politicians thought that the measures to recover debts were too harsh and sought to mitigate their provisions. In 353/2 a politician named Timocrates enacted a law about those in debt to the public treasury allowing them to avoid prison if they could provide three credit-worthy sureties. A man named Diodorus attacked the law by bringing a public action for passing an inexpedient law, charging that the statute was contrary to several other laws, and Demosthenes wrote the speech that Diodorus delivered at the trial later that year. The speech reflects the concerns about public finances during this period.

Another major concern of the Athenians was the security of their grain supply from the Black Sea. Because the resources of Attica could not supply all the needs of the population, the Athenians imported grain from the north shore of the Black Sea, Egypt, and Sicily.[18] Leucon, the king of the Cimmerian Bosporus, had granted the Athenians special privileges to facilitate the export of grain from his territory.[19] To ensure that this grain reached the Piraeus, the Athenians had either to maintain friendly relations with the communities along the Dardanelles or to control cities in the area. When the Spartans seized control of the Chersonese in 405 after the battle of Aegospotamoi, they were able to cut off the grain supply to Athens, which helped to bring about the city's surrender the following year. The Spartans also cut off the grain supply in 387/6 during the Corinthian War, an action

---

(10.35–41) defends the fund against criticism, and after the battle of Chaeronea he was elected supervisor of the fund (Aes. 3.24). See E. M. Harris 2006: 120–139.

[17] See Dem. 22.47–58, with E. M. Harris 2008: 186–190.

[18] For Athenian imports from Egypt, see [Dem.] 56.5–8. For imports from Sicily, see Dem. 32.18–20 and [Dem.] 56.9. On the grain trade in general, see Garnsey 1998 and Whitby 1998. The study of the grain trade by Moreno 2007 should be used with caution.

[19] For the privileges granted by Leucon and the honors given to him by the Athenians, see Dem. 20.29–40 with Harris 2008: 30–34; Kremmydas 2012: 241–264; and especially Canevaro 2016: 240–265.

that forced the Athenians to sue for peace.[20] In 362 the Byzantines, Chalcidians, and Chalcedonians forced the ships carrying grain to Athens through the Bosporus to their ports ([Dem.] 50.6), which caused a panic in Athens. The Athenians sent several generals to the area to protect Athenian interests and concluded a series of treaties with Cersebleptes, the king of eastern Thrace, to ensure safe passage of ships carrying grain (see *Against Aristocrates* 167–173). As part of their attempts to secure the Chersonese, the Athenians granted citizenship to the mercenary Charidemus, who commanded the troops of Cersebleptes and was married to the sister of his father Cotys (*Against Aristocrates* 129). When Aristocrates proposed a decree granting special protection to Charidemus, a politician named Euthycles attacked the measure as illegal; Demosthenes wrote the speech for him to deliver in court.

The speeches *Against Aristocrates* (23) and *Against Timocrates* (24) also discuss important aspects of the rule of law and its importance for Athenian democracy. The rule of law was one of the most important Athenian cultural values and has its roots in the Archaic period with the laws of Draco and Solon.[21] There is no reason to think that the Athenians believed in popular sovereignty in the fifth century BCE and in the sovereignty of the law (or the courts) in the fourth century BCE; throughout the Classical period, the Athenians believed that democracy and the rule of law went hand in hand.[22] Widespread throughout the Greek world, the ideal of the rule of law provided the Greeks with some of the core beliefs that shaped their cultural identity.

---

[20]Xen. *Hellenica* 5.1.25–31.

[21]For the rule of law in the legislation of Solon and in the city-states of the Archaic period, see E. M. Harris 2006: 3–28. The evidence in this essay refutes the claim of D. Cohen 1995: 34–57 that the basic features of the rule of law varied from one city-state to another.

[22]For the view that the Athenians believed in popular sovereignty during the fifth century and the sovereignty of law in the fourth century, see Hansen 1974 and Ostwald 1986. For the evidence showing that the Athenians believed in, and attempted to implement, both democracy and the rule of law throughout the Classical period, see E. M. Harris 2016b.

There were several aspects to the rule of law.[23] First, there was the ideal of equality before the law. This meant that no one was above the law and that everyone, citizens and free foreigners, were on the same footing in legal disputes. Second, there was the principle that all officials are accountable to the people and can be tried and punished for violating the law. Third, the rule of law meant that all those put on trial were judged according to consistent principles and not by whim or by ad hoc judgments. Fourth, the law must be accessible to all those who are subject to its provisions. This requirement has two main features: the laws should be easy to find and consult and they should also be easy to understand (see, for instance, Dem. 20.93). Fifth, there can be no punishment without law or without a trial. Sixth, the adjudicative procedures followed by the courts should be fair. This aspect of the rule of law has several features, but prominent among them are the requirements that cases should be judged by impartial judges and that litigants should have the right to present evidence and witnesses to support their claims.

The best evidence for understanding how the judges at Athenian trials approached their task are the terms of the judicial oath, which are mentioned several times in each speech.[24] First, the judges swore to judge according to the laws and decrees of the Athenian people, which meant that in effect they would decide cases according to consistent rules, not on an ad hoc basis. This pledge showed how the Athenian reconciled the ideals of democracy and the rule of law: they instructed their judges to enforce

---

[23]For the basic aspects of the rule of law in the modern world see Bingham 2010. For the basic features of the rule of law in Classical Athens see E. M. Harris 2013a: 4–11 and *passim*.

[24]*Against Aristocrates* 19, 96, 101, 194; *Against Timocrates* 2, 35–36, 58, 78, 90, 148, 151, 175, 188, 191. On the Judicial Oath, see E. M. Harris 2013a: 101–137. The document at *Against Timocrates* 149–150, which purports to give the text of the Judicial Oath is a forgery and its contents are not reliable as evidence. See Canevaro 2013a: 173–180 and *Against Timocrates* 149nn and 150nn. There is no reason to believe that the Athenians viewed litigation as a form of feuding. See E. M. Harris 2013a: 60–98.

rules enacted by the Athenian people who had right to vote on all public matters through democratic institutions. Second, the judges swore to vote in accordance with their most just judgment, which meant in general that they would vote honestly and not swayed by either personal favor or enmity (see *Against Aristocrates* 97).[25] Third, the judges pledged to listen to both sides equally. Fourth, the judges swore to cast their votes only about the charges made in the plaint brought by the accuser.[26] The plaint submitted by the accuser to the relevant official had to state what laws the defendant had violated and how the defendant had violated them. This meant that the judges could vote only about the issue: did the defendant violate the law or not? As a result, the judges did not take public service into account when making their decisions unless it was somehow relevant to the charges in the indictment.[27]

Some scholars think that the Athenians could not have implemented the rule of law because the citizens who decided cases in the court were "amateur."[28] For this reason the Greek term *dikastes* is sometimes mistranslated with the English term "juror."[29] It would be a serious mistake to consider Athenian judges "ama-

---

[25] This part of the oath may have included a clause instructing the judges to vote according to their most just judgment in cases "where there are no laws." This clause however was hardly ever invoked. Above all, it did not grant the judges the right to ignore the laws if they wished. See E. M. Harris 2013a: 110–114. Lanni 2006: 72 misrepresents this part of the oath and further claims that this clause occurs "in most (. . .) citations of the oath." This is very far from the truth: for the actual evidence, see E. M. Harris 2013a: 353–357.

[26] On this part of the Judicial Oath, see E. M. Harris 2013a: 114–136. There is no reason to believe that the courts for homicide had a different standard of relevance than the other courts (*pace* Lanni 2006: 75–114). See E. M. Harris 2009/2010: 325–328.

[27] For a list of all mentions of public service in the preserved forensic speeches of the Attic Orators and their relevance, see E. M. Harris 2013a: 387–399.

[28] For this view, see Gagarin's Series Introduction. This paragraph draws on my comments in E. M. Harris, Leão, and Rhodes 2010: 1–2.

[29] Most of the authors of volumes in this series translate the term in this way, with the exception of the speeches I have translated.

teurs" for several reasons. Each year 6,000 Athenian citizens were selected to judge cases in court and swore the judicial oath. In the fourth century there were probably around 30,000 citizens and roughly 20,000 or more qualified to judge cases; this means that the average Athenian over the age of thirty spent one year in every three or four hearing legal cases. When an Athenian was selected to judge cases, he did not hear one or two cases, but dozens each year. It has been estimated that the courts held trials between 175 and 225 days a year, and anywhere between 1,500 and 2,000 men might be needed to hear cases on any given day. If a citizen were assigned to a public case, he would hear only one case, but were he assigned to private cases, he would hear up to four. This would mean that the average citizen sitting in the courts would hear around 125 cases in a year. This made the Athenian *dikastes* very different from modern jurors, who may hear only two or three cases in an entire lifetime. Even though the average citizen serving in the courts received no formal training, he would have acquired an extensive legal education from hearing dozens of cases a year. It should come as no surprise that the litigant Nicobulus speaking in court assumed that the judges knew about the relevant law about releases without his telling them about it (Dem. 37.18). The average citizen would also learn about laws and decrees from serving in the Council and from attending meetings of the Assembly where legislation was discussed and approved.

The speeches *Against Aristocrates* and *Against Timocrates* show how the Athenians incorporated these features of the rule of law into their legal procedures. One of the main charges against the law of Aristocrates is that it deprives the person who might kill Charidemus of the right to a trial (see *Against Aristocrates* 22–27) and is not consistent with several other laws. The law also removes the protections afforded those who have been convicted of murder and go into exile (37–43). In *Against Timocrates* the accuser Diodorus states that the rule of law is central to Athenian power and prosperity and that Timocrates' law seriously threatens the legal system (5). One of the crimes Timocrates has committed is his failure to make a text of his law available to all Athenians before they voted about it (18, 25). If his law is allowed to remain in force, it will threaten the consistency of the laws and lead to contradictory statutes (32, 34–38). Diodorus claims that Timocrates has enacted *ex post facto* legislation in violation of Athenian legal principles (59, 72–74).

## THE DOCUMENTS IN *AGAINST ARISTOCRATES* (23) AND *AGAINST TIMOCRATES* (24)

In the forensic speeches of the Attic orators, there are many passages in which the litigant discusses a law, a decree, the statement of a witness, or some other document and then asks the secretary to read the document to the court. In many cases, the manuscript has only the word *nomos*, *psephisma*, or *martyria* at the point where the document was read aloud. But in some cases, however, there is a text inserted into the speech, which appears to contain the contents of the document that the litigant is discussing. There are several found in Andocides' *On the Mysteries*, in Aeschines' *Against Timarchus*, and in many speeches in the Demosthenic corpus—in particular, *On the Crown*, *Against Meidias*, *Against Aristocrates*, *Against Timocrates*, *Against Lacritus*, *Against Macartetus*, and the two speeches *Against Stephanus* and *Against Neaira*. There are shorter quotations from documents found in *Against Leptines*, *Against Pantaenetus*, and *Against Dionysodorus*. There are also short documents in three speeches of other orators.

There was much debate about the authenticity of these documents among German scholars in the nineteenth century, but this debate ended for the most part with the publication of Engelbert Drerup's study of the documents published in 1898, which came to the conclusion that although some were not authentic, most were.[30] This view for the most part prevailed in the twentieth century and was followed by scholars of Athenian law such as A. R. W. Harrison, D. M. MacDowell, M. H. Hansen, P. J. Rhodes, M. Gagarin, and D. Phillips.[31] Recent studies of many of

---

[30] Drerup 1898.

[31] For instance, Phillips 2013 appears not to know Drerup's work and includes many documents shown to be forgeries such as And. 1.83–84 (Phillips [2013] 66), And. 1.96–98 (Phillips [2013] 479–480), Dem. 21.8 and 10 (Phil-

these documents by M. Canevaro and myself have demonstrated that many of these documents are forgeries and do not contain reliable information about Athenian law and legal procedure.[32]

When studying these documents it is important to pay close attention to the evidence provided by the stichometry.[33] Stichometry is a system of measurement of texts used in antiquity. It consisted of alphabetic marks, *A B Γ Δ* etc., added in the margin of a papyrus typically every one-hundred lines of text (partial stichometry), and a final count of lines written at the end in Attic acrophonic numerals (total stichometry). These numbers were then uncritically transcribed from copy to copy of the speeches next to the same passages of the texts, without any regard for the length of the lines of each new copy. We have stichometric numbers extant for many Demosthenic speeches (which contain the vast majority of extant documents) in some medieval manuscripts. The stichometric marks were written in a very early copy of the corpus, perhaps the first, and, as Canevaro has shown elsewhere, this edition should be dated to the end of the fourth century BCE or to the beginning of the third, and placed in Athens. If one measures the number of characters per 100 lines of a stichometric section, the sections are remarkably consistent in length both within the same speech and within different speeches

---

lips [2013] 417–418), Dem. 21.47 (Phillips [2013] 92), Dem. 24.103–105 (Phillips [2013] 356).

[32]On these documents, see in general Canevaro and Harris 2012, Canevaro 2013a; and E. M. Harris 2013/2014, which provides a detailed refutation of Sommerstein 2014 and additional arguments, which show that the case against the authenticity of the document at And. 1.96–98 is overwhelming. The studies of some documents by Scafuro are not reliable and should be used with much caution. On Scafuro 2004, see E. M. Harris in Canevaro 2013a: 211–223; on Scafuro 2005, see Canevaro 2013a: 157–173. Canevaro and I plan to publish a detailed refutation of Scafuro 2006 in the near future. The attempt of Hansen 2015 and 2016a to defend the authenticity of the documents in And. *On the Mysteries* is not convincing. See Canevaro and Harris forthcoming.

[33]For a discussion of stichometry in the Demosthenic corpus, see Canevaro 2013a: 10–27, with references to earlier scholarship.

of the same category. The measurements are consistent among sections that do not contain documents and with sections that do contain documents, if we take the documents out of the calculation. On the other hand, if we include them, the results are widely inconsistent, which indicates that they were inserted at a later date. What careful analysis of the documents in the public speeches of the Demosthenic corpus has revealed so far is that the documents that lie outside the stichometry contain both mistakes about Athenian law and legal procedure and language and formulas that are not consistent with those found in contemporary inscriptions, whereas those that lie within the stichometry tend to deviate less from contemporary evidence, though are not completely free from errors. Several of the documents in *Against Aristocrates* lie within the stichometry and appear to contain reliable information. By contrast, the majority of the documents in *Against Timocrates* lie outside the stichometry and are forgeries composed in either the Hellenistic or Roman periods (see 20–23nn, 33nn, 54nn, 59nn, 71nn, 105nn, 149–151nn; for discussion of the document at 45, see the notes), though some that are within the stichometry appear to contain reliable information (see 39nn, 42nn, 50nn, 63nn).

The translations in this volume follow the Oxford Classical Text of Dilts, except where indicated.

# 23. AGAINST ARISTOCRATES

## INTRODUCTION

Demosthenes wrote the speech *Against Aristocrates* for a public prosecution against an illegal decree (*graphē paranomōn*). According to the ancient hypothesis of the speech, a man named Euthycles, who is otherwise unknown, brought the charge and delivered the speech in court.[1] Aristocrates had proposed a decree granting special protection for the general Charidemus, whose career is discussed at length in the speech (144–211).[2] Because Euthycles is attempting to prove that Charidemus does not deserve the honors that Aristocrates has proposed, he is clearly a biased source, and one should be skeptical about much of the information he provides about Charidemus' career.[3] Even though Euthycles delivered the speech, many of the views and arguments are similar to those found in speeches that Demosthenes wrote for himself for delivery in the Assembly and the courts.[4] For in-

---

[1] For Euthycles as the prosecutor, see Dionysius of Halicarnassus *Ad Ammaeum* 1.4; *hypothesis* I.2; II.2. Plutarch (*Dem.* 15.2) says that the speech was written for someone else, but he does not give the name. Sealey 1993: 131 argues that Demosthenes himself must have delivered the speech, but see MacDowell 2009: 196, note 111. Dover 1968b: 161–163 thought that the speech was written by two different authors, but see Usher 1976.

[2] On the career of Charidemus, see Parke 1933: 125–32; Davies 1971: 571–574; Pritchett 1974–1991: 2.85–89; Bianco 2014.

[3] For the method of evaluating statements found in forensic oratory, see E. M. Harris 1995: 9–16.

[4] See Papillon 1998: 91–104. Note that Demosthenes used sections 207–210 in his *Third Olynthiac* (3.26–31) and 196–200 for *On Organization*

stance, the criticism of the use of mercenaries is similar to an argument in the *First Philippic* (Dem. 4.19–27). Demosthenes also did not oppose (and may have actually supported) the exclusion of Cersebleptes from the Peace of Philocrates, which contributed to his defeat by Philip of Macedon in 346.[5]

Charidemus was born probably in the early 390s in the city of Oreus on the island of Euboea (213).[6] Charidemus started his career as a light-armed soldier; Euthycles' charge that he fought against the Athenians and raided the territory of their allies early in his career is hard to evaluate because too little is known about politics on Euboea at the time.[7] From 368 to 365 Charidemus was hired by the Athenian general Iphicrates, who had been sent to recapture the former Athenian colony of Amphipolis in northern Greece (149). According to Euthycles, Charidemus received some hostages from Amphipolis from Harpalus and released them despite orders that they be sent to Athens, but Euthycles is probably distorting events (see 149n). Charidemus served briefly under Timotheus, who took over command in Northern Greece after Iphicrates was recalled. Charidemus then joined Cotys, the king of Thrace, before returning to the Chalcidice to serve under the Olynthians, who were fighting against the Athenians. After being captured by Timotheus, he switched his allegiance once again and fought for the Athenians (150, 152). Euthycles puts these moves in the worst possible light, and one must bear in mind that Charidemus was a mercenary at the time and owed his loyalty to the people who paid him. At some point he offered to help the Athenians take the Chersonese, but the negotiations do not appear to have gone anywhere (153).

Charidemus left Timotheus' service around 360, hired himself to Mentor and Memnon, the brothers-in-law of Artabazus, who

---

(13.21–24), though some scholars have doubted the authenticity of the latter speech.

[5] See Aes. 2.81–93, with E. M. Harris 1995: 74–76.

[6] See also [Arist.] *Oeconomica* 1351b; Aelian *Varia Historia* 2.41; Athenaeus 10.436b. For Euthycles' allegations about his father, see 213n. For the year of his birth, see Davies 1971: 571–572.

[7] For discussion, see Bianco 2014: 9–10.

had been the Persian satrap of Hellespontine Phrygia, and seized the cities of Scepsis, Cebren, and Ilium (154). Euthycles claims that Charidemus then abandoned these cities because Artabazus was about to attack, but Artabazus was persuaded to allow Charidemus to depart under a truce (156–157). He then took up service again with Cotys, who was at war with Athens, and laid siege to Crithote and Elaeus in the Chersonese (158–159). Charidemus appears to have married a sister of Cotys in this period (129).[8] Cotys was assassinated around 360, and Cersebleptes, Amadocus, and Berisades fought each other to gain his kingdom (8–9).[9] Charidemus threw his lot with Cersebleptes, who was very young at the time (11, 163). Athenodorus, a mercenary supporting Berisades, compelled Cersebleptes to conclude a treaty by which the kingdom was divided among the brothers (170). Cersebleptes received the eastern part of the kingdom, Amadocus received the central part of the kingdom, and Berisades received the western part of the kingdom.

Cersebleptes' kingdom posed a potential threat to Athenian interests because it lay close to the Thracian Chersonese and the Hellespont (110), which controlled the route to the Black Sea and the Bosporan kingdom from which the Athenians imported large amounts of grain (see Dem. 20.31).[10] According to Euthycles, Charidemus attacked the Chersonese and the Athenians who had settled there (167). The Athenian general Cephisodotus came to an agreement with Charidemus, which the Athenians considered against their interests (167–169, 175). Chabrias relieved Cephisodotus and negotiated another treaty with Cersebleptes, but the Athenians also found this treaty unsatisfactory (172, 176–177). In 357 Chares was sent to the Chersonese and was able with the help of Charidemus to conclude a treaty with the Thracian kings that the Athenians considered satisfactory (173). Fragments of this

---

[8] For the date, see Davies 1971: 571.

[9] One finds the spelling "Cersobleptes" in literary texts and the spelling "Cersebleptes" in inscriptions (e.g., *IG* ii² 126, lines 10, 20).

[10] The extent of the contribution made by imports from the Black Sea regions to Athens is the subject of debate. See Garnsey 1988: 144–210; Whitby 1998; and Moreno 2007: 89–164.

treaty have been preserved; its terms provided that the Greek cities along the coast of the northeastern Aegean were to remain free and autonomous as long as they paid tribute to the kings and to Athens. The kings pledged that if any of the cities were to revolt from Athens, they would support the Athenians.[11] Around this time, it appears that Charidemus was given Athenian citizenship (23, 65, 89) as a favor to Cersebleptes (141, 203).[12] After this Charidemus used Cardia as his base in the Chersonese (182).

Charidemus was elected general at Athens for the year 353/2, and Aristocrates proposed a decree granting him certain protections, among which was a clause making anyone who killed Charidemus subject to arrest (*agōgimos*). Euthycles brought a public action against Aristocrates for proposing an illegal decree before the Assembly ratified the decree, and the case came to trial in 352/1.[13]

The public action against illegal decrees could be brought by any Athenian citizen against a decree (*psēphisma*) that violated a written law (*nomos*). Laws were provisions that applied to all people or to broad categories of people and were permanently valid (Arist. *Nicomachean Ethics* 1137b13–14, 27–29; [Plato] *Definitions* 415b). In fact, after 403 it was illegal at Athens to pass a law directed at a single individual.[14] By contrast, a decree was concerned with some specific issue or individual. A law might make it illegal for magistrates to receive gifts; a decree might grant honors to a particular person or conclude an alliance with another

---

[11] *IG* ii² 126; Rhodes and Osborne 2003, no. 47 (Greek text and English translation).

[12] See Parke 1928 and Davies 1971: 571.

[13] Papillon 1998: 11, note 41, places the speech in the late summer of 352 because Philip's presence at Hieron Teichos, which he dates to the autumn of 352 (Dem. 3.4), is not mentioned in the speech, which therefore must have been delivered before that time. But see Jaeger 1938: 235–236, who argues that the speech could have been delivered in late 352 or early 351. Lane Fox 1997: 183–186, followed by Roisman 2006: 165–167, attempts to date the speech to 353/2, but his arguments are not convincing. See 9n, 103n, 121n, 124n.

[14] See 86 and the note there and *Against Timocrates* 59.

community. Before 403 the Assembly passed both laws and decrees by a simple majority vote, but after 403 the Athenians created a separate and more elaborate procedure to pass laws. Proposals for laws were still made in the Assembly, but they now required final approval by a board of *nomothetai* (see the introduction to *Against Timocrates*). The *graphē paranomōn* was created to ensure that laws took precedence over decrees of the Assembly and that all decrees conformed to the basic provisions of the laws (Dem. 20.86).

One could bring a *graphē paranomōn* against a proposed decree either before (Xen. *Hellenica* 1.7.12–14) or after the Assembly voted to ratify it (Dem. 22.9–10). If the action was brought after ratification, the decree was held in abeyance until the court made its decision. If the proposer was convicted, the decree was annulled (Lyc. *Against Leocrates* 7); if he was acquitted, the decree went into effect immediately (Dem. 18.103). In this case, however, Euthycles brought his action against Aristocrates before the Assembly voted on his proposal (14, 16, 18, 92, 186). If Aristocrates had been convicted in court, his proposal would have been dropped and never come to a vote. It is uncertain what happened when a *graphē paranomōn* was brought against a motion not yet passed by the Assembly and the proposer was acquitted during the subsequent trial. It has been suggested that in this case the motion went into effect without being sent back to the Assembly for ratification. Although the sources do not provide a clear answer to this question, it is unlikely that a proposal could become a decree of the people without receiving the approval of the Assembly, since all extant decrees begin either with the phrase "the People has decided" or "the Council and the People have decided."[15]

The action was an *agōn timētos*, which meant that after a defendant was convicted, both the prosecutor and the defendant proposed a penalty and the court chose which one to impose (Aes. 3.210). The penalties could range from a small fine to permanent exile or execution (Dem. 22.1, 4, 7; 23.62), but there is no known case where the defendant was put to death. Two men Sciton and

---

[15] *Pace* Hansen 1987.

Smikros are said to have been fined ten talents each for convictions on this charge (Dem. 21.182; cf. Dem. 58.1, 31, 32, 70). If the infraction was minor, the fine might be as small as twenty-five drachmas (Hyp. 3.18). Someone who was convicted three times on this charge suffered a form of disenfranchisement and lost his right to propose measures in the Assembly (Diodorus 18.18).

One could bring a *graphē paranomōn* on various grounds both procedural and substantive. Euctemon indicted Androtion for his proposal to award honors to the Council for three reasons: first, the proposal had not received prior approval from the Council; second, it violated the law that forbade honors for the Council when a certain number of triremes had not been built; and third, Androtion was barred from making proposals, since he had been a prostitute (Dem. 22.5–7, 8–20, 29–32).[16]

There is some controversy about the constitutional significance of the *graphē paranomōn*. The orators who discuss the nature of the action describe it as a means of enforcing the laws and also as a way of preventing the Assembly from making rash and hasty judgments under the influence of unscrupulous demagogues. This power to overrule the decisions of the Assembly might appear to indicate that the courts were in principle superior to the Assembly and thus were the sovereign body in the Athenian constitution. As a result, they exercised not only the judicial function of enforcing the laws but also a political function of serving as a check on the excesses of demagogues in the Assembly.

Several of the arguments presented by prosecutors in *graphē*

---

[16]de Brauw 2001–2002 claims that litigants in court cite laws primarily to demonstrate their law-abiding character, but this is not convincing. In *graphē paranomōn* speeches such as *Against Aristocrates* and in speeches against inexpedient laws such as *Against Timocrates*, the litigants cite laws to show that a decree or a law violates one or more laws. The claim of Lanni 2009 that the main aim of the *graphē paranomōn* was to protect democratic deliberation is not convincing. In cases such as *Against Aristocrates*, the aim is clearly to protect the rights of individuals to a trial and to protect the community's monopoly of legitimate force. In the *graphē paranomōn* brought by Aeschines against Ctesiphon, one of the main aims was to protect the accountability of officials. See Aes. 3.9–31.

*paranomōn* cases would appear to support this view of the courts' role: orators sometimes claim that the decree being attacked not only violates the laws but also is detrimental to the interests of the community. Prosecutors might thus inject political considerations into their arguments, and several modern scholars think that these points carried a great deal of weight in the court's decision.[17] In general, however, the courts appear to have judged cases involving illegal decrees primarily on legal grounds. In fact, Euthycles recalls how a defendant in a recent case admitted that he was guilty of proposing an illegal decree but argued that his proposal was made to advance Athenian interests (100). Euthycles rightly calls this argument "shameless" and observes that it was against Athenian interests for the judges to confirm an unjust proposal when they had sworn to vote in accordance with the laws (101).

When litigants in court mention verdicts in *graphē paranomōn* cases, they always state that the defendant was convicted because his proposal was illegal or that the defendant was acquitted because his proposal was not illegal (see, for example, *Against Timocrates* 14).[18] For instance, Archinus brought a *graphē paranomōn* against Thrasybulus for a decree that would have granted citizenship to all those who helped to restore the democracy in 403 BCE. One source reports that the decree had not received preliminary approval from the Council, which was legally necessary for all decrees (Plutarch *Moralia* 835f–836a); another reports that the decree would have granted citizenship to several men who were slaves (*Ath. Pol.* 40.2). When Philocrates in 346 proposed that the Athenians elect ten ambassadors to negotiate with King Philip about peace, a certain Lycinus brought a *graphē paranomōn* against him, probably for political reasons. Philocrates was acquitted by a large margin because there was nothing illegal about a decree to send ambassadors, which was one of the recognized powers of the Assembly (Aes. 2.13–15; 3.62).

---

[17]See, for instance, Yunis 1988. A similar view is found in Lanni 2009.

[18]On the reasons for verdicts reported by litigants, see E. M. Harris forthcoming a.

Because judges in these cases tended to focus primarily on legal issues, the courts were generally reluctant to overturn a decree and convict a proposer. Aeschines (3.194) reports that the politician Aristophon boasted that he was indicted seventy-five times on the charge of proposing illegal decrees, yet never once convicted. He also claims that Cephalus, who moved more proposals than any other politician, was never once indicted on this charge. Hyperides claims that Diondas brought fifty charges of passing illegal decrees and did not win one conviction.[19] The most political decrees were those granting honors to generals and politicians for their services to the community. In these decrees the Assembly in effect voted to endorse the policies of the political leaders who received honors. Not surprisingly, rival politicians often brought a *graphē paranomōn* against these decrees as a way of attacking the reputation of the leaders they honored. For instance, honorary decrees for the politicians Chabrias (Dem. 20.146), Timotheus (Aes. 3.243), and Iphicrates (Dem. 23.130, 136) were all challenged in this way. Yet the courts tended to have respected the judgment of the Assembly in these cases for they rarely voted to invalidate a decree of honors unless they had a good legal reason for doing so. In only two known cases did the courts vote to overturn a decree of honors, and in each case the decree contained technical violations of the law (Dem. 58.1, 30–34, 70; Athenaeus 251b).

Euthycles brought a *graphē paranomōn* against Aristocrates' proposal on several grounds. His main charge was that Aristocrates' decree deprived the person who might kill Charidemus of the right to a trial. Euthycles interprets the word *agōgimos* ("subject to arrest" or "subject to extradition") in Aristocrates' decree to mean that anyone could seize the person who killed Charidemus and do with him whatever he wished, including murder (15–17, 28). As several scholars have noted, this interpretation is highly questionable; all this clause meant was that if someone killed Charidemus, he could be arrested anywhere in order to be sent to Athens for trial.[20] In fact, Euthycles states that Aristocrates would cite many

[19] See Horváth 2014: 79.
[20] See Gernet in Gernet and Humbert (1959) 99–103; Lonis 1988b; MacDowell 2009: 199–202.

decrees containing a similar clause voted by the Assembly (95), which would indicate that this kind of clause was not normally regarded as illegal.

Relying on this questionable interpretation, Euthycles argues that Aristocrates' proposal violates several Athenian laws about homicide that involved granting a trial to all those accused of crimes.[21] First, it violates the law providing that all those accused of deliberate homicide be tried by the Areopagus (22–27). Second, it violates the law forbidding anyone to maim or demand ransom from someone accused of murder (28–36). Third, it contravenes the law protecting from deadly violence those convicted of murder who have gone into exile (37–43). Fourth, it violates the law protecting from enslavement or seizure of their property murderers who have gone into exile (44–50). Fifth, it contravenes that law protecting from prosecution for homicide those who report murderers who have returned to Attica (51–52). Sixth, it violates the law absolving from guilt those who kill during athletic contests against their will or during war in ignorance or who kill those caught having sex with their wives, daughters, sisters, mothers, or concubines (53–58). Seventh, it contravenes the law absolving from guilt those who kill someone taking their property against their will (60–61). Eighth, Euthycles claims that Aristocrates and his family should be disenfranchised for attempting to overturn the laws about homicide (62). Ninth, Euthycles claims that Aris-

---

[21] Sections 22–81 of the speech are one of the richest sources for Athenian homicide law and are drawn on extensively by MacDowell 1963, which despite its errors remains the most reliable work on the subject. For analysis of the errors in this work see Tulin 1996 (on the right to prosecute homicide), E. M. Harris 2006: 391–404 (on *bouleusis* of homicide) and Harris 2015a (on the role of pollution in procedure for homicide). The works of Carawan 1998 and Phillips 2008 should be used with caution. The inscription *IG* i[3] 104 contains a republication of Draco's homicide law made in 410/9 but is very fragmentary. Köhler 1867 (followed by Stroud 1968) restored many of the gaps in the text with phrases drawn from the document found at Dem. 43.57–58, but this document is a forgery, and the information contained in it is not reliable. Mirko Canevaro, Robert Pitt, and I are preparing a new, more reliable text of the inscription.

tocrates is attempting to abolish the powers of all the courts with jurisdiction over cases of homicide (65–81). Finally, Euthycles argues that Aristocrates' decree violates the law prohibiting laws directed at an individual (86) and the law stating that no decree should take precedence over a law (87).

Euthycles states that even if the decree were illegal but somehow in Athenian interests, the court should vote against the decree (95–101), yet he still devotes a large part of his speech to showing that the decree is not in Athenian interests and that Charidemus does not merit special treatment (102–203). Euthycles argues that it is not in Athenian interests to allow Cersebleptes to grow too powerful (111–116). He recalls how several foreign leaders whom Athens honored later turned against them (118–125). The Athenians should not allow Charidemus to become so powerful that he can harm Athenian interests (126–134) and should be suspicious of his patron Cersebleptes (135–137). To show that Charidemus does not deserve special honors, Euthycles reminds them that Charidemus is a mercenary like Philiscus, who was also untrustworthy (141–143) and reviews his entire career, which demonstrates that he often acted against Athenian interests (144–190). These facts justify a cautious attitude toward Cersebleptes and Charidemus (191–194).

The final part of the speech starts with criticism of the new Athenian tendency to grant lavish honors to individuals and reminds the court how their ancestors did not reward successful leaders in the same way (196–204) and punished harshly those who broke the law and were disloyal (204–206). In the good old days, leaders did not profit from public office; now politicians profit at the expense of the Treasury (207–210). The Athenians should be more like their neighbors Aegina and Megara, communities that do not grant citizenship so easily to foreigners (211–214). At the very end, Euthycles summarizes his legal arguments against Aristocrates' decree (215–220), which clearly indicates that he expected the judges to vote about the legality of the decree and not to take political considerations into account.

We do not know the outcome of the case, but Euthycles' dire warnings about Charidemus' dubious loyalty did not turn out to be accurate; the general was a trustworthy citizen until Alex-

ander demanded his exile.[22] In 351/0 Charidemus was sent with
ten ships and five talents to Thrace to counter Philip's presence
there (Dem. 3.5). In 349/8 he was sent with eighteen triremes, four
thousand peltasts (light infantry), and one hundred and fifty cavalry to defend Olynthus against Philip's attacks (Dionysius of
Halicarnassus *Letter to Ammaeus* 1.4; Athenaeus 10.436b-c). Although he was not successful in preventing the fall of Olynthus,
the Athenians do not appear to have held him responsible for the
defeat because he was not prosecuted. He was later given a crown
for donating shields to the state (Dem. 18.114); the inventories of
the treasurers of Athena record three other crowns awarded to
him (*IG* ii² 1496, lines 28, 32, and 36). He also served as trierarch
several times (*IG* ii² 1624, line 321; 1627, lines 207, 217). After the
rout of the Greek army at Chaeronea, certain politicians wanted
to elect Charidemus general and give him extensive powers, but
Phocion was given the command, presumably because the Athenians thought that Charidemus would be viewed as too hostile
to Macedonia (Plut. *Phocion* 16.3). The Athenians trusted him
enough to send him abroad on a mission shortly afterwards (Aes.
3.77). Alexander obviously considered Charidemus such a dangerous patriot that he demanded that the Athenians surrender him
along with several other anti-Macedonian politicians after the fall
of Thebes in 335 (Plut. *Phocion* 18.2–4 and *Demosthenes* 23; Arrian
*Anabasis* 1.10.4–6). Phocion and other ambassadors were able to
convince Alexander to relent, but the king still demanded that
Charidemus be sent into exile. He therefore left Athens for the
court of the Persian King, where he was first honored, then later
put to death on suspicion of treason (Diodorus 17.30.2–4; Quin-
tus Curtius 3.2.10).[23]

The speech was highly regarded in antiquity. Dionysius of
Halicarnassus (*De compositione verborum* 25.3) considered it one of

---

[22]Cf. Pritchett 1974–1991: 2.89: "The epigraphical record, his frequent
election to the generalship, and the patriotic close to his Athenian career, go
a long way to discount the orators' allegation that Charidemos was permanently disloyal towards Athens."

[23]Diodorus (17.30.2) says that Charidemus had served on campaigns
with Philip, but this is clearly a mistake.

Demosthenes' best speeches. A rhetorical treatise called the "Aristides Rhetoric" praised the speech for combining all three types of oratory:

> Accordingly, although there are three genres of oratory and the circumstances determine the form in these genres, I assert that all three genres, which one must include and mix together, fall into the same space; for example, the speech of Demosthenes <about> granting protection to Charidemus shares in the three genres. For the part dealing with illegality immediately at the outset is judicial, criticizing Aristocrates for speaking in violation of the law; but further on, the part about advantage has a certain deliberative stance, for example, that the Athenians must not allow Charidemus to become stronger; the third part in this is appropriate for an encomiastic style: abuse of Charidemus. The judicial nature unites all these in one place, and there results a blending and mixture of them, yet the one part is not the same as the other part, but insofar as the situation requires, each section differs. Yet the genres do not split apart from each other; as a result, the whole is one unified speech, although not stating the same thing in each part.[24]

## 23. AGAINST ARISTOCRATES

[1] None of you, men of Athens, should think that I come to accuse Aristocrates because of private enmity or that I am eager to incur his hostility because I saw him committing some minor or trivial offense.[25] On the contrary, if my reasoning and thoughts

---

[24]For the Greek text of the passage and a translation, which I have modified slightly here, see Papillon 1998: 17–18.

[25]Although some accusers in public actions admit that the defendant is a personal enemy (for example, Aes. 1.1; Dem. 24.7), the Athenians did not look favorably on cases brought only to take personal vengeance (see 190n), and most public cases were not brought for this reason (Rubinstein 2000: 179–180). Allen 2000 claims that Lycurgus was unusual for claiming that he brought his charge against Leocrates in 331 as a public duty and not for personal reasons, but passages like this one show that Lycurgus was drawing on

are correct, my overriding aim in this case is for you to retain secure possession of the Chersonese and not to lose it again by being deceived. [2] If you wish to gain a correct understanding of this case and to judge the charge justly in accordance with the laws, you must all not only pay attention to the words written in the decree but also consider their consequences.[26] If you could perceive the crimes committed the minute you heard the decree, you might not perhaps be misled in the first place. [3] But there is one type of crime committed by some that consists in proposing and writing decrees in such a way that you hardly suspect anything and let down your guard. You should not therefore be surprised if we show that the decree has been written so that ostensibly it grants physical protection to Charidemus, but in reality it deprives the city of its rightful and secure protection of the Chersonese. [4] You would be justified, men of Athens, in paying attention to me and to listening favorably to what I say.[27] I am not one of those people who pester you, nor am I one of those politicians who enjoy your confidence.[28] Because I promise to demonstrate how serious their crimes are, if you show me as much

---

traditional ideas (cf. Dem. 20.1). There were several laws discouraging litigants from using the courts to pursue feuds. See E. M. Harris 2006: 405–422; E. M. Harris 2013a: 72–76. On motivation in lawsuits, see Kurihara 2003. To justify his prosecution, therefore, Euthycles states that he brought his charge against Aristocrates for harming the public interest, not out of personal hostility.

[26]Euthycles reminds the judges of their oath, which bound them to follow the laws when reaching their verdict, to judge only the charge in the indictment and to ignore irrelevant issues. On the judicial oath, see E. M. Harris 2013a: 101–137. Note that Euthycles equates a just vote with one according to the laws, which shows that the court considered law and justice one identical standard, not two distinct standards (*pace* Christ 1998: 195). Euthycles stresses the consequences of the decree as a way of impressing on the judges the importance of their task.

[27]Euthycles reminds the judges of their oath to listen to both sides impartially.

[28]Euthycles attempts to gain the judges' goodwill by claiming that he is not a politician. For suspicion of politicians, cf. Dem. 21.189. Statements like this make it unlikely that Demosthenes delivered the speech.

support as you can and are ready to hear me, you will save the situation and avoid discouraging those of us who think they can help the city in some way.²⁹ This will be their attitude if they do not find it difficult to get you to listen to them. [5] As it is now, many men are afraid to address you; they may not be not talented speakers, but they are still better men than those who are. The thought of public service does not even occur to them. Speaking for myself—I swear by all the gods—I would have hesitated, as you well know, to bring this indictment by myself if I did not consider it quite shameful now to keep quiet and remain silent when I saw certain men plotting to harm the city and earlier when I sailed as trierarch to the Hellespont to denounce and accuse men who I thought were doing you wrong.³⁰

[6] I am not unaware that some people consider Charidemus the city's benefactor. If I can tell you what I wish and what I know he has done, I believe that I will show not only that he is no benefactor but also that he is our greatest enemy in the world and that his aims are the very opposite of what they should be. [7] If then, men of Athens, the greatest crime Aristocrates had committed were to show so much concern in his decree for such a man as I promise to show Charidemus to be that he has granted him a special and illegal form of punishment if anything happens to him,³¹ I would try to tell you this right now so that you would know that he is far from deserving to obtain the benefits of this decree. But in fact there is another still greater injustice contained in this decree; you should learn about this first and be on your guard.

[8] First of all, it is necessary to tell you and to show what is responsible for your secure control of the Chersonese.³² By under-

---

²⁹Because Athens relied mostly on volunteer accusers, Euthycles argues that it is important not to discourage them from bringing charges.

³⁰Euthycles may have sailed as trierarch during the campaign mentioned at 165.

³¹This is a euphemism for "if he should die." Cf. Dem. 20.159.

³²Sections 8–17 form a kind of narration. The aim of this part of the speech is to discuss Aristocrates' motive for proposing his decree. (Cf. the similar use of the narrative in *Against Timocrates* 11–16 and Papillon 1998: 27: "The relevant items are not just the legality of the decree, but the mo-

standing this, you will clearly see their crime. This, then, men of Athens, was the situation after the death of Cotys: there were three kings of Thrace instead of one—Berisades, Amadocus, and Cersebleptes.[33] As a result, they fell out with each other and courted you and tried to win your favor. [9] Well, now, men of Athens, some people wished to put an end to this rivalry, to dethrone the other kings, and to hand over the entire kingdom to one man, Cersebleptes. They worked together to have passed a preliminary motion, which avoids the appearance of accomplishing anything like this, but in reality achieves this result above all, as I will demonstrate.[34] [10] After one of the kings, Berisades, died, Cersebleptes violated his oaths and the agreement that he concluded with you and started to attack Berisades' sons and Amadocus.[35] It was obvious that Athenodorus was going to support the sons of Berisades, and Simon and Bianor were going to support Amadocus. Athenodorus was the son-in-law of Berisades; Simon and Bianor, the sons-in-law of Amadocus. [11] They therefore looked for a way to force them to remain at peace while Charidemus, acting on behalf of Cersebleptes, would deprive them of support and gain safe control of the entire kingdom for him.

---

tivations of it behind the scene.") The analysis of the motive allows Euthycles to introduce his discussion of Thracian affairs both here and later in the speech.

[33] The Thracian king Cotys died in 360/59. See Badian 1983: 54. Berisades inherited the western part of the kingdom, which stretched from the river Nestus to the river Hebrus; Amadocus, the central part of the kingdom, which stretched from the river Hebrus to Maroneia; and Cersebleptes, the eastern part of the kingdom, which stretched from Maroneia to the shores of the Black Sea. Euthycles goes into greater detail about these events later in the speech (170–180). For the history of Thrace in this period, see Archibald 1998.

[34] Lane Fox 1997: 183–184 mistakenly believes that this passage places the proposal to grant privileges to Charidemus to 356 and belongs to an earlier draft of the speech, but as the following passage makes clear, it belongs several years later.

[35] Berisades appears to have died in early 356 because his son Cetriporis was on the throne by the summer of 356. See *IG* ii² 127, lines 2, 9 (restored), 11, 15 (partially restored), 39–47.

(. . .) if their first step would be to pass a decree in your Assembly to make anyone who killed him subject to arrest, the second to get you to elect him general.[36] [12] Neither Simon nor Bianor was eager to take up arms against your general.[37] They had become citizens and were otherwise looking out for your interests. Nor was Athenodorus, who was a citizen by birth, ready even to plot against you.[38] Nor by this decree would the escape the blame that would clearly attach to them if something were to happen to Charidemus. Once these were deprived of allies in this way and after immunity was given to Charidemus and Cersebleptes, the latter would easily drive out the former and take control of the kingdom. [13] The facts themselves accuse them of having these intentions and making such plots. They tried to do this during the war, and Aristomachus came as their representative, this man here from Alopeke, who gave other speeches in public, praising Cersebleptes and Charidemus and describing how they were on your side.[39] [14] He said that Charidemus was the only man who could return Amphipolis to the city and advised you to elect him general. This preliminary motion had been prepared and ar-

---

[36]There appear to be some words missing at the beginning of this sentence.

[37]The only information we have about the soldiers Simon and Bianor comes from this speech.

[38]Athenodorus appears to have been born on Imbros (Plut. *Phocion* 18.4; Aelian *Varia Historia* 1.25). As a private citizen, he founded a city in Thrace (Isoc. 8.24). Around 340 he was honored by the citizens of Kios in Asia Minor (*IK Kios* 2 = Tod 1947, no. 149). Later he served under the Persian King and was captured by Alexander at Sardis in 334 but released at the request of Phocion (Plut. *Phocion* 18.5; Aelian *Varia Historia* 1.25). He is also mentioned at 170.

[39]Aristomachus was the son of Critodemus, who was killed in 405 by the Spartans during the Athenian defeat at Aegospotamoi (Lys. 19.16). He was a witness for Apollodorus about events around 378/7 ([Dem.] 59.25) and was a trierarch shortly after (*IG* ii² 1605, lines 30–31) and possibly before (*IG* ii² 40, lines 8–9). Around 343 he was accused of bribing Theocrines to pass a decree in favor of the people of Tenedos. See Davies 1971: 61–62. The wording implies that Aristomachus was present in court and may have intended to testify for Aristocrates.

ranged so that if you should be taken in by their promises and the hopes that Aristomachus held out, the people would ratify it immediately, and nothing would stand in their way.

[15] Yet what more deceitful or dishonest plot could these men have invented to get rid of the two other kings and to place the entire kingdom under the control of the one king they wish than by intimidating the men supporting the two and by putting them on the defensive against baseless charges,[40] and on the other by giving the man aiming at power and acting contrary to your interests the power to act with impunity?[41] [16] These actions are certainly not the only thing that makes it obvious that this was the motive behind the preliminary motion. No, the decree itself also provides overwhelming testimony. After writing: "If someone kills Charidemus" and omitting how he does it, whether in our interests or not, he has immediately afterwards written: "he is subject to arrest from the territory of the allies."[42] [17] Certainly none of our enemies or none of his would ever come into the territory of our allies whether or not he killed Charidemus; he has therefore not proposed this punishment for these men. On the other hand, one of our friends who became his enemy when he tries to do something against your interests would be intimidated by this decree and be careful not to be forced into a position where he would alienate you. In this group are Athenodorus, Simon, Bianor, the kings of Thrace, and anyone who might regard the act of preventing him from acting against your interests as a way of doing you a favor.

[18] Their intent in proposing the preliminary motion was to trick the Assembly into passing the measure, and our aim in bringing this indictment is to stop them, men of Athens.[43] I have

---

[40]Manuscripts add the phrase "which they would reasonably have expected to have confronted them as a result of this decree here," but this is deleted by Dobree, followed by Dilts.

[41]The king they wish to take control of the entire area is Cersebleptes.

[42]For a similar expression in an Athenian decree, see *IG* ii³ 399, lines 15–16.

[43]Sections 18–21 form what later rhetoricians called the *partitio* (*prokataskeuē* in Greek), in which the speaker outlines the topics he is going to

promised to show three things: first, that the decree was proposed
in violation of the laws; second, that it is not in the city's interest; and third, that the person for whom it has been proposed
does not deserve to gain these privileges.[44] Perhaps it is right to
give you who are about to hear these points a choice as to which
point you wish to hear first, second, and last. [19] Think about
what you actually want to hear so that I discuss this first.[45] Do
you wish me to start with the violations of the law? We will discuss that first. What I am in fact asking and requesting all of you
to grant is justified in my opinion: do not, men of Athens, let
your mistaken views about Charidemus and your impression that
he is your benefactor make you hostile and cause you to give me
a less favorable hearing when I present my arguments about the
laws. Do not allow this to prevent you from fulfilling your duty
to cast a vote in obedience to your oath or to prevent me from instructing you about the case in the way I wish.[46] Listen to me in
the following way and observe how fairly I am going to present
my case. [20] When I discuss the laws, pay no attention to whose
benefit the decree has been proposed or what sort of person he is;
consider whether it has been proposed in violation or in accordance with the laws and nothing else. When I examine what he
did and explain how he has tricked you, decide whether I am tell-

---

cover in the proofs. See Papillon 1998: 27–30.

[44]Volpis 1936: 52 believes that these three points were the charges in the
indictment submitted to the magistrate. This is unlikely: the charges in the
indictment would have pertained only to the laws that the decree violated
(cf. the end of the speech, 215–220, where the charges in the indictment are
listed). Euthycles is clearly referring to the points he has made in the preceding sections of the speech.

[45]By giving a choice, the speaker shows consideration for his audience
and acts as if he is speaking spontaneously and not from a written text. As
the scholion on 18 observes, Euthycles gives the impression that he is following the judges' wishes.

[46]Euthycles reminds the judges about their oath to listen to both sides
impartially. He argues that this requires them to allow him to present his
arguments in the order he chooses. For a similar interpretation of this clause
of the oath, see Dem. 18.2.

ing the truth or lying.[47] [21] When I examine whether it is in the city's best interests to pass this proposal or not, disregard everything else and consider only this question: are the arguments I am making about this topic correct or not? If you listen to me in this frame of mind, you will reach an excellent understanding about what should be done by examining each issue separately and not considering them all together at the same time.[48] I will also have a very easy time making the points I wish to make. My arguments about all these topics will be brief.[49]

[22] Take then the laws themselves and read them so that I may use them to show that his proposal violates them.[50]

[LAW]

The Council of the Areopagus judges cases of homicide, deliberate wounding, arson, and drugs if anyone kills by administering them.

[23] Stop. You have heard the law and the decree, men of Athens. What do I think is the easiest way for you to understand the arguments that it is illegal? I will tell you: if you consider the cat-

---

[47]Euthycles makes a clear distinction between questions of law and questions of fact.

[48]Euthycles claims that his division of topics is aimed at making his points clear and easy to understand. He thereby enhances his credibility by portraying himself as honest and straightforward in contrast to the deceit of his opponents.

[49]For this promise to be brief, cf. *Against Timocrates* 10 and the note there. Usually this promise precedes the narrative, but here it precedes the proofs.

[50]The text of this document is very close to the paraphrase at 24, which, however, lacks the phrase "at the Areopagus," and contains similar information to that found at *Ath. Pol.* 57.3 and Pollux 8.117 (cf. Din. 1.6). The heading "Law from the Laws about Homicide from the Areopagus" is found in some manuscripts but not others and was probably added at a later stage in the manuscript tradition. This law probably came from a general law about the powers of the Areopagus, not from a collection of laws about homicide. For discussion, see Canevaro 2013a: 40–47.

egory into which the person for whom the proposal was made belongs, whether a foreigner, a metic, or a citizen. To start, if we will say he is a metic, we will not state the truth. On the other hand, if we say he is a foreigner, we will not do him justice. After all, it is just for the grant of the people that made him a citizen to remain valid.[51] We must therefore make our arguments, it seems, as if we were dealing with a citizen.[52] [24] By Zeus, consider how simply and justly I make use of the argument, I who place him in this rank in which he would obtain the most honor.[53] On the other hand, I do not think that he should illegally receive privileges that not even those of us who are citizens by birth possess. What are these privileges? Those that this man here has proposed. For it is written in the law that "the Council is to judge cases of homicide and intentional wounding and arson and drugs if anyone kills by administering them." [25] By adding the phrase "if he kills," the man who established the law, however, provided for a trial and did not state what must happen to the offender before the trial. This is good, men of Athens, because he was concerned about protecting the city's respect for religion.[54] How did he do this? It is not possible for all of us to know who the killer is. If anyone makes a charge, he thought it terrible to accept it on trust without a trial. On the other hand, he believed that when we are going to avenge the victim, we should be persuaded and, after learning the facts, be certain that he is guilty after learning the facts.[55] The righteous thing to do is to punish after you know

---

[51]Euthycles refers to the law requiring that all grants made by the people of Athens must remain valid, that is, cannot be revoked by a subsequent measure. See Dem. 20.96.

[52]Euthycles admits that Charidemus has been granted citizenship, but his way of expressing himself suggests that he did not deserve the award. For the date of the award, see the Introduction.

[53]Euthycles says this to give them impression that he is trying to be fair to Charidemus and has no personal grudge against him.

[54]Homicide was an offense that incurred pollution. A failure to grant the man accused of murder a fair trial would therefore risk the wrath of the gods. On the role of pollution in homicide law, see E. M. Harris 2015.

[55]For the right to a fair trial in Athenian law, see the Introduction.

the truth, not before. [26] In addition, he reasoned that all terms like these, such as "if someone kills," "if someone commits sacrilege," "if someone commits treason," and all such terms are the names of charges brought before the trial takes place,[56] but when someone comes to trial and is convicted, are types of offenses. He did not think it necessary to add then the punishments after the name of the charge, but the type of trial.[57] For this reason he wrote that if anyone kills someone, the Council is to judge the case, but did not state what was to happen to him if the defendant was convicted. [27] That man framed the law in this way, but how has this man written his decree? "If anyone kills," he says, "Charidemus." He uses the same description of the deed by writing "if anyone kills" as the lawgiver. Yet after this he no longer uses the same language, but eliminates the requirement to stand trial and makes him immediately subject to arrest. He passes over the legally designated court and hands him over without trial to his accusers for them to do whatever they want to him, even if his guilt is not obvious. [28] Those who catch him have the right to torture, maim, and collect money.[58] And yet the law cited below explicitly and clearly forbids all these things and does not permit this to be done even to those convicted and judged to be murderers. Read the actual law, the next one.[59]

---

[56]Some Athenian laws take the casuistic form of conditional sentences with the substantive offense named in the protasis and the legal procedure to be followed in the apodosis. Other laws simply give orders and do not mention legal procedures. In general, Athenian laws contain more rules about substantive matters than about procedural ones. On the forms of Athenian laws, see E. M. Harris 2013a: 138–174.

[57]Euthycles makes a firm distinction between the substantive and procedural aspects of law.

[58]Euthycles gives a tendentious interpretation of Aristocrates' decree, which provided only for the arrest of anyone who murdered Charidemus. There is no reason to assume that his decree gave his accusers the right to torture, maim, or collect money. An *axon* was a wooden pillar on which laws were inscribed. See Davis 2001 with earlier bibliography.

[59]The text of this law contains several problems. Euthycles quotes the phrases "it is permitted to kill and to arrest murderers" (29, 30) and "not to

[LAW]

It is permitted to kill murderers or to arrest them in our territory, as stated in the *axon*, but not to maltreat them, nor to
demand ransom; otherwise he will owe double the amount
of damages. The officials who have jurisdiction for the judges
are to introduce the case for anyone who wishes. The Heliaea
(court) is to decide.

[29] You have heard the law. Consider, men of Athens, and look
at how fairly and very piously the lawgiver framed the law. He
says "murderers." First, he calls this man, who has already been
convicted by the court's decision, a murderer. No one is given this
description until he is proven guilty and convicted. [30] Where
does it make this clear? In the first law and in this one. In the
first one he wrote, "If anyone kills, the Council is to judge"; in
the latter he calls him the murderer and indicates the punishment
he must suffer. He stated the decision for which the action is the

---

maltreat or to demand ransom" (33). In phrase about the *axon*, the document uses the verb *agoreuei* and the text of the speech *eirētai*. Novotny 2014:
344 observes that the former verb is not found in legal contexts, whereas
the latter is (cf. *IG* ii² 37, line 13; *IG* ii² 111, line 20; *IG* ii² 223B, line 8; *Sup-
plementum Epigraphicum Graecum* (hereafter, *SEG*) 26: 72, line 44), but
we do not know enough about the language of Archaic statutes to rule out
the possibility that it could have been used with this meaning in the sixth
century. Köhler noted that the inscription recording Draco's homicide law
mentions the "first *axon*" (*IG* i³ 104, line 11) and restored the ordinal "first"
before *axon* in the text of document, even though the quotation of this provision does not contain the number (31). In the discussion of the law, Euthycles states that the *thesmothetai* are to put to death (31), but the document
does not mention these officials. The term *eispherein* in the document appears to be used in the sense of "introduce a case to court," but the standard
term is *eisagein*, and the phrase "anyone who wishes" appears out of place
in this context. The phrase about "officials who have jurisdiction for the
judges" is also without parallel. Different officials had different jurisdictions
for different types of cases (see, for example, Dem. 35.47); there was not one
set of officials who had responsibility for charges brought before judges in
court. For discussion with a survey of earlier attempts to emend the text, see
Canevaro 2013a: 48–55. It is difficult to determine whether the text of the
document is genuine or not.

cause and indicated with this term the punishment to which the
convicted man is liable. He means those people who have been
found guilty. What does it say? "It is permitted to kill or to arrest
him." [31] To one's own custody? In any way someone wishes? Far
from it. But how? It says "as is stated in the *axon*." What is this?
All of you know this. The *thesmothetai* have the power to execute
men in exile for murder.[60] Last year you all saw a man arrested
by them and taken out of the Assembly. It is to them therefore
that one must bring him. [32] What is the difference between this
and arresting the man into one's own custody? The one who arrests and takes him to the *thesmothetai* gives the laws power over
the guilty man; a man who takes him into his own custody gives
himself power over him. In the former way, the offender is punished as the law orders; in the latter, as the person who arrests
him wishes. It certainly makes the greatest difference whether the
law or a personal enemy has the power to punish. [33] The law
states "not to maltreat or to demand ransom (*apoina*)."[61] What
does this mean? The meaning of "not to maltreat" I think is obvious; it means not to flog, not to imprison, not to do things like
this. "Not to demand ransom" means "not to collect money." The
ancients used to call money "compensation."[62] [34] The law provided how the murderer and the man convicted must be punished
and where by indicating the country of the victim and explicitly
stated no other method than this one and no other place except
here. But the man who proposes this decree does not do this: he
has stated quite the opposite. After writing "if anyone kills Charidemus," he says, "let this man be subject to arrest anywhere."
[35] And what do you say? Although the laws do not allow arrest

---

[60] Euthycles interprets the reference to the rule in the first *axon* as a reference to a rule granting only the *thesmothetai* the power to kill exiles who illegally return to Attica, but the text of the law makes clear that the power to
kill such exiles is granted to everyone. Euthycles wishes to limit the power
to the *thesmothetai* because he is arguing that it is wrong for Aristocrates' decree to give anyone the power to kill the person who murders Charidemus.

[61] The word *apoina* is the term for ransom in the *Iliad*. See Wilson 2002.

[62] This is unlikely because the practice of receiving compensation origi-
nated before the first coins were struck in Attica in roughly the middle of
the sixth century BCE. For the date, see Kroll and Waggoner 1984.

even of convicted men, except in our territory, do you write that a man is subject to arrest without trial in all the territory of our allies? The laws do not allow for arrest even in our territory; are you allowing it anywhere at all? Indeed in making him subject to arrest, you have allowed all these things that the law has forbidden: to exact money, harm him while alive, maim him, even kill him. [36] How then would anyone be convicted of proposing a more illegal decree or formulating it in a more shocking way than this? There are two terms provided, one for those who are charged ("if anyone kills"), the other for the convicted ("if anyone is a murderer"). But in your version you have taken the designation of the person who is charged, and you have written this punishment, which the laws do not even allow against men who have been convicted, for men who have not been tried.[63] What lies between these two, you have eliminated. Between the charge and the verdict there is the trial, which this man has mentioned nowhere in his decree.

[37] Read the laws in order.[64]

[LAW]

If anyone kills or is responsible for killing a murderer, who is keeping away from the border market (*agorâs ephoriâs*), the games, and the Amphictyonic sanctuaries, he is subject to the

---

[63] It was illegal to put citizens to death without a trial.

[64] The text of the document is very close to the version given in the text of the speech (35). The terms of the law have been restored in *IG* i³ 104, lines 26–29 by Köhler 1867: 34–35, followed by Stroud 1968: 53–54. The terms of the law are puzzling because the murder of an exile who returned to Attica would be classified as intentional homicide, but the law at 22 makes the Areopagus responsible for judging this kind of case, not the *ephetai*. Gagarin 1981: 133–135 and Carawan 1998: 161 believe that this was part of Draco's law and that in this period the *ephetai* judged all cases of homicide (cf. Pollux 8.125). Wallace 1989: 17–18 claims that the Areopagus was equivalent to the *ephetai*, but this is not convincing because most sources clearly differentiate the two bodies. By the late fourth century the *ephetai* were responsible for trials at the Palladium, the Delphinium, and the shrine in Phreatto (*Ath. Pol.* 57.3). For discussion, see Canevaro 2013a: 55–58.

same provisions as apply to the person who kills an Athenian. The *ephetai* are to decide his case.

You must understand the intention of the lawgiver. You will see how carefully and legally he arranged everything. [38] "If anyone kills," he says, "or is responsible for killing a murderer who is keeping away from the border market, the games and the Amphictyonic sanctuaries,[65] he is subject to the same provisions as apply to the person who kills an Athenian. The *ephetai* are to decide his case." What does this mean? The lawgiver thought that the person who was tried and convicted on a charge of homicide, if he went into permanent exile and was safe, it was right to ban him from the victim's country but not at all righteous to kill him anywhere. What was his intention? If we kill men who have fled abroad, others will kill those who have fled here.[66] [39] If this happens, the one source of safety left for all unlucky men will be eliminated. What is this? The possibility of emigrating from the land of their victims to the country of those whom they have not wronged and live there without fear. To prevent this from occurring and to stop the cycle of revenge going on forever, he wrote: "If anyone kills a murderer keeping away," he says, "from the border market." What does he mean by this? The boundaries of the country.[67] There, I think, in earlier times citizens living on the

---

[65]It is uncertain whether the adjective "Amphictyonic" modifies the words for "games" and "sanctuaries" or just the latter. This appears to refer to the Amphictyony of Delphi, which consisted of members from many regions of Greece (including Athens) and controlled the shrine of Apollo at Delphi. In the Classical period, the Amphictyony met twice per year, once at Delphi, once at Anthela. For its history and institutions, see Lefèvre 1998 and Sánchez 2001.

[66]This analysis of the lawgiver's intent is speculative. The rule is probably better explained in terms of beliefs about pollution. Once the killer went out of the victim's country, the community had no reason to fear pollution and could allow the killer to go free. Permanent exile from the community was a punishment virtually equivalent to death (see, for example, Sophocles *Oedipus Tyrannos* 100–101).

[67]Like all states, the Greek *polis* had fixed borders. On the borders of Greek states, see Daverio Rocchi 1988 and Rousset 1994. The meaning of the term "border market" or "market by the *horoi*" may not have been known at

border and those in the neighboring area used to meet, which is why he called it "the border market." [40] And again "from the Amphictyonic sanctuaries"? Why did he ban the murderer from these? He bans the killer from all these places to which the victim had access during his life, first from his country and all that is sacred and holy in it, adding the border market, then from shrines in the Amphictyons.⁶⁸ The reason was that the victim, if he was a Greek, would have access to these too. And "the games." For what reason? Because games in Greece are open to everyone. On the principle of access for all, the victim had access to these too. So let him also keep away from these. [41] The ban applies to the man banned from these places. If anyone kills him in any other place besides these, the lawgiver has provided the same penalty as for killing an Athenian. The lawgiver does not designate the exile by the name of the city (he no longer has any rights in the city) but by the name of the action that is the reason for his punishment. For this reason, he also says, "If anyone kills the murderer." But after indicating the places from which he is banned, when it comes to inflicting the legal penalty, he gives the name of the city and writes that "he is subject to the same provisions as apply to the person who kills an Athenian." Men of Athens, this is different from what the author of this decree stated. [42] Yet isn't it shocking for someone to propose that those exiles whom the law allows to live in safety as long as they stay away from the places I mentioned are to be subject to arrest? And to take from them the benefit of pardon that rightly existed for unlucky men from those who have no complaints against them? One cannot know who will benefit from all these one day because it is impossible to know what will happen to them in the future. Let us imagine the following possibility: a man kills Charidemus and flees into exile, keeping away from the legally designated places, but some people

---

the time, and this explanation may be speculative. In the Classical period, the penalty for involuntary homicide was exile from Attica until the relatives pardoned him (see 72; Dem. 21.43, 37.59). If a person charged with intentional homicide went into exile, before the court voted, he could be condemned to permanent exile (Dem. 21.43).

⁶⁸This sentence appears to interpret the phrase "Amphictyonic shrines."

catch him after he is extradited and kill him in retaliation. These people would be liable to a charge of murder and so would you. [43] Because it has been written: "if anyone is responsible," you too will be responsible by giving them the right to do this by your decree.[69] Then certainly if we absolve you from responsibility for what happened, we will still come in contact with men who are polluted.[70] Yet on the other hand if we bring charges, we will be forced to do the opposite of what we decided.[71] Is the reason why it is necessary to repeal this decree trivial or insignificant?

[44] Read the next law.[72]

------

[69] A charge of murder could be brought not only against the person who committed deadly violence against the victim but also against those who were in any way responsible for the victim's death. See E. M. Harris 2006: 391–404. Euthycles means that Aristocrates would be responsible for the victim's death by proposing this decree, which (on his interpretation) allows anyone to kill the person who murders Charidemus. The argument is far-fetched but aimed at the judges' fear of incurring pollution.

[70] If the Athenians did not convict Aristocrates, they would be in contact with the person who is responsible for allowing the person who murders Charidemus to be killed while remaining away from Attica and who would therefore incur pollution. Like other passages in the speech, this shows that concern about pollution existed in the 350s.

[71] This means that if the Athenians allow a charge of murder to be brought against the person who kills Charidemus, they would be acting against the terms of Aristocrates' decree. For concern with consistency in Athenian statutes, see Sickinger 2008; E. M. Harris 2013a: 246–247, Canevaro 2013b; and Canevaro 2016b.

[72] This document appears to give the text of a genuine statute or a document composed by someone who knew the laws about homicide, but its meaning is not clear. For discussion, see Canevaro 2013a: 58–61. MacDowell 1963: 121–122 thinks that it refers to the arrest of the convicted killer, who would be brought back to Athens (cf. 28, but the term there is *apagein*, which is the normal term for "arrest" and not *agein*; for a similar idea, see Phillips 2008: 64, 79). Westermann 1865: 3 suggests that it refers to taking the goods of the exile, but the object of the verbs is the exile, not his goods, which are mentioned in the relative clause (cf. Ruschenbusch 2010: 46). Moreover, in the discussion of the law, Euthycles believes that it concerns seizing the murderer. The verbs *agein* and *pherein* can be used to de-

[LAW]

If anyone pursues or seizes and carries away beyond the border any of the murderers in exile whose goods are not confiscated, he is to owe the same penalty as one who did this in our own territory.

Here is another law, men of Athens, which is humane and good. This man has obviously violated this law in a similar way. [45] "If anyone [pursues or seizes] a murderer in exile," it states, "whose goods are not confiscated." He means those who have left the country on a charge of involuntary homicide. What makes this clear? His use of the phrase "who has gone abroad" and not "who has gone into exile" and the qualification "whose goods are not confiscated" because the property of those who commit deliberate homicide is confiscated.[73] He would therefore be speaking about involuntary homicide. [46] What does it say? "If beyond the border," it says, "someone pursues or seizes or carries away."[74] What does this mean, the phrase "beyond the border"? For murderers this is the border of the country of their victims, from which they are excluded. The law allows him to be driven out or carried away from this place, but does not allow anyone to do either of these things beyond this limit. If anyone violates this rule, he has imposed the same penalty that would apply if he were to harm someone remaining here by indicating that he owes the same penalty as if he committed the offense right here. [47] Suppose, then, someone were to ask this Aristocrates here (do

---

note carrying off slaves (e.g., Euripides *Trojan Women* 1310 and section 61 in this speech, where it clearly refers to enslavement), and the law is more likely to protect the exile from enslavement, just as the law protects him from murder.

[73]For the confiscation of goods belonging to those convicted on a charge of intentional homicide, see Dem. 21.43. For the goods of involuntary murderers not being confiscated, see Theophrastus *On Laws* fr. 9 (Szegedy-Maszak).

[74]For the expression "bear off or carry away" (*agein kai pherein*), see Dover 1968a: 129.

not consider the question naïve), first, if he knows whether anyone will kill Charidemus or if he will die in some other way. I
think he would say that he does not know. Well, now, we will assume someone is going to kill him. Next, do you know whether
he will do it willingly or unwillingly, and whether the person who
will do it is a citizen or a foreigner? It is impossible to say that you
know. [48] Surely, then, when writing "if anyone kills," he should
certainly have indicated whether unwilling or willing, unjustly or
justly, foreigner or citizen, so that whoever committed the crime
would have his legal rights, instead, by Zeus, of just writing the
name of the offense and adding the phrase "let him be subject
to arrest." What limit have you left with this clause when you
allow the murderer to be pursued anywhere at all, although the
law quite explicitly does not allow him to be seized outside the
borders?[75] [49] The law does not allow anyone to arrest him or
even to pursue him beyond the borders. As a result of your decree,
anyone who wishes will seize the man who commits involuntary
homicide and has been surrendered to him and will take him to
the country of the victim. Aren't you overturning all the laws of
humanity? Aren't you eliminating any concern for intention, the
factor that determines whether each action is good or shameful?[76]
[50] You see that this is the case in all the laws, not just those
about homicide. "If anyone strikes someone," it states, "and is the
first to strike an unjust blow."[77] Because if someone strikes back,
he does no wrong. "If anyone utters slanders," the law has added,
"which are false" because if they are true, it is appropriate.[78] "If
anyone kills," the law adds the qualification, "deliberately" be-

---

[75] This argument is specious. The law was concerned with those who had
fled into exile and been convicted of murder. Aristocrates' decree concerned
the extradition of those accused of murder but not yet tried.

[76] For the importance of intention in Athenian law, cf. Dem. 21.42–44.

[77] As the argument makes clear, the phrase "first to strike an unjust
blow" does not come from the law about homicide but from the law about
assault and battery ([Dem.] 47.40). It should not be restored in Draco's homicide law (*IG* i³ 104, lines 33–35). See Harris 2016b (*pace* Gagarin 1978).

[78] On slander in Athenian law, see Lys. 10, with Loomis 2003.

cause if he does so against his will, it is not the same.[79] "If anyone harms someone," the laws adds, "willingly and unjustly."[80] In
every case, we will find that the intention determines the nature
of the action. But not for you! You simply write: "If anyone kills
Charidemus, let him be arrested," whether he does so against his
will, or justly, or striking back in retaliation, or in any of the ways
permitted by the laws or in any way whatsoever.

[51] Read the next law.[81]


[LAW]

There are to be no private actions for homicide anywhere
against those who denounce exiles if he returns where he is not
allowed.

This is the law of Draco, men of Athens, and there are all the
other laws about homicide that I have written in the indictment.[82]

---

[79]The person who committed deliberate murder (*phonos ek pronoias*) was
put to death and his property confiscated. For the meaning of the term *phonos ek pronoias* (which is often mistranslated "premeditated homicide" by
writers such as Stroud 1968; Wallace 1989; and Pepe 2012), see E. M. Harris 2013a: 182–189. If he left Attica before the court found him guilty, he was
sentenced to permanent exile. In both cases his property was confiscated.
The person who committed involuntary homicide was sent into exile until the relatives of the victim granted him pardon and purification was performed. See Dem. 21.43, 37.59.

[80]If harm was done unwillingly, that is, through negligence, the offender paid only simple damages (Dem. 21.43), but if deliberately, double
the value of the damage.

[81]The terms of the law in the document are very close to those in the
quotation of the law that follows, but the order of the clauses is different,
and the document has the term "exiles" but the quotation "murderers." The
word "anywhere" is not in the quotation. It is impossible to know which
version is correct. For discussion, see Canevaro 2013a: 62–64.

[82]When the accuser drew up his indictment in a case against an illegal
decree, he had to include all the laws the decree violated. The indictment
was then kept on file after the trial. On the indictment, see E. M. Harris
2013a: 114–136 and 2013b.

We must examine what it says. "Against those who denounce," it says, "murderers who return where it is not permitted there are no private actions for homicide."[83] Right here the lawgiver clearly establishes two rights (both of which this man has violated by proposing this decree): first, it allows anyone to denounce the murderer but not to seize and carry him off and, second, if someone returns where it is not permitted, it grants him the same right, but not in any place someone wishes. [52] Where is it not permitted to go? To the city from which one is in exile. Where does it make this very clear? In the phrase "if someone returns." It is impossible to apply this to any other city except that from which one is in exile. After all, one can surely not return to that city from which he was not in exile to begin with. This law has granted the right to make a denunciation and allows this: "if anyone returns where it is not allowed." But he has written right here: "Let him be subject to arrest" where no law prevents the exile from going.

[53] Read another law.[84]

---

[83]On the procedure of *endeixis*, see MacDowell 1963: 122 and Hansen 1976: 100–103, 111–118. For those who denounce a person who is later executed as a result of the denunciation being accused of homicide, see Lys. 13.41–42, 87, with E. M. Harris 2006: 396–397.

[84]This document concerns the categories of just homicide (or "homicide according to the laws"), and some of its provisions are quoted verbatim in the discussion that follows. Similar categories are found in *Ath. Pol.* 57.3 (killing a *moichos*; killing in war, in ignorance; and killing in an athletic contest), but for killing in an athletic contest, the document adds the word "involuntarily." One should not read anything into this variation because the *Constitution of the Athenians* is not giving a verbatim quotation of the law. Carawan 1998: 92–96 claims that Draco's laws (and Archaic law in general) did not pay attention to intent and that the document is therefore a forgery or a later version of the law. Draco's law did, however, take account of intent (*IG* i[3] 104, line 17), and Carawan's view is not convincing. The category of "killing on the road" is not mentioned in Euthycles' discussion but is explained by Harpocration (s.v. ἐν ὁδῷ), the Suda, and *P.Berol.* 5008 as killing someone who attacks from an ambush. For discussion of the term "ambush" and the meaning of this clause, see E. M. Harris 2010: 132–133, 141–142. Sosin 2016 claims that this clause refers to homicide committed by someone driving a chariot on a road, but this is not convincing because this

[LAW]

If anyone kills in athletic games involuntarily, or taking him on the road or during war in ignorance, or with his wife, or with his mother, or with his sister, or with his daughter, or with his concubine whom he keeps for the purpose of free children, one is not to go into exile because he has killed for one of these reasons.

There are many laws, men of Athens, that the proposed decree violates, but it violates none more seriously than the law read out just now. This law grants so clearly and states under what conditions killing is permissible. This man has overlooked all these provisions and provided a penalty without specifying the manner in which the murder is committed. [54] Yet look at how piously and carefully the man who originally created these distinctions made them. If anyone kills someone in an athletic contest, the law specifies that this man does no wrong.[85] Why? It does not consider what happened, but the intent of the accused. What is this? To remain alive and gain victory, not to kill. If the victim was too weak to undertake the strain of competing for victory, he considered him responsible for his own death. For this reason he did not allow any punishment to avenge him. [55] Next, the law states that this man who kills "during war in ignorance" is ritually pure.[86] This is right: if I have killed someone thinking that he is an enemy, I do not deserve to go on trial, but to gain sympathy. "Or with his wife," it states, "or with his mother or with his sister or with his daughter or with a concubine whom he keeps for

---

case would have been covered by one of the other categories of homicide; moreover, his view has no support in the ancient sources. See Harris 2016b. For discussion of the text, see Canevaro 2013a: 64–70.

[85] Gernet 1959: 124 believes that this law applies to Antiphon's *Second Tetralogy*, but this law applied only to those competing in a contest; the victim in the *Second Tetralogy* is a bystander.

[86] For the expression "ritually pure" (*katharos*) being equivalent to "innocent," see E. M. Harris 2010: 128–129. Like other passages in this speech, this one shows that beliefs about pollution shaped the laws about homicide. See E. M. Harris 2015.

the purpose of free children" and makes the person who kills in these cases free from punishment and very rightly, men of Athens, releases him from guilt.[87] [56] Why then? In the case of those whom we fight the enemy to protect so they do not suffer insult and humiliation,[88] he has granted the right to kill even friends if they commit outrage and corrupt them in violation of the law. One is not born a friend or an enemy; it is the actions that determine each of these categories. The law therefore allows the punishment of those who commit hostile actions as if they were enemies of the community.[89] There are so many circumstances in which it is permitted to kill; wouldn't it be terrible if this man Charidemus were the only one whom it was not permitted to kill even in these circumstances? [57] Let us assume that what has happened to others happened to him and that he returns from Thrace and comes to settle somewhere in the city. At that point he will no longer have the power that allows him to do many things forbidden by the laws, but his habits and desires will encourage him to try these things.[90] Will everyone have to submit to Charidemus' violent insolence without speaking a word? It will not be in fact safe to kill him and to impose the punishment that the law

---

[87]This law is also quoted and discussed at Lys. 1.30–35, where the speaker claims that it applied only to cases of seduction. This passage, however, makes it clear that the law applied both to those who seduced the female relatives and to those who used violence. See E. M. Harris 1990 (= E. M. Harris 2006: 283–295), which is now widely accepted. Carey 1995 follows all of the points in E. M. Harris 1990 but attempts to argue that seduction was viewed as a more serious crime than rape. For a detailed refutation, see E. M. Harris 2006: 293–94. The views of Omitowoju 1997 (repeated in Omitowoju 2002) about sexual violence are not convincing. See E. M. Harris 1998.

[88]Euthycles alludes to the common practice of raping the women of a defeated city.

[89]Normally the law did not allow the use of deadly force against fellow citizens even if they were personal enemies. An exception is made in this case.

[90]Euthycles insinuates that Charidemus has been raping women in Thrace and would continue to do this if he were to return to Athens.

grants because of this very decree. [58] Well, now, if someone replies, "Where would this happen?" what prevents me from asking, "Who would kill Charidemus?" But let us not think about this. Yet since the decree on trial does not concern some event in the past, but the sort of eventuality that no one knows whether it will happen, let us assume that the chances of this happening in the future are equal. On the basis of what we as human beings can reasonably expect, let us assume that one or the other might possibly occur. [59] If we overturn the decree and something happens to this man, there are punishments provided in the laws.[91] But if we allow it to go into effect, and that man wrongs anyone while he is alive, the victims of his abuse lose their right to a trial according to the laws.[92] From all points of view, therefore, the decree is contrary to the laws, and it is in our interest to repeal it.

[60] Read the next law.[93]

[LAW]

If anyone kills by striking back immediately against someone carrying or dragging away his property wrongfully by force, he is to die without compensation.

These are the circumstances in which it is permitted to kill. "If anyone kills by immediate retaliation someone carrying or dragging away his property wrongfully by force, he is to die without compensation."[94] By Zeus, look at how good this rule is. After indicating the circumstances in which it is permitted to kill, by adding "immediately," he removes the interval for plotting any harm.

---

[91] The point is that there is no need for the special protection given in the decree because there are already legal procedures to bring murderers to trial.

[92] This is misleading. Anyone who killed Charidemus would still have the right to a trial and could defend himself by claiming that Charidemus was acting unjustly.

[93] For discussion, see Canevaro 2013a: 70–71.

[94] The Greek word *amunomenos* is sometimes translated "in self-defense," but it can denote any violent retaliation whether or not in self-defense. See, for example, Thuc. 1.96; Ant. 4.4.4.

By writing the term "striking back" it clearly permits the victim the right, not anyone else. The law grants the right to kill immediately by striking back, but this man stated nothing but simply "if anyone kills" even if the laws permit it. [61] But, by Zeus, we are quibbling. Whom will Charidemus carry off and drag away unjustly by force?[95] Everyone in the world. You surely know that all men who lead an army demand property and carry and drag it away from those over whom they think they have the upper hand. Wouldn't it be shocking, Earth and gods, and clearly illegal not only against the written law but against the common law of mankind if it were not permitted for me to strike back against the person who is carrying off and dragging away my property like an enemy (this would be the case if it is not permitted to kill Charidemus even in these circumstances), but if Charidemus unjustly and by force loots someone's property and carries it off, the killer will be subject to arrest although the law provides that he is innocent in such circumstances?

[62] Read the next law.[96]

[LAW]

Let any official or private citizen who is responsible for overturning or changes this law be without rights and his children and his property.

You have heard the law, men of Athens, stating directly that "let any official or private citizen who is responsible for overturning the law or changes it, be without rights and his children and his property."[97] Do you think the lawgiver has little or hardly

---

[95] Euthycles insinuates that Charidemus will attempt to enslave Greeks during his campaigns.

[96] The text of the document is close to that of the quotation in the following section, with minor differences (the infinitive *einai* for the imperative *esto*). It is impossible to determine which version is correct. For discussion, see Canevaro 2013a: 71–73.

[97] This is an entrenchment clause, which was often added on to laws to ensure that they were not changed or abolished. For examples and an analy-

any concern that the law remain in effect and not be overturned or changed? But this man Aristocrates here hardly cares about it and changes and overturns it. What else does changing the law mean other than inflicting punishment outside the established courts and outside the boundaries one must respect and extraditing them and taking away their right to speak in their own defense? What else does it mean to "destroy" than when someone proposes one measure after another contrary to the rules contained in the laws?

[63] He has violated not only these laws, men of Athens, but many others that we did not copy in our indictment because there are so many.[98] But I am giving a summary: all the laws about the courts for homicide, about issuing a summons, about giving testimony, about the oaths to be sworn by litigants or any other rules, all of these he has violated. This decree here that he has proposed violates all of them. There is no summons,[99] no testimony of those knowing the facts,[100] no swearing of oaths,[101] but the punishment has been written straight after the charge and this is a penalty that the laws forbid. What else could one call this? Yet all

---

sis of their role, see E. M. Harris 2006: 23–25. For examples from Athenian inscriptions, see Lewis 1997: 136–149. Some have claimed that the Greek word *thesmos* used here to denote "law" is archaic and had a different significance from the word *nomos* (e.g., Ostwald 1969), but the two terms are used as virtual synonyms. See Hölkeskamp 2002: 123–126. The argument here is fallacious. Enacting a decree that contravened the laws about homicide would not overturn those laws, which would still remain in effect.

[98] In the plaint for a *graphē paranomōn* submitted to the *thesmothetai* who were responsible for these cases (*Ath. Pol.* 59.2), the accuser had to list all the laws the decree violated. See E. M. Harris 2013b: 161–162.

[99] The manuscripts add the term *krisis* after "summons," but the word is deleted by Reiske.

[100] Todd 1990 claims that the main function of witnesses was to show support for the litigant who called on him. This passage shows, however, that the witness in Athenian law was to provide evidence about the facts based on their knowledge of the relevant facts. See Rubinstein 2005.

[101] For the oaths sworn in homicide cases, see MacDowell 1963: 90–100.

these procedures are required by law for the five courts.¹⁰² **[64]** By
Zeus, perhaps one would say that these procedures are worthless
and created for no good reason, whereas what this man has proposed is just and good. Far from it: I do not know of anything
more shocking to have taken place in your city than this decree.
Out of all the courts in the world one will find none more righteous and just. I want to tell you briefly about the courts I have
mentioned, which bring respect and honor to our city. You will
enjoy hearing about them. I will begin where it is easiest for you
to learn, then return to the award granted to Charidemus.

**[65]** Men of Athens, we made Charidemus a citizen, and
through this award we gave him a share in the sacred and holy
rites,¹⁰³ legal rights, and all the rights that we ourselves share. We
Athenians enjoy many rights not similar to those elsewhere. One
that is the most distinctive and hallowed is the court of the Are-
opagus.¹⁰⁴ One could tell more stories about this court, both old
stories handed down in myth and events that you yourselves have
witnessed as about no other court. It is worth hearing one or two
of these stories as a sample. **[66]** There is a story from long ago
handed down by oral tradition that in this court alone the gods
thought it right to be accusers or defendants and to be judges for
their disputes with each other. Poseidon obtained justice for his
son Halirrhothius from Ares.¹⁰⁵ The twelve gods decided that

---

¹⁰²Euthycles discusses the five courts at 65–79. This passage therefore
serves as a transition to the next section.

¹⁰³Citizenship did not just grant political and legal rights but also the
right to participate in the religious rites of the city.

¹⁰⁴The Areopagus was the most respected court in Athens. See Xen.
*Memorabilia* 3.5.20; Lys. 6.14, 12.96; Aes. 1.92; Lyc. *Against Leocrates* 12;
Diodorus 1.75.3. There is no reason to consider it an "aristocratic" body
(*pace* Wallace 1989). For a good recent discussion of its role, see Zelnick-
Abramowitz 2011. Some scholars have argued that its powers were increased
in the late fourth century, but see E. M. Harris 2016a: 74–78.

¹⁰⁵According to myth, Ares caught Halirrhothius raping his daughter
and killed him. When Halirrhothius' father, Poseidon, prosecuted Ares before the Areopagus, the court acquitted him. See Euripides *Electra* 1258–

case between the Eumenides and Orestes.[106] These are the stories from long ago. More recently no tyrant, no oligarchy, no democracy has dared to take trials for homicide away from this court alone. All men think that in such cases what they consider just is less robust than the standard of justice maintained by this court. In this tribunal alone no defendant who has been convicted or accuser who has lost has ever proved that his case was wrongly decided.[107] [67] The man who wrote this decree has overlooked this safeguard and the legal penalties contained in it and has proposed to give Charidemus while still alive the right to do whatever he wishes and, if something happens to him, grants his relatives the right to bring unjust charges.[108] Consider the question in the following way: all of you certainly know that on the Areopagus, to which the law grants the right to judge cases of murder, the accuser making such a charge calls down curses on himself, his descendants, and his family. [68] Next, he does not swear just any oath but one that no one else has ever sworn about anything, standing on sacrificial cuts of a goat, a ram, and a bull,[109] which have been slaughtered by the correct officials and on the prescribed days so that in regard to the correct times and per-

---

1263; Apollodorus 3.14.2; Pausanias 1.21.4; Din. 1.86–87 Hellanicus *Fragmente der griechischen Historiker* (hereafter, *FGrHist*) 323a F 22. This passage shows that the members of the Areopagus could be called judges when deciding cases (cf. Aeschylus *Eumenides* 743) (*pace* Wallace 1989: 101).

[106]According to Aeschylus, Athena appointed human judges to decide the dispute between the Erinyes and Orestes (Aeschylus *Eumenides* 487–489). For a similar version of the myth, see Euripides *Orestes* 1650.

[107]For a similar view, see Aes. 1.92.

[108]Only relatives of the victim had the right to bring a private charge of homicide (*dike phonou*) against the killer. See Dem. 47.69–70, with Tulin 1996.

[109]When one swore an oath in ancient Greece, it was customary to cut an animal in pieces (*tomia*) and stand in the middle of them. On this ritual, see *Ath. Pol.* 55.5; Aes. 2.87; Ant. 5.88; Plato *Laws* 753d. For a parody of the practice, see Aristoph. *Lysistrata* 181–238. For a Hebrew parallel, see Jeremiah 34.18–19. Stengel 1910: 78–85 argued that the *tomia* were the testicles of the animal, but see Casabona 1966: 211–215.

sons involved, everything has been done in as righteous a manner as possible.[110] Even after this the man who has sworn such an oath is still not considered trustworthy. No, if he is shown not to speak the truth, he will gain no advantage but transfer his perjury to his children and descendants. [69] If he is judged to have made an honest accusation and he convicts the guilty man on a charge of murder, not even then does he gain power over the convicted man. No, the laws and the officials assigned to this task have the power to punish him. The accuser can witness the penalty inflicted by law, nothing more. These are the rules for the accuser. The rules for the defendant are the same, but it is permitted for him to leave after giving his first speech. Neither the accuser, nor the judges, nor anyone else in the world has the power to prevent him. [70] Why is this so, men of Athens? Because those who originally established these rules, whether they were heroes or gods, were not too insistent on punishing misfortunes, but were humane in alleviating their suffering as much as was morally right.[111] These are all the rules, which are so good and based on the law that the man who proposed this very decree has clearly broken. There is not even a single one of them contained in this man's proposal. This is the first court whose written and unwritten rules the decree has violated.[112]

[71] Next, it will be clear that he is doing away with a second court, the one for involuntary homicide at the Palladium, and violating its rules.[113] Here too the same procedures have been es-

---

[110]Normally accusers did not take such an oath. Because homicide was considered the most serious crime against an individual, the laws provided special rituals to mark its importance. See E. M. Harris 2015.

[111]For the gods as the authors of the laws of Athens, see E. M. Harris 2006: 52–54.

[112]The Athenians believed that there were unwritten laws made by the gods, which provided by general principles on which the laws of the city were based. They were not two separate and potentially conflicting sources of authority. On the unwritten laws and their relationship to the laws of the city, see E. M. Harris 2006: 54–57 (correcting Ostwald 1973).

[113]On this court, see *Ath. Pol.* 57.3; Pausanias 1.28.8. This court also tried cases involving the murder of slaves, metics, and foreigners and cases in-

tablished, first, the swearing of oaths; second, presentation of speeches; and third, the decision of the court, none of which is mentioned in his decree. If the defendant is convicted and found guilty, neither the accuser nor any one else has power over him except for the law. [72] What, then, does the law provide? That the man convicted of involuntary homicide will depart at a stated time by a fixed route and remain in exile until he comes to a settlement with one of the victim's relatives. At that time the law allows him to return not in any way, but after performing sacrifices and being purified and the rest of the required procedures, men of Athens.[114] The law is correct in providing all these rules. [73] For it is right to assign a lesser penalty to involuntary homicide than to homicide committed willingly.[115] It is also right for the law to provide safety to a man to go off into exile and for the man returning from exile to be purified in the manner prescribed by law and for the laws to have power over everything. All of this is good. By proposing his decree, this man here has violated all these rules that have been so justly enacted by the original legislators. This is how shamelessly he has ignored these two courts, which are so old and so respected, and these rules, which have been handed down from time immemorial.

[74] There is another court, a third one, in addition to these, which is the most solemn and awe-inspiring of all: if one admits killing but says that he has done so legally. This is the court at the Delphinium.[116] Judges, I think that the men who originally set up these procedures examined first the question whether no killing should be considered sanctified or some category of homicide should be considered sanctified. They reasoned that because Orestes, after admitting that he killed his mother, had his case tried before the gods as judges and was acquitted, it is necessary

---

volving attempted murder (*bouleusis phonou*). On the last charge, see E. M. Harris 2006: 391–404.

[114]Cf. Dem. 37.59. The requirement of purification reveals the concern about pollution in homicide law.

[115]Cf. Dem. 21.43.

[116]On this court, see *Ath. Pol.* 57.3, with MacDowell 1963: 70–81. For the categories of just homicide, see E. M. Harris 2013a: 50–53.

to consider some form of homicide to be just. After all, the gods would not have cast an unjust vote. When they decided this, they wrote down and clearly specified the circumstances in which killing is permissible. [75] But this man makes no exception, but simply makes him subject to arrest if anyone kills Charidemus even if he kills justly, even if he kills as the laws permit. There are certainly two ways of qualifying all actions and words: they are either just or unjust. No single action or word can have both labels at the same time (how could the same actions be just and unjust at the same time?), but each is tested and found to have one or the other qualification. If it appears unjust, the action is judged evil; if just, honest and good. You have assigned neither of these qualifications by writing "if anyone kills." By leaving the charge unqualified and immediately adding the phrase "he is subject to arrest," you have clearly violated this third court and its rules.

[76] Now there is a fourth court in addition to these, the one at the Prytaneum.[117] It has jurisdiction if a stone or a piece of wood or iron or some other similar object falls on a person and strikes him, or if someone does not know who threw it but knows what caused the killing and possesses it; these cases are brought there. If religious considerations forbid inanimate objects without intelligence that cause death to go without trial, then certainly these same reasons make it sacrilegious and terrible to make an innocent man, or even if he may be guilty, a man who is still a human being and shares the same nature as us, subject to arrest for such a crime without any discussion or decision.[118]

[77] Consider how he has violated yet another court, the fifth one, that at Phreatto.[119] Men of Athens, the law allows cases to be brought here "if anyone has gone into exile on a charge for involuntary homicide and those who have sent him into exile have not yet granted pardon, he is charged with voluntary homicide."

---

[117] On this court, see Pollux 8.120, with MacDowell 1963: 85–89.

[118] Pollution for homicide arose when the victim who had been unjustly killed was not avenged. This principle extended both to those killed by other human beings and to those killed by animals and inanimate objects.

[119] On this court, see *Ath. Pol.* 57.3; Pausanias 1.28.11, with MacDowell 1963: 82–84.

The fact that he is not able to return here was not a reason for the man who formulated each of these rules to overlook his case. Nor was the fact that he had committed a crime like this a reason to give credence to another similar charge. [78] No, he found a way to satisfy the claims of religion yet did not take away his right to speak and be judged.[120] What then did he do? He had the men assigned to judge his case go to a place where the defendant could come, specifying a certain place in the countryside near the sea called Phreatto. The defendant sails up in a boat and pleads his case without touching land, and the judges listen and give judgment on land. And if he is convicted, he rightly pays the penalty for having committed voluntary homicide. But if he is acquitted, he is released free of this charge, but he still is subject to punishment for his previous conviction. [79] What, then, is the reason why he took this matter so seriously? The man who made these distinctions thought that allowing the guilty man to go free was just as impious as surrendering the innocent before trial. And yet if he was so serious about granting those judged guilty of murder the right to speak, the benefit of a trial, and all their other rights about subsequent charges, it is quite shocking to propose a decree ordering a man who has not been convicted, or judged guilty or not, or to have acted unwillingly or willingly, to be surrendered to his accusers.

[80] In addition to all of these, there is still a sixth method of punishment, which this man violated when he proposed his decree.[121] If anyone is ignorant of all these things or the time has

---

[120]A man who had been convicted of involuntary murder and had not yet been pardoned was considered polluted and could not therefore set foot in Attica. The boat the defendant stands in is not tied to the shore because the rope would bring the polluted man in contact with the land and spread his pollution to Attica. Even though he could not return to Athens, the lawgiver still thought he should not lose his right to a trial. Cf. Pollux 8.120.

[121]The normal procedure for prosecuting a murderer was a private action for homicide (*dike phonou*), which could be brought only by the relatives of the victim. This procedure provided for the arrest and imprisonment of a murderer (*apagoge phonou*, which should be distinguished from *apagoge kakourgon*, on which see E. M. Harris 2006: 373–390). Like other public ac-

expired in which it is necessary to do each of these things[122] or he does not wish for some reason to proceed in these ways, but sees the murderer going around the sanctuaries and in the agora, it is possible to lead him away to prison, not to his house or anywhere else he wishes in the way that you allow him. After being taken there, nothing will happen to him before his trial, but if he is convicted, the defendant will be punished with death, but if the accuser does not gain one-fifth of the votes, he will owe an additional one thousand drachmas.[123] [81] But this man did not write this in his decree. Instead he orders that the accuser suffer no penalty and the accused be surrendered immediately without trial. And if any individual or even an entire city should protect all those laws that I have enumerated from being destroyed and

---

tions, it could be brought by "anyone who wished," not just the relatives of the victim. For discussion, see MacDowell 1963: 130–140 and more recently Volonaki 2000. This was the procedure followed in Lysias' speech *Against Agoratus*. The document at Dem. 24.105 is a forgery and should not be used as evidence for this procedure. See the discussion there with Canevaro 2013c.

[122]This phrase has given rise to debate. It might appear to indicate that there was a statute of limitations for private charges of homicide as there was for other private cases (see Dem. 36.26–27 with Charles 1938: 3–20). This is the view of Lipsius 1905–15: 853, note 24, and Glotz 1904: 429. For the view that the passage of time purifies pollution for homicide, see Aeschylus *Eumenides* 286. Some scholars, on the other hand, think that the statute of limitations did not apply in private cases of homicide because these cases involved pollution, which could not be removed except by punishment (for intentional homicide) or by purification (in cases of involuntary homicide). It is noted that in the case *Against the Stepmother* (Ant. 1.30) the victim died when his son, who brought the case as an adult, was only a child. Lys. 13.83 has been interpreted to mean that there was no statute of limitations for homicide, but this may apply only to *apagoge phonou*. Passow 1890, followed by Charles 1938: 31–32, believes that the period mentioned would be the first nine months of the year when the *basileus* could accept charges of homicide. In the last three months of the year, he could not accept charges (Ant. 6.38, 42), and this action was provided to allow prosecution during that time.

[123]On this penalty for failing to gain one-fifth of the votes in a public action, see E. M. Harris 2006: 405–422. The unsuccessful prosecutor also lost the right to bring any public action in the future.

all the courts that I have discussed from being demolished, courts that the gods have established and that men have used ever since, and should stop someone from being abused and wronged, he has written that this person is to be banned. He has not given this man a chance to speak or a right to a trial, but punishes this man immediately without a trial. How could a decree be more shocking or more illegal than this one?

[82] Is there any law still left? Show it to me; this one here. Read this one.[124]

[LAW]

If anyone dies by a violent death, his relatives have the right to take hostages for him until they undergo trial for homicide or surrender the killers. One can seize up to three hostages, no more.

---

[124]The wording of the document is very close to the wording of the quotation in the text except that the former uses the term *androlepsia* (seizure of a hostage) and the latter uses *androlepsion* (the right to seize a hostage). This statute granted the relatives of the victim the right to seize up to three hostages and may have applied to hostages in foreign communities in which the murder had occurred. See Lipsius 1905–1915: 267; Bravo 1982; Todd 1993: 331. On the other hand, there is no reason to rule out the possibility that it applied both to those who murdered Athenians in foreign cities and also to those who murdered an Athenian in Attica, then fled abroad. Euthycles stresses the former because it is relevant to his argument about the decree for Charidemus. Ruschenbusch 1960: 140–142; Ruschenbusch 2010: 40–42; and Carawan 1998: 43 believe that it may have applied to murders in Attica and was intended as a way of putting pressure on the killer to submit to justice or for his family to pay compensation, but the following paraphrase, in sections 82–83, and the lexicographers indicate that it applied to murderers to be extradited from foreign cities. There is no reason to think that the phrase "by a violent death" indicates that the provision dates to the fifth century. We know too little about the language of Archaic statutes to rule out an earlier date (*pace* Gagarin 1981: 143 and Phillips 2008: 241–247, which is mostly speculation). Moreover, the practice of seizing hostages or goods (*sylan*) is well attested in the Archaic period: see Bravo 1982 and more briefly Lintott 2004. For discussion of the text of the document, see Canevaro 2013a: 73–74.

There are many excellent laws, men of Athens, but I do not know of any better or more just than this one. Look at how fair and very humane it is. [83] "If anyone dies by a violent death," it says. First, by adding this word "violent," he has given a sign allowing us to understand that he means "unjustly." He says, "His relatives have the right to take hostages for him until they undergo trial or surrender the killers." Look at how well formulated this is. First, it requires that the hostages undergo trial, and then, if they do not agree, it orders the surrender of the accused. If they refuse to do either of these things, it says, "One can seize up to three hostages, no more." The decree he proposed violates this entire law. [84] First, by writing "if anyone kills," he did not add "unjustly," "violently," nor anything at all. Next, before requiring a trial, he immediately wrote that he may be seized. Moreover, if the city in which the murder took place provides no legal procedures or does not surrender the accused, the law grants the right to seize up to three hostages. [85] The decree leaves the city without a penalty and pays no attention to it, but, as for those who receive a man who has gone into exile (I will assume this) and follow the common law of humanity about sheltering exiles, the decree states that they are excluded from the alliance if they do not surrender the suppliant.[125] By not specifying the circumstances of the killing, not mentioning any trial, not requiring a legal procedure, allowing the accused to be seized anywhere, and punishing those protecting him and not those in whose territory the murder occurred, for all these reasons the decree clearly violates this law.

[86] Read the next one.[126]

---

[125] Supplication was a Greek ritual by which a suppliant made a request to a person or a community, who then decided whether or not to accept his request. Once the request was granted, the person or community was obligated to protect the suppliant. Euthycles is misleading here because a city would be unlikely to accept a suppliant who had committed murder and was sought by another city. On the expulsion of suppliants, see Naiden 2006: 161–162, 168–169.

[126] The text of this law differs in only one minor way from the quotation in the text (*epi pasin Athenaiois* as opposed to *eph'hapasin*) and is also found at And. 1.87, on which see Canevaro and E. M. Harris 2012: 116–117.

[LAW]

It is not permitted to enact a law about an individual unless it is the same for all Athenians.

The law that was read out just now, men of the court, is no longer concerned with homicide but is no way inferior to any of the others. Just as each man has an equal share in the rest of political life, the man who made this law thought that all must have an equal share in the laws.[127] For this reason he wrote, "It is not permitted to enact a law about an individual unless it is the same for all Athenians." Because it is agreed that decrees be proposed in accordance with the laws, the person who proposed this private decree for Charidemus, which will not apply to you and everyone else, clearly violated the law. Obviously, whatever one cannot put even in a law, one cannot legally put this in a decree.[128]

[87] Read the next law. Is that all?

[LAW]

No decree of the Council or Assembly prevails over a law.

Put it down. I think that a few words about this are enough, men of the court. It is easy to show that the decree violates this law. When a man has proposed a decree violating so many laws and inserts a private matter in a decree, what else will one say he has done except to ask that a decree prevail over a law?

[88] Well, now I wish to show you one or two decrees proposed for genuine benefactors of the city so that you see how easy it is to make a correct proposal when one's aim is to honor someone

---

For detailed discussion of the law and the different versions, see the note on *Against Timocrates* 59.

[127] For the Athenian ideal of equality before the law, see E. M. Harris 2013a: 5–6, 136–137.

[128] This *a fortiori* argument is fallacious. While laws could not be passed about an individual, decrees often granted honors or privileges to individuals. A decree could not violate the rules found in the laws but could deal with specific matters. See Hansen 1978 (= Hansen [1983] 161–176).

and grant him a share of our rights and not to give the appearance of doing so while wishing to commit fraud and deceit. Read these decrees here. To reduce the length of what you are about to hear, I have extracted those sections that are relevant to my charge. Read.

[DECREES]

[89] You see that all have written their decrees in the same way: "Let there be the same punishment as if he killed an Athenian."[129] They have allowed your laws about these matters to remain in force and have respected them because they have granted them privileges by way of a reward. But Aristocrates does not. Instead, he insults the laws as much as he can, treating them as worthless in his effort to create a special privilege, and belittles that award of citizenship you gave to Charidemus. As if you approve this and owe him an additional favor, he has added that you protect him so that he can do whatever he wishes with impunity. Isn't he bringing about the result I am discussing?

[90] Men of Athens, I know that because Aristocrates will not be able to show that he has not clearly violated the law in proposing his decree, he will try to suppress his most serious crime of all, which is to make no provision in his entire decree for a trial on such a charge.[130] I do not think that I have to say much about this. From the decree itself I will clearly prove that Aristocrates thinks there will be no trial for the accused. [91] He has written, "If anyone kills Charidemus, let him be subject to arrest, but if anyone, either a city or private individual, removes him, let them be banned from the alliance," not "if he does not surrender for trial the person who has been removed." No, the rule is absolute.

---

[129]For this kind of formula in Athenian decrees, see *IG* i³ 27, lines 15–17; 57, lines 9–12; 156, lines 14–17; 162, lines 9–12; 227, lines 22–24; 228, lines 9–14; *IG* ii² 32, lines 9–14; 38, lines 2–6. All of these appear to be decrees honoring foreign benefactors.

[130]Sections 90–99 form the *refutatio*, conclude the legal arguments against the decree, and provide a transition to the deliberative section of the speech (100–143). See Papillon 1998: 34–35.

If the decree provided for a trial but not for removal, he would not have added the penalty for those who removed him whenever they do not provide a trial for the person they have removed.

[92] I think that he will also present the following argument and attempt in this way to mislead you: the decree is not in effect. It is a preliminary motion, but the law provides that decrees of the Council are in effect for one year.[131] As a result, if you vote against it, the city will not suffer any serious harm because of this decree. [93] In my opinion, you should reply in this way: this man proposed this decree not so that nothing unpleasant would happen to you because the decree would not go into effect. To begin with, it was possible for him not to propose the decree if his intention was to aim at what is best for the city. No, his intention was to mislead you and allow certain people to accomplish what is against your interests. We the accusers are responsible for the delay and the reasons why it did not go into effect.[132] It would be strange if the reasons why you should feel gratitude to us were to serve as a way of protecting them! [94] Moreover, the matter is not so simple as one thinks. That might perhaps be the case if no one else in the future were going to propose decrees with so little regard for your interests. But when there are many such people, it would not be right to avoid overturning this decree. Who will not have the courage and propose a decree when this decree is acquitted? Who will not put it to the vote? Who will indict it? The question is not whether the decree is not in effect because time has passed but whether you will grant immunity to those who wish to do you wrong if you now acquit him.

[95] Now, I have not failed to notice that Aristocrates will not have any straightforward or honest nor any defense at all to present but will make some points like this to distract you: there

---

[131] On this rule, see Rhodes 1972: 62–63.

[132] The choice of when to bring a case to trial lay in the hands of the accusers, who might request delays for various reasons. Apparently Euthcyles brought the charge against Aristocrates, then delayed bringing the case to court. An accuser might choose to delay bringing a case to court for many years. See, for example, E. M. Harris 1995: 139–142 for Aeschines' delay in bringing his case against Ctesiphon to court.

have been many similar decrees for many people.[133] This is no indication that this man has proposed a legitimate decree, for there are many reasons that have caused you to be deceived. [96] For instance, suppose that one of the illegal decrees was not indicted. It would certainly have gone into effect, but it still would remain an illegal decree. Suppose that the proposal was acquitted because the accusers were bribed or were unable to prove their case. That still does not prevent it from being illegal. Did the men who judged the case not abide by their oath? Yes. How? I will show you. They have sworn to judge according to their most just opinion, but their decision based on this opinion relies on what they hear.[134] When they have cast their vote in this way, they respect their oath. [97] Everyone who casts his vote without enmity or favor or any other unjust motive and not contrary to his honest opinion respects his oath. If someone learns about something but still does not understand it, he does not deserve punishment for his failure to understand. But if someone knowingly betrays or deceives them, this man is subject to the curse. For this reason

---

[133]Although the Athenian legal system had no doctrine of binding precedent as in Common Law, litigants in Athens often appeal to judgments in prior cases to support their legal arguments and show that other judges have interpreted the law in the same way that they do. Athenian courts also tended to side with litigants who followed the standard interpretation of the law and showed some concern for applying statutes consistently and had the means to do so (*pace* Gagarin [2012]). See E. M. Harris 2013a: 246–273. For consistency in the application of the law about the award of crowns, see E. M. Harris forthcoming b, providing further evidence against Gagarin 2012. This is one of the rare cases in Attic oratory in which a litigant argues against the validity of arguments based on precedent. For another example, see Dem. 22.6.

[134]The judges in Athenian courts swore to vote according to their most just judgment. This was not a license to ignore the law (which they also swore to follow) but was a pledge to vote honestly, that is, showing impartiality to accuser and the defendant, as is made clear in the following section. The judges could rely on their own judgment alone only in cases where the laws did not provide clear guidance (*pace* Kästle 2012), but this rarely, if ever, occurred. See Dem. 20.118–119 and 39.39–40, with E. M. Harris 2013a: 109–114.

the herald pronounces the curse at every meeting of the Assembly not against those who have been deceived but against those who in their speeches deceive either the Council or the Assembly or the court.[135] [98] Do not allow them to tell you that this has happened but that this is right to happen, not that other judges have ratified these decrees but demand instead that they prove to you that their case is more just than ours. If they cannot do this, I think that it is not good for you to make their decree more binding than your own judgment. [99] In my opinion, moreover, such an argument that there have been similar decrees for other men is quite shameless. If an offense against the laws was ever committed, and you followed this example, you should not be acquitted for this reason but quite the opposite: this is all the more reason to convict you. You would never have made this proposal if one of them had been convicted. By the same token, no one else will propose a decree like this if you are convicted now.[136]

[100] I do not think that Aristocrates can say that he has not proposed a decree that violates all the laws. Recently I saw a man on trial for proposing an illegal decree. Although he was guilty in terms of the laws, he tried to argue that his proposal was in your interests and in this way to exert pressure on you. This argument was naïve, in my opinion, or rather shameless. [101] For even if the proposal was to your advantage in all other regards, it would still be against your interests for him to ask you, men who have sworn to decide according to the laws,[137] to confirm what not even he himself can show is a just proposal because every judge should regard obedience to his oath as his most important duty.[138] "Be that as it may, there might still be some logic in

---

[135]For the curse uttered by the herald before meetings of the Assembly, see Aes. 1.22–23.

[136]This passage shows that the courts did not render ad hoc judgments but enforced the law to shape the conduct of individuals.

[137]Euthycles alludes once more to the judicial oath.

[138]This passage is crucial for understanding the role of the procedure against illegal decrees. It shows that the aim of the procedure was not to provide another chance to discuss the political merits of a decree of the Assembly but to decide about its legality (*pace* Yunis 1988). See also the end of

this impudent argument."[139] In fact, however, this man will not be able to make even this argument because his decree, which violates the laws, is even more contrary to your interests than illegal. [102] This is what I wish to show you right now. To make this point as briefly as possible, I will cite an example well known to all of you. You know that it is not in the city's interests that either the Thebans or the Spartans grow strong, but the Phocians act as a counterweight to the former and other powers to the latter.[140] This situation allows us to remain powerful and secure. [103] You consider that the same holds true also for your citizens living in the Chersonese, namely, that none of the Thracian kings be strong.[141] Their chaotic politics and mutual distrust provide the greatest and most secure protection for the Chersonese. This

---

the speech, where Euthycles makes it clear that the judges will vote about the issue of legality, not the political merits. The passage also shows that the Athenian courts did not occasionally ignore the law in their verdicts and decide cases in terms of what was considered political advantageous (*pace* Wallace 2012; see the decisive criticisms of Ismard 2012). In fact, when litigants describe the reasons for verdicts, they never say that the judges voted for a litigant because they considered his case stronger on political grounds. See, for instance, *Against Timocrates* 14, where Euctemon was accused of proposing an illegal decree and acquitted when the decree is shown to be in accordance with the laws.

[139] Euthycles imagines someone making an objection to his point.

[140] At the time, the Thebans were fighting the Phocians in the Third Sacred War, which began in 356, and the Spartans were opposed by the Arcadian League and other city-states in the Peloponnese. On the Third Sacred War, see Buckler 1989. On the situation in the Peloponnese, see Dem. *On the Megalopolitans* (16), where the same concept of the balance of power is found.

[141] Lane Fox 1997: 186 believes that the Athenian citizens living in the Chersonese mentioned in this passage must be the cleruchs placed in Sestos after its capture by Chares in 353/2 (Diodorus 16.34.3; *IG* ii² 1613, lines 297–298). But Timotheus had captured several cities for the Athenians in the Chersonese between 365 and 360. Alopeconnesus was also an Athenian possession before 353: see 166. One of these, Crithote, was still in Athenian hands at the time the speech was delivered. There is no reason to believe that there were not other Athenians living in the area before 353/2. See 161.

decree here, which grants protection to the person looking after Cersebleptes' interests and creates terror and fear for the generals of the other kings lest they cause him offense, makes the generals weak and one man alone powerful. [104] Do not be at all surprised if the decrees have such a powerful effect. I will remind you about an event in the past, which is well known to all of you. About the time Miltocythes revolted from Cotys, when the war had already lasted a long time, when Ergophilus had left and Autocles was about to sail out as general, another decree like this one was proposed that caused Miltocythes to flee in panic, thinking that he no longer had your support, and placed Cotys in control of the Sacred Mount and its treasures.[142] In fact, men of Athens, after this Autocles was put on trial for destroying Miltocythes, but the time limit for prosecuting the men who proposed the decree had passed,[143] yet it had damaged the city's position. [105] Yet you are well aware that should you not overturn this decree, the kings and their generals will get discouraged. They will think that they have been shoved aside and that you are leaning toward Cersebleptes. If this knowledge causes them to give up their power the moment Cersebleptes attacks, consider once more what will happen. [106] By the gods, let us imagine that Cersebleptes wrongs us, which he is more likely to do now than when

---

[142]Miltocythes revolted in late 362 and sent ambassadors to Athens seeking an alliance ([Dem.] 50.4–6). The Sacred Mount appears to have been the main city of Cotys' kingdom (cf. Aes. 2.90). Cotys also sent a letter to Athens asking for an alliance (see 115), which appears to have made the Athenians change their mind. Ergophilus was general in 363/2 ([Dem.] 50.12). Demosthenes (19.180) states that he was convicted and punished with death or a large fine; Aristotle (*Rhetoric* 2.3.13.1380b) says that he was acquitted. Autocles was removed from his command ([Dem.] 50.12) and prosecuted by Apollodorus (Dem. 36.53), probably in 360. Hansen 1975: 94–96 believes that the procedure in both cases was *eisangelia*, but the evidence is inconclusive. On these events, see Heskel 1997: 70–94.

[143]There appears to have been a statute of limitations of one year for prosecutions of illegal decrees. See Giannadaki 2014. Euthycles is trying to explain why the decree similar to that of Aristocrates was not indicted even though it was against Athenian interests.

he had no power.[144] Will we not take their side and try to weaken him with their help? Then suppose they say to us, "You, men of Athens, not only failed to help us when we were wronged but also made us incredibly afraid to defend ourselves by passing a decree providing that if anyone kills a person acting contrary to your interests and ours, he is subject to arrest. You certainly have no right to call on us for help in a situation in which you made a bad decision both about your own interests and about ours." Tell me, if they say this, won't they be more justified than we are? I think that they will be.

[107] You certainly cannot even claim, by Zeus, that there was good reason for you to be tricked and deceived. If you could not predict the future, and you were not capable of understanding the situation, there was the example of these Olynthians here to consider. How did Philip treat them, and how did they treat him? Philip did not return Potidaea to them when he could not take it away from them as Cersebleptes did with you in the Chersonese. No, he spent much money fighting you; then after he took it and could have kept it for himself if he had wished, he surrendered it to them and did not try to do anything else.[145] [108] Nevertheless, when they saw him in a position in which they could trust him, they were his allies and fought against us because of him. Yet when they saw him growing too powerful for them to trust him, they refrained from voting a decree granting extradition for anyone who kills those who helped him gain power. [109] Instead, they went so far as make you, whom they knew would look more kindly than anyone else in the world on those who killed his friends and Philip himself, their friends and say that they will also make you their allies.[146] The Olynthians then know how to

---

[144]This prediction was not fulfilled. During the rest of his career Charidemus was a loyal Athenian citizen. See the Introduction.

[145]According to Plutarch (*Alexander* 3.4–5), Philip captured Potidaea in 356 at time of Olympic games. He then expelled Athenian colonists there and made a gift of its territory to Olynthians (Diodorus 16.8.2–3; Dem. 2.7, 6.20). See Psoma 2001: 242, with notes 444 and 448.

[146]These negotiations between the Olynthians must have occurred not long before 352/1. Philip appears to have made a demonstration against

predict the future; will you who are Athenians not do the same thing? It would be shameful for men renowned for knowing how to make well-informed decisions to be seen paying less attention to their vital interests than the Olynthians.[147]

[110] Now, I hear that he is going to make another argument like the one Aristomachus[148] made earlier in the Assembly: it is impossible that Cersebleptes would ever decide to become your enemy by trying to take the Chersonese. Even if he were to take and hold it, he would gain nothing. When there is no war in the area, its revenue does not exceed thirty talents, but if there is war, not even a single talent.[149] On the other hand, the ports that would be closed in that case bring in more than two hundred.[150] What therefore would be his motive for choosing to gain little and go to war when it is possible for him to gain more and remain your friend? One cannot help but wonder, they will say. [111] I have plenty of arguments that I believe would reasonably persuade someone to distrust Cersebleptes rather than to believe these speakers and allow him to grow powerful. Nevertheless, I am going to tell you what occurs to me right now. You certainly know Philip, men of Athens, the Macedonian. It was certainly more to his advantage to receive the revenue from all of Macedonia without interference than to receive those of Amphipolis with risks.[151] It was also preferable for him to keep us as his tra-

---

Olynthus shortly before 352/1 (Dem. 4.17). See Griffith in Hammond 1972–1998: 2.296–304.

[147]The Athenians had a reputation for their intelligence, which Herodotus (1.60.2) mentions. In the Mytilene debate, Cleon criticizes the Athenians for their intellectual sophistication (Thuc. 3.37.4).

[148]On Aristomachus, see the note on 13 above.

[149]Greek cities charged merchants a tax, usually two percent, for using their harbors. See E. M. Harris 1999 and Migeotte 2014: 248–263, especially 261–263, for these revenues.

[150]The phrase is slightly elliptical; he refers to the ports in Cersebleptes' kingdom, which would be closed as a result of war.

[151]Amphipolis was a colony founded by Athens in 437/6 (Thuc. 4.102). The city was taken by the Spartan general Brasidas in 424 (Thuc. 4.103–108). The terms of the Peace of Nicias in 421 awarded the city to Athens

ditional allies rather than the Thessalians, who earlier drove his father into exile.[152] [112] Apart from this example, there is also the following one: you, men of Athens, have never betrayed any of your allies, but the Thessalians have never had an ally whom they did not betray.[153] Yet, although this is the way things stand, you see that Philip has chosen to receive a small amount of revenue, keep untrustworthy friends, and run risks instead of living in safety. [113] What is the reason? There is no rational explanation available. All people, men of Athens, have two options: the first is the greatest of all, success. The other is not as good, but better than the rest: making sound decisions. Men do not acquire both at the same time: no one who is successful sets a limit or bound to his desire for gaining more. For this reason men often lose what they possess because of their desire to gain more.[154] [114] Yet why should one mention Philip or anyone else? Whenever Cotys, the father of Cersebleptes, was engaged in a civil war,

---

(5.18.5). Athenian attempts to recover the city in 417 and 414 were unsuccessful (Thuc. 5.83.4, 7.9). The Athenians renewed their claims to the city around 370 (Aes. 2.32, with Jehne 1992). For Iphicrates' attempt to retake the city between 368 and 365, see Aes. 2.27 and 149. For Timotheus' attempt to retake the city between 365 and 359, see 149 with E. M. Harris 2006: 355–364. Philip took the city in 357 (Diodorus 16.8.2–3). In the *Second Olynthiac* Demosthenes (2.6) alludes to a secret deal between Athens and Philip, which is explained by Theopompus (*FGrHist* 115 F 30). Whatever took place, Athenian democratic institutions made such secret agreements impossible. See de Ste. Croix 1963 (*pace* Trevett 2011: 44–45, with note 4).

[152]Philip agreed to support the Thessalians against the Phocians in the Third Sacred War in return for the revenues from their ports. See Dem. 2.7. Some scholars think that Philip was elected archon of the Thessalians at the time, but this view is based on a misreading of Justin's *Philippic History* (11.3.1–2). See E. M. Harris 1995: 175–176 and Dmitriev 2011: 411–420. Euthycles is mistaken when he says that the Thessalians drove Amyntas, the father of Philip, into exile (for the same mistake, see the scholion to Aes. 2.26). Amyntas was driven out of his kingdom by the Illyrians and helped by the Thessalians (Diodorus 14.92.3–4; 15.19.2). On the reign of Amyntas, see Hammond 1972–1988: 2.172–180 and Borza 1992: 180–197.

[153]It is impossible to know what incidents are alluded to here.

[154]On attitudes to greed in ancient Greece, see Balot 2001.

he sent ambassadors and was ready to do anything because at the time he realized that it was not in his interest to wage war against the city. But when he had Thrace under his control, he captured cities, committed injustice, and in his drunken rage damaged his own interests, then also acted against us. He seized territory; the situation was impossible. Everyone who seeks to commit unjust aggression does not normally take into account the worst consequences but only what he will gain from success. [115] This, then, is the way I think you should make your policy: if Cersebleptes adopts the right attitude toward you, you should do him no wrong, but if he tries to harm you for no reason, he will not be too powerful to be punished. I will read you the letter that Cotys sent when Miltocythes revolted, and the one that he sent to Timomachus when he held complete power and took your territory away from you.[155]

[LETTERS]

[116] Men of Athens, you have seen this example of his actions. You also know that when Philip was besieging Amphipolis, he claimed that he was doing so in order to hand it over to you, then after he took it, he also took Potidaea from you.[156] If you believe me, you will wish to have the same amount of trust that they say Philocrates, the son of Ephialtes, said he had toward the Spartans.[157] [117] They say that when the Spartans were trying to deceive him and offering any assurance that he wished to accept,

---

[155] Euthycles alludes to Cotys' capture of Sestos in early 360: see 158. Miltocythes revolted in late 362: see [Dem.] 50.5. Greek city-states usually conveyed messages to other city-states by sending ambassadors. Foreign kings such as Philip of Macedon often sent letters to Greek city-states. On these letters, see Ceccarelli 2013 and Sickinger 2013.

[156] On Potidaea, see 107n. On Amphipolis, see 111n.

[157] Philocrates, the son of Ephialtes, sailed from Athens with ten ships to help King Evagoras of Cyprus in his revolt against the Persian King around 390 but was captured by the Spartan Teleutias (Xen. *Hellenica* 4.8.24). Nothing more is known about him.

Philocrates replied that he thought that there would be trust only if the Spartans should demonstrate that they would not be able to do wrong if they wished because he knew for certain that they would always want to do so. As long as they were capable of doing harm, therefore, there would be no trust. If you take my advice, you will maintain this kind of trust toward the Thracian and not have to discover in the future what attitude he would have toward you if he should rule all of Thrace.

[118] One would have to be out of one's mind to propose decrees like this and to grant people rewards like these. Many examples make this easy to understand. You surely know as well as I do, men of Athens, that you once made Cotys a citizen clearly because you thought him friendly at the time.[158] In fact, you also gave him gold crowns, which you would not have done if you thought he was actually an enemy. [119] Just the same, when he was a god-forsaken scoundrel and was doing you much harm, you made the men who killed him, Pytho and Heraclides from Ainos, citizens, called them benefactors, and gave them gold crowns.[159] If someone had proposed when Cotys appeared to be on your side, that if someone kills Cotys, he is to be extradited, would you extradite Pytho and his brother or would you violate this decree and make them citizens and honor them as benefactors? [120] Another example: when Alexander of Thessaly held Pelopidas as his prisoner and was the Thebans' worst enemy, he was so

---

[158]Cotys gained the throne of Thrace in 384/3 and presumably given citizenship shortly after this. Cf. [Dem.] 12.9.

[159]On these grants of citizenship, see M. J. Osborne 1981–1983: 58–59. The Athenians gave the tyrannicides Harmodius and Aristogeiton heroic honors and granted special privileges to their descendants. See Taylor 1991. On their statues, see Azoulay 2014. The Athenians passed a decree moved by Demophantus after the fall of the Thirty in 403 granting the same honors to anyone who killed a tyrant or someone attempting to overthrow the democracy. See Dem. 20.159 and Lyc. *Against Leocrates* 124–127. The document found at And. 1.96–98 is a forgery, and the information contained in it not reliable as evidence. See E. M. Harris 2013/2014 (*pace* Teegarden 2012; Teegarden 2014: 15–53; J. L. Shear 2007; and Sommerstein 2014).

friendly to you that he asked you to send him a general, and you sent him support, and Alexander was everything.[160] By Zeus, if someone had written, "If someone kills Alexander, he is subject to arrest," would it have been safe to attempt to punish him for his subsequent acts of arrogance and abuse?[161] [121] Why should one cite other examples? The man who now appears to be your greatest enemy is this man Philip.[162] When he captured some of our citizens who were trying to restore Argaeus, then released them and returned all the property they lost, he sent a letter announcing that he was ready to make an alliance and renew our ancestral friendship.[163] If he had asked to receive these honors, and

---

[160]In 368 Alexander of Pherai took the Thebans Pelopidas and Hismenias prisoner at Pharsalos (Diodorus 15.71.2; Plut. *Pelopidas* 27.5–7 and *Moralia* 194D; Polybius 8.35.7–9; Pausanias 9.15.1). Alexander appealed to Athens for support and concluded an alliance (*IG* ii² 116, lines 39–40; Diodorus 15.71.3). The Athenians erected a bronze statue of him (Plut. *Pelopidas* 31.4). On this episode, see Buckler 1980: 123–129.

[161]In 362 Alexander seized the island of Tenos, an Athenian ally; enslaved its inhabitants (Dem. 50.4); and fought the Athenians at Peparethos (Diodorus 15.95.1–3). In 361/0 the Athenians concluded an alliance with the Thessalians against him (*IG* ii² 116, especially lines 31–34). He was later murdered by his wife (Plutarch *Pelopidas* 35.7). On Alexander of Pherai, see Sprawski 2006.

[162]Lane Fox 1997: 185 believes that Euthycles is alluding to Philip's victory at Crocus Field and his attempt to seize Thermopylae in 352, but this is unconvincing. The Athenians had many good reasons to consider Philip a serious enemy before 352, especially after his capture of Amphipolis, which the Athenians claimed; his conquest of their bases at Potidaea, Methone, and Pydna; and his defeat of the Athenian allies Lyppeius, Grabus, and Cetriporis in Northern Greece.

[163]When Philip II acceded to the Macedonian throne in 360/59, the Athenians supported his rival Argaeus and sent the general Mantias with 3,000 hoplites and ships (Diodorus 16.2.6). To deprive Argaeus of Athenian support, Philip withdrew the Macedonian garrison from Amphipolis and declared the city independent. He then defeated Argaeus near Aegae (Diodorus 16.3.3–6; cf. 16.4.1–2). For Philip's release of Athenian prisoners after the battle, see Libanius 15.42 and 20.23; Justin 7.6.6. On this incident, see Heskel 1996. Euthycles says that such an award to Philip would have been

one of the men he released proposed that if someone kills Philip, he is subject to arrest, we would have been quite humiliated. [122] Don't you see and understand, men of Athens, what a great penalty you would have paid for your foolishness in each case if you had actually voted some decree like this? Men who are not in their right mind, I think, do one of two things: either when they make a friend, they trust him so much that they throw away the chance to defend themselves if he tries to wrong them; or when they think someone an enemy, they hate him so much that if he ceases his hostility and wishes to become a friend, their attitude prevents any reconciliation.[164] There should be limits, I think, to friendship and hatred; in each case one should not go beyond the right measure.[165]

[123] Now, I certainly cannot see what would stop all those people who can claim to have done you a service from asking for the same privileges if you will give them to Charidemus, for example, if you wish, Simon, Bianor, Athenodorus, and thousands of others. If we are going to vote the same privileges for all, we are likely to start acting like mercenaries without realizing and serving as bodyguards for each of these men. Yet if we grant them to one and not the others, those who don't receive them will have a right to complain. [124] Look, if Menestratus of Eretria[166] asks

---

an embarrassment after Philip turned against the Athenians. The "ancestral friendship" could mean the ties the Athenians had with the Macedonian kings Alexander, Perdiccas, and Archelaus in the fifth century or the Athenian alliance with Philip's father Amyntas III (Aes. 2.26).

[164]This is similar to an idea found in Sophocles *Ajax* 678–682: "Our enemy must be hated as one will sometime become a friend and in helping a friend I shall aim to assist him as one assists a man who will not remain a friend forever" (trans. Lloyd-Jones). A similar maxim was attributed to Bias of Priene, who lived in the sixth century. See Arist. *Rhetoric* 2.13.1389b23–25 and Diogenes Laertius 1.87. For other examples, see Tziatzi-Papagianni 1994: 404–405.

[165]For the idea that there is a limit to enmity, see Sophocles *Ajax* 1332–1373.

[166]Menestratus ruled Eretria on the island of Euboea in this period and was replaced by Plutarch, another tyrant (Plut. *Phocion* 12, 13.7, 14.2, with

you to vote the same privileges for himself, or Phayllus of Pho-cis[167] or some other dynast (circumstances often cause us to be-come the friends of dynasts), will we vote such privileges for all of them or not? By Zeus, we will vote them. And what will we say, men of Athens, if we claim to defend the freedom of the Greeks yet also clearly serve as bodyguards for those who possess private armies hostile to democracy? [125] If something like this must be granted to anyone (which I say it should not), it should be given, first, to someone who has done us no wrong; second, to someone who will not be in a position to harm us even if he wishes; then to someone who will clearly be devoted to protecting all men from suffering injustice and not for the purpose of harming others with impunity. I will pass over the fact that Charidemus is not among those who have done us no wrong nor among those who are seek-ing this privilege to protect themselves. But listen to me when I say that he will not be trustworthy in the future and see if you think that my analysis is correct.

[126] In my opinion, men of Athens, all those who aspire to share our values and laws and are eager to become citizens, obtain those rights, and at the same time live with us and exercise the rights they wanted.[168] But all those who have no desire or ambi-tion to obtain these rights but seek the advantages that they reap by appearing to win your esteem, these men, I think, no, in fact, I know for certain, when they see hope of greater gain elsewhere, they will turn their backs on you and will pursue that option. [127] For example, so that you know what I have in mind when

---

Picard 1979: 240–241).

[167] Phayllus, the brother of the Phocian leader Onomarchus (Diodorus 16.35.1), succeeded his brother after the latter's death at the battle of Cro-cus Field in the summer of 352 (Diodorus 16.37.1) and died not long after in 351 (Diodorus 16.38.6). Phayllus could not be described as a dynast before this date because he commanded only troops. This would place the date of the speech after the middle of 352 and rule out an earlier date for the speech (Sealey 1955: 118; *pace* Lane Fox 1997: 184–186).

[168] For a noncitizen to obtain citizenship at Athens, the Assembly had to vote that he was worthy of the privilege. As a result, relatively few grants of citizenship were made. See M. J. Osborne 1981–1983.

I say this, this man Pytho I just mentioned, after he killed Cotys and thought it was not safe for him to go just anywhere, came to you and asked for citizenship and placed you ahead of everyone. But when he thinks Philip's affairs are better suited to his interests, he completely turns his back on you and takes Philip's side. There is nothing, men of Athens, there is nothing secure nor honest in men whose sole aim in life is greed. On the contrary, any person with good sense must be on his guard against them and not trust them first, then later complain.

[128] Let us assume, men of Athens, the opposite of the truth, namely, that Charidemus has been, is now, and will be devoted to your interests and will never change his attitude. It still is not a good idea to vote this decree for him. If he obtained the immunity granted by the decree for some other reason than our relations with Cersebleptes, there would be less danger. But as it is, I have thought about it and found that this man on whose behalf he will exercise the advantage of this decree deserves neither your trust nor his. [129] Just look at how fairly I am examining each topic and how completely justified are my fears. I notice that Cotys was a relative of Iphicrates by marriage in the same way that Cersebleptes is related to Charidemus, and I see that Iphicrates has done much more for Cotys—and deserved far more gratitude—than Charidemus has done for Cersebleptes.[169] [130] Let us consider what happened: you certainly know, men of Athens, that you granted Iphicrates the honor of a bronze statue and the right to dine in the Prytaneum and other rewards and honors, which were the source of his good fortune, yet he dared

---

[169]The Athenian general Iphicrates married a relative of Cotys in the early 380s. The marriage is described in detail by the comic poet Anaxandrides (Athenaeus *Deipnosophistai* 4.131 = Anaxandrides fr. 42 Kassel-Austin). Athenaeus and Nepos (*Iphicrates* 3.4) report that Iphicrates married Cotys' daughter, but Davies 1971: 249 argues that it must have been his sister because Cotys was not old enough in the 380s to have had a daughter of marriageable age. His son Menestheus by this marriage was married to Timotheus' daughter in the early 360s ([Dem.] 49.66). See E. M. Harris 2006: 362–363, correcting Davies 1971: 250–251. For the date of Charidemus' marriage, see the Introduction.

to fight for Cotys' interests and against your generals.[170] He considered Cotys' safety more important than the honors that you gave him. If you had not shown more moderation in your anger than he did in his rashness, nothing would have prevented him from being the most wretched man in the world. [131] And yet after Cotys was saved and had real proof of his friendship, just when he thought that he was safe and secure, he was not eager to repay the favor nor to perform any act of generosity for you to gain forgiveness for his previous actions, but demanded that Iphicrates join in his campaign against the rest of your possessions. [132] When he refused, Cotys took the army of barbarians that Iphicrates had recruited and took Charidemus into his pay, then attacked your territories and placed Iphicrates in such an impossible position that he departed and lived in Antissa and later in Drys, thinking it was not a good idea for him to return to your city after he had taken the Thracian's side instead of yours.[171] Yet he also did not think it safe to remain at the court of Cotys, who, as he saw, showed so little concern for his safety. [133] If, then, men of Athens, Cersebleptes grows more powerful because of the immunity granted to Charidemus, then abandons him, and stirs up trouble and marches against you, will you be satisfied, if Charidemus' hopes are disappointed, with having strengthened the Thracian against you? I do not think that would be right. This is what I think is right: if Charidemus realizes this possibility and sees it coming, then succeeds in obtaining these decrees, [134] put an end to his plotting. But, if he has not realized it, the more one considers him loyal to you, the more you should look out both

---

[170]The statue of Iphicrates was on the Acropolis (Pausanias 1.24.7) and was the subject of a lawsuit in 372/1 (Dionysius of Halicarnassus *Lysias* 12). This and his other honors were probably for his victories in 373/2, especially at Cephallonia and Corcyra (Xen. *Hellenica* 6.2.32–38; Diodorus 16.57.2; Polyaenus *Strategemata* 3.9.55).

[171]Iphicrates retreated to Antissa and Drys probably because he did not wish to return to Athens through fear of prosecution for not retaking Amphipolis. See E. M. Harris 1989; Bettalli 2013: 375. Drys was an *emporion* located on the coast of Thrace opposite Samothrace. See Hansen and Heine Nielsen 2004: 878.

for your interests and for his. What good friends should do for their friends is to avoid doing them favors that will cause harm to their friends and to themselves, but to cooperate with them in doing what will benefit both parties, but when one sees into the future better than the other, to make good plans and not to sacrifice one's future interests for the pleasure of the moment.

[135] Even when I think about it, I still cannot understand how Cersebleptes, an unreliable barbarian, would not intend to wrong Charidemus. When I consider how much Cotys almost caused Iphicrates to lose without caring in the least, I think that Cersebleptes would not care about what Charidemus would lose. [136] Cotys thought that he would deprive Iphicrates of his honors, his right to dine the Prytaneum, his statue, and the country that made him an object of envy, I might almost say all those things without which life would not have been worth living for Iphicrates; he showed no restraint.[172] But what in fact might Cersebleptes have a reason not to take away from Charidemus? He has neither children, nor a statue, nor relatives, nor anything else in our country. [137] If Cersebleptes has no natural loyalty, if his record in the past gives us good reason to distrust him, if there is nothing in the situation that would cause him to change his attitude and character and to show any concern for Charidemus, what reason is there for us to cooperate with him out of simple and absolute stupidity in gaining what he wants, which is also against our interests? I do not see any.

[138] The decree brings no advantage to our foreign policy. Nor does it help our city's reputation to be seen passing such a decree. You need to understand this. Men of Athens, if the decree had been proposed for someone living in our city and obeying its laws, it would be less dangerous but still shameful. But in fact it has

---

[172]The right to dine in the Prytaneum (*sitesis*) was the highest honor awarded in Classical Athens. On the right, see M. J. Osborne 1981. The location of the Prytaneion is a matter of debate. Schmalz 2006 places it at Hagia Aikaterini Square northeast of the Acropolis, but see Kavvadias and Matthaiou 2014, who place it on the Street of Tripods about 150 meters east of the cave of Aglauros. On the rationale for honorary decrees in the fourth century, see Lambert 2011b.

been proposed for Charidemus, who lives in no city at all, serves as general for a Thracian,[173] and through his kingship does injustice to many. [139] Certainly you know that all mercenary leaders aim at gaining power by taking Greek cities. But all those who wish to live in their own country free and under the rule of law consider these men who wander around the whole world, if one can tell the truth, as their common enemies. Is it honorable or fitting for you, men of Athens, to be seen voting to grant protection like this for a man who plots against anyone he meets to serve his own greed and to announce in advance that anyone who defends his own freedom will be banned from the territory of your allies? [140] I find this neither honorable nor worthy of you. You blame the Spartans for decreeing that the Great King could do anything he wishes to the Greeks living in Asia;[174] isn't it shameful for you to surrender to Cersebleptes not only the Greeks living in Europe but also those whom Charidemus thinks he will conquer? This decree will have no other effect when it does not specify what must be done and what not for Cersebleptes' general and creates so much intimidation for anyone who defends himself.

[141] Look, now, men of Athens, I would like to tell you about an event in the past that will make it even more obvious to you that this decree must by all means be nullified. At a certain period and in certain circumstances you made Ariobarzanes a citizen and Philiscus because of him just as you are now making Charidemus a citizen because of Cersebleptes.[175] Philiscus followed

---

[173]The manuscripts add the word *basilei* (king) after *Thraki anthropo*, but this is probably an intrusive gloss and has been deleted by Cobet.

[174]By the terms of the Peace of Antalcidas in 386, the Spartans compelled the Greeks to make a peace treaty, which granted the King of Persia control over the Greek cities of Asia Minor (Xen. *Hellenica* 5.1.25–29). See Badian 1991. In the following years Isocrates (4.120–124, 12.59–61) criticized the treaty as a betrayal of Greek freedom.

[175]Around 369 Ariobarzanes, the satrap of Phrygia (Diodorus 15.90.3), sent the mercenary captain Philiscus to Delphi to attempt to make peace between the Thebans and their allies and the Spartans. When he did not succeed, Philiscus started to hire mercenaries to fight for the Spartans (Xen. *Hellenica* 7.1.27; Diodorus 15.70.2). The award of citizenship to Ariobarzanes

the same profession as Charidemus and through Ariobarzanes' power was conquering Greek cities. In every city he entered, he did many shocking things, raping free boys and women and doing everything a man who was raised without the benefit of law or civilized life would do when he came to power. [142] There were two men in Lampsacus: one was named Thersagoras; the other, Execestus. Both of them shared our attitude toward tyrants and killed Philiscus, an act of justice, with the intention of liberating their country.[176] Let us imagine that when Philiscus was leading the mercenaries he hired in Perinthus, held the entire Hellespont, and was the most powerful satrap, one of the men who spoke for him proposed a decree just as this man has, that if anyone killed Philiscus, he was subject to extradition in the territory of the allies. By Zeus, do you see how shameful that would be for our city? [143] Thersagoras and Execestus came to Lesbos and lived there. If one of Philiscus' friends or children laid a hand on them, they would have been surrendered to them thanks to your decree. How is it not shameful and shocking, men of Athens, for you to be seen setting up bronze statues of men who do such things and granting them the greatest honors, but voting to surrender those who elsewhere have the same attitude about their own country? In that case, everything turned out well, and you were not deceived and suffered no embarrassment. In this case, if you follow my advice, you will avoid this. If a decree is not specific but simply states: "if anyone kills Charidemus," the same kind of thing could happen at any time.

[144] At this point I would like to examine Charidemus' past in a few words and to reveal how thoroughly shameful are those who praise him. I promise you one thing, and let no one be angry with my promise: I will show you not only that he does not deserve the protection this man has proposed but also that he should justly pay the greatest penalty if it should be right to pun-

---

and Philiscus probably dates to this time and before the revolt of the former from the Persian King in 366 (Dem. 15.9). See M. J. Osborne 1981–1983: 3.50–53. On relations between Ariobarzanes and Athens, see Weiskopf 1989.

[176]The death of Philiscus appears to have occurred between 363 and 361. See Heskel 1997: 117. On Athenian attitudes about killing tyrants, see 119n.

ish those who are your enemies, who deceive you, and who act against your interests. [145] Perhaps some of you have begun to wonder how you could have been so easily deceived when he was first made a citizen, then again when he was given gold crowns for being our benefactor. Rest assured, men of Athens, that you were deceived. I will tell you the reasons why this justifiably happened to you. Many times, men of Athens, you have good ideas but do not carry them out to the end. [146] What sort of thing I am talking about? If someone were to ask you what is the most dishonest group in the city, you would not answer the farmers or the merchants or those who work the mines or any men like this.[177] But if someone were to answer those who make a habit of speaking and proposing decrees for a fee, I am certain that you would all agree. Up to this point you have judged well; from this point on, you go wrong. [147] You think that these men are the most corrupt, but you have trusted them when it comes to evaluating each person's character. When they tell you that someone is good or bad, they judge him according to their own interests, not in terms of justice and truth. This is exactly the way the politicians have always treated Charidemus. You too will agree after I tell you about his past.

[148] I do not count as a crime all the campaigns he fought against you from the beginning as a soldier in the ranks of the slingers and the light-armed troops.[178] I omit the fact that he maintained a pirate ship and raided your allies. Why? Because, men of Athens, pressing needs remove all rational calculations about right and wrong. If one is to judge a person rightly, one should not get too caught up in these details. But listen to me as I tell you about the harm he did to you from the point when he started to lead mercenaries and to command some troops. [149] First of all, this man was hired by Iphicrates and served under him for more

---

[177]This passage is important for showing that there was no prejudice in democratic Athens against those involved in trade and crafts. For the numerous Athenian citizens involved in trade and crafts, see E. M. Harris 2002.

[178]Charidemus probably fought among light-armed soldiers called peltasts, which came from Thrace. On these troops, see Best 1969.

than three years.[179] After you removed Iphicrates from the office of general and sent Timotheus as general against Amphipolis and the Chersonese,[180] he turned over to the people of Amphipolis the hostages from their city, which Iphicrates had received from Harpalus and given to him to guard after you voted that he send them to you.[181] This is what prevented you from taking Amphipolis.[182] Second, after Timotheus hired him and his troops, he did not serve Timotheus but sailed off with your light triremes to Cotys, who he clearly knew was your greatest enemy in the world. [150] After that, when Timotheus decided to wage the campaign against Amphipolis before the one against the Chersonese, Charidemus, unable to do you any harm in that area, hired himself to the Olynthians, your enemies, who held Amphipolis at the time.[183] He sailed from there, leaving from Cardia, to fight against the city and was captured by our triremes.[184] Because of circumstances and the need for mercenaries in the war against Amphipolis, instead of being punished for not returning the hostages and for deserting to Cotys, who was your enemy, and taking your

---

[179]Iphicrates was sent to capture Amphipolis around 369 (Aes. 2.27).

[180]Timotheus replaced Iphicrates around 365. See Heskel 1997: 28.

[181]The name Harpalus is Macedonian, and these hostages appear to have been given by the people of Amphipolis to the Macedonian king Ptolemy as part of an alliance. See Heskel 1997: 28. Euthycles does not explain why Harpalus gave these hostages to Iphicrates. Because he is not an impartial source, it is possible that Euthycles is misrepresenting events and that Charidemus may have had a good reason to return the hostages. It is possible that Iphicrates may not have paid Charidemus and that Charidemus raised money for his troops by handing the hostages over in return for payment.

[182]This explanation is implausible. Iphicrates may have tried to blame his failure to take Amphipolis on the incident as a way of evading responsibility. It is more likely that the Athenian failure to take Amphipolis in these years was caused by Olynthian support for Amphipolis. See the next section and Psoma 2001: 231, with note 362.

[183]Euthycles naturally interprets all of Charidemus' actions as motivated by hostility to Athens, but his reason for sailing to help the Olynthians may have been that the Olynthians had offered to hire his mercenaries.

[184]Cardia was an independent Greek city on the Thracian Chersonese. In the late 340s it was the site of a conflict between Athens and Philip II.

triaconters, he exchanged assurances and fought on your side.[185]
[151] He should have been grateful to you for not executing him
as he deserved: in return for his crimes, the city acted as if it owed
him something and gave him crowns and citizenship and those
privileges all of you know. To show that I speak the truth, read for
me the decree about the hostages, and Iphicrates' letter and the
one from Timotheus, then this testimony. You will see that what I
say is not mere words or allegations but the truth. Read.

[DECREE, LETTERS, TESTIMONY]

[152] First of all, he hired himself out to places where he knew
he would fight against you when it was possible for him to seek
work in many other places. Later, when he could not do you any
harm there, he sailed back here where he could fight against the
city and was the main reason why we did not take Amphipolis.
You have heard this from the decree and the testimony. This is
what Charidemus' early career was like; you will see what happened next. [153] After some time passed and there was already a
war against Cotys, he sent a letter to you (actually not to you but
to Cephisodotus; he would not have done that if he thought he
could hoodwink the city, aware of what he did). In this letter he
promised to return the Chersonese to the city, although he had
decided to do just the opposite. You need to hear about the business with the letter (it is short) and think about the way this man
has dealt with you from the beginning. [154] When he was ca-
shiered by Timotheus, he left Amphipolis, crossed to Asia, and because of Artabazus' arrest by Autophradates, he hires himself and
his troops to the brothers-in-law of Artabazus after exchanging

---

[185]Triaconters ("thirty-oared" ships) were smaller than triremes, which
normally had about two hundred rowers. They were used for irregular operations (Thuc. 4.9; Xen. *Anabasis* 5.1.16). According to Polyaenus (3.9.63),
Iphicrates had one hundred triaconters when raiding Phoenice in the Adri-
atic. Their gear is recorded in *IG* ii² 1629, lines 91–164, 330–335, but they
are not listed among the ships in the naval registers. See Gabrielsen 1994:
128–129.

guarantees with them.[186] He paid little attention to his oaths and, taking advantage of the people in the area who had let down their guard because they considered him a friend, he seizes Scepsis, Cebren, and Ilium from them.[187] [155] After gaining control of these places, he suffered the kind of reverse that one would not expect to happen to someone who claimed to be a general, nor even to an ordinary person. He did not have even a single place along the coast where he had access to a good supply of grain for his soldiers, and he had no grain in his area. Instead of looting these places and retreating, he stayed inside the walls because he was set on doing injustice. When Artabazus had collected a force and arrived there after being released by Autophradates, he gained access to a supply of grain from upper Phrygia, Lydia, and Paphlagonia, which belonged to him.[188] Charidemus, on the other hand, had no other prospect than to face a siege. [156] He realized the danger he was in and figured that he was about to be reduced to starvation if nothing else. Either at someone's suggestion or by his own decision, he saw that there was only one path to safety, that which is open to all men. What is this? Your generous nature or whatever else you must call it.[189] With this thought in mind,

---

[186]Autophradates was the satrap of Lydia (Diodorus 15.90.3). Artabazus was the son of Pharnabazus (the satrap of Hellespontine Phrygia) and Apame (the daughter of the Persian King Artaxerxes; Xen. *Hellenica* 5.1.28) and was probably born around 388. He married the sister of the Rhodians Mentor and Memnon (Diodorus 16.52.4; *IG* ii² 356). Artabazus appears to have taken over his father's satrapy around 363 after the revolt of Ariobarzanes (see 141n). On his career, see Weiskopf 1989: 54–64. Euthycles does not give the reason for the arrest. The two satraps may have disagreed about how to deal with the supporters of the rebels Ariobarzanes and Orontes. See Weiskopf 1989: 61–63.

[187]These cities are in the Troad near the Aegean and the Hellespont and would have formed part of Artabazus' satrapy.

[188]Artabazus controlled these territories by virtue of his satrapy in Phrygia.

[189]On the generous nature of the Athenians, see Dem. 21.184; 22.51; 24.51, 170, 190.

he sends you a letter, which is worth hearing. What he wanted by promising to return the Chersonese to you and giving the impression that Cephisodotus, who was an enemy of Cotys and Iphicrates, had this intention, was to obtain some triremes from you and escape from Asia to safety.[190] [157] What happened immediately after his guilt was clearly proven? Memnon and Mentor, the brothers-in-law of Artabazus, young men enjoying unanticipated good fortune because of their relationship with Artabazus, wished to rule the country without delay and in peace, to receive honors, and to stop fighting and facing danger.[191] They persuade Artabazus to give up his effort to punish Charidemus and to send him away under a truce by convincing him that you would transport him across even against his wishes and that he would not be able to prevent it. [158] When Charidemus gained safety contrary to any reasonable expectation, he crossed to the Chersonese on his own thanks to the truce; then far from attacking Cotys after writing that Cotys would not stand firm if he attacked him or that he would work with you to recover the Chersonese, he hired himself out again to Cotys and laid siege to the rest of your possessions, Crithote and Elaeus.[192] He decided to do this and to deceive you when he was in Asia and sent the letter to you. You will understand this from the route he followed when he crossed over. Leaving from Abydos, which had always been hostile to you, the place from which those who captured Sestos set out, he crossed to Sestos, which Cotys held.[193] [159] Yet do not think that the people of Abydos and those at Sestos would have welcomed him after he sent that letter to you, unless they were aware that he was deceiving you and were collaborating in his deception. Their aim was to get you to provide security for the transport of his army and, once it was across, which happened because Artabazus granted them

---

[190]Cephisodotus was an Athenian general sent to the Chersonese in late 360.

[191]On Memnon and Mentor, see 154n.

[192]Timotheus captured these cities during his campaign in the area around 361. See Xen. *Agesilaus* 2.26 and Nepos *Timotheus* 1.2.

[193]Cotys had captured Sestos around 361/0.

free passage, to make use of it to help themselves. To show that these are the facts, read the letters, both the one that Charidemus sent and those from the commanders in the Chersonese. You will see from them that these are the facts.

[LETTER]

[160] Recall the place from which he departed, from Abydos to Sestos. Do you think the people of Abydos or Sestos would have welcomed him if they were not participating in his deception when he sent the letter to you?

Read the actual letter. Note, men of Athens, how he exaggerates as he sings his own praises when writing to you about what he has done and what he promises to do.

[LETTER]

[161] Excellent, isn't it? Men of Athens, what he wrote would deserve much gratitude if it were actually true. In reality, when he did not think that he was going to obtain a truce, he wrote this to deceive you. When he did obtain it, read the kind of things that he did.

[LETTER]

After Charidemus promised to restore the lost territories and crossed over, the commander at Crithote said that the danger to the territory still in our control had become more serious than before.[194] Show them another letter and read a passage from it.

[LETTER]

Read from another letter.

---

[194]The letter of the commander may have stated only that the situation was desperate without naming Charidemus' actions as the cause.

[LETTER]

[162] You see that the facts are verified by testimony from all sides: after crossing over, he marched not against Cotys but joined with him and marched against you. Read for me only one more letter, this one, and leave aside the others. It has become clear, I suppose, that he has deceived you. Read.

[LETTER]

Stop. Notice that after writing that he would give back the Chersonese, he hired himself to your enemies and tried to take away the rest of your territory; then after writing that he had not received the ambassador sent by Alexander, he clearly acted the same way Alexander's pirates did.[195] A true friend, isn't he? And one who is straight with you, I suppose, who would never send a dishonest letter or deceive you?

[163] These are not the only facts proving (although it is plainly clear) that none of his professions of loyalty to our city can be trusted; this will be even more obvious from what happened next. Pytho did a fine deed by killing Cotys, who was your enemy and dishonest. Cersebleptes, who is now king, was a mere child and so were all the sons of Cotys, and Charidemus, profiting by his presence there and from having an army, seized control of the situation. Cephisodotus then arrived as general, the man to whom Charidemus sent that letter, along with the triremes that were about to protect him in the event that Artabazus did not give his consent when it was unclear how he was going to escape. [164] What should a man who was truly sincere and friendly have done, men of Athens? The general was there, and he

---

[195] On Alexander of Pherai, see 120nn. This embassy must have occurred before the death of Alexander of Pherai in 358. The decision of Charidemus not to receive the ambassador of Alexander, who was the enemy of Athens at the time, would indicate that Charidemus was pro-Athenian at the time, but Euthycles does not stress this point. Euthycles says that Charidemus offered to help the Athenians in the Chersonese but does not say if they accepted his offer.

was not one of those who Charidemus could have said bore him a grudge but was a person whom he had chosen as a friend in Athens. He had sent him that letter, and after Cotys had died, he was in control of the situation. Shouldn't he have given the territory back to you right away, joined with you in setting up a king of Thrace, and shown his goodwill toward you when an opportunity like this presented itself? I would say so. [165] Did he then do any of these things? Far from it. For seven months he spent all his time fighting against us, was openly hostile and without a single kind word for us. Initially we were anchored at Perinthus with only ten ships and heard that Charidemus was nearby so that we could meet with him and discuss the situation.[196] Watching for the moment when our troops were taking their meal, he tried to seize our ships, killed many sailors, and drove all the others into the sea with some cavalry and light troops. [166] Then after we sailed away, not to any place or territory in Thrace—one could not even say, "By Zeus, he did some harm because he was defending himself to avoid suffering any harm himself." That is not possible: we did not come to any place in Thrace but to Alopeconnesus, which is and was then part of our territory in the Chersonese, a cape extending toward Imbros, far away from Thrace, a place full of pirates and cutthroats. We arrived there and laid siege to these men. [167] Charidemus, after marching through your entire part of the Chersonese, attacked us and helped the pirates and cutthroats.[197] Through his persistence he partly convinced, partly compelled your general not to pursue your best interests instead of being persuaded to do what he had agreed and promised to do. He then drew up a treaty with Cephisodotus that made you so angry that you removed the general from office and fined him five talents. Only three votes prevented him from being sentenced to death.[198] [168] How absurd must it appear, men of Athens, when

---

[196]Euthycles was serving as a trierarch during this campaign. See 5.

[197]Euthycles blackens the reputation of the people of Alopeconnesus and criticizes Charidemus for supporting them, but he skips over the Athenian invasion of Thracian territory.

[198]The trial of Cephisodotus must have taken place around 359. Euthycles may have been the prosecutor. For the sources, see Hansen 1975: 98–99.

for the same actions we see one man so harshly punished as guilty and another is still even now honored as a benefactor? You witnessed what happened to the general and can testify that I am telling the truth. You put him on trial, removed him from office, and expressed your anger. You know all the facts about this. Call as witnesses the trierarchs at Perinthus and Alopeconnesus.

[WITNESSES]

[169] Later, when Cephisodotus was relieved of his command, you did not think the treaty concluded with him was good or just. Then Miltocythes, who was always loyal to you, this good man Charidemus arrests after he was betrayed by Smicythion.[199] Because it was illegal for the Thracians to put one another to death, Charidemus knew that Miltocythes would be safe if he were brought to Cersebleptes, and he turns him over to the people of Cardia, your enemies. They took him and his son and sailed with them out to sea in a boat, then cut his son's throat and threw him into the sea as he watched this happening to his son. [170] All the Thracians were furious about this, and Berisades and Amadocus joined forces.[200] Seeing this opportunity, Athenodorus made an

---

[199]The Athenians had sent support to Miltocythes in late 362. See [Dem.] 50.5. Even though Euthycles puts Charidemus' actions in the worst possible light, one must recall that Miltocythes had rebelled from Cotys and that Charidemus was at the time supporting Cotys' son Cersebleptes. Charidemus may have had nothing to do with the decision of the Cardians to put Miltocythes to death. The claim that Charidemus gave Miltocythes to the people of Cardia because the Thracians were not permitted to kill each other is quite implausible and probably invented to explain why Charidemus himself did not have Miltocythes executed. It is equally implausible that Miltocythes, who had rebelled against Cotys, would have been safe had he been surrendered to his son Cersebleptes.

[200]Euthcyles blames the outbreak of war between Cersebleptes and his brothers on the death of Miltocythes, but it is hardly credible that Berisades and Amadocus would have objected to the execution of someone who had rebelled against their father. The rivalry of the three brothers, each striving

alliance with them and was prepared to go to war.[201] With Cersebleptes intimidated, Athenodorus concluded a treaty by which he
compelled him to swear an oath to you and to the kings that the
entire kingdom be divided into three parts and that all of them
would return your territory to you. [171] When you appointed
Chabrias at the elections to carry on that war, Athenodorus had
to dismiss his troops because he had no money from you or any
resources, and Chabrias had to sail out with just one ship. What
was this Charidemus doing? He renounced the agreement that he
had concluded with Athenodorus and persuaded Cersebleptes to
do the same. Then, he concludes one with Chabrias that was even
more dreadful than the one with Cephisodotus.[202] Chabrias was
forced to put up with this, I suppose, because he had no forces
with him. [172] When you heard this, there were many speeches
in the Assembly, and treaties were read out; without showing any
respect for Chabrias' reputation or any of his supporters, you rejected this agreement too and voted a decree on the motion of
Glaucon to elect ten ambassadors from among your citizens and
instructed them to receive the oath from Cersebleptes again if he
was abiding by the treaty with Athenodorus and, if not, to receive the oaths from the two kings and make plans to wage war
against Cersebleptes.[203] [173] After the ambassadors sailed away,
time passed and the situation progressed to the point where, because of their delays and their unwillingness to do anything
straightforward or honest, we sent help to Euboea,[204] and Cha-

---

for complete control of Thrace, is a more likely explanation for the outbreak
of hostilities.

[201] On Athenodorus, see 12n.

[202] These events are to be dated around 358.

[203] The Athenians and other Greeks often sent embassies of as many as
ten ambassadors on important missions to foreign communities. See Mosley 1973: 55–62.

[204] In 357 the Athenians supported the Euboeans in their revolt against
Thebes and gained them as allies. See Diodorus 16.7.2; Aes. 3.85. For the alli-
ance between the Euboeans and the Athenians, see *IG* ii² 124. On events in
Euboea during this period, see Brunt 1969; Picard 1979: 237–240.

res returned with mercenaries and sailed out to the Chersonese as your general with full powers.²⁰⁵ In this case he concluded a treaty with Chares in the presence of Athenodorus and the kings, the one that is the best and the most fair.²⁰⁶ His actions proved that his attitude toward our city was opportunistic and that he never decided to do anything sincere or honest. [174] Next, you see that he is your friend by necessity and that he adjusts his loyalty according the amount of power you hold. Do you think that we should allow him to grow more powerful and do so through your own actions? You have not taken the right decision. So that you know that I am telling the truth, take for me the letter that arrived after the first treaty; next, the one from Berisades. This is the best way for you to learn and grasp the point.

[LETTER]

And read the letter of Berisades.

[LETTER]

[175] This is the way the alliance with the kings was arranged after the chicanery surrounding the treaty with Cephisodotus. Miltocythes had been eliminated; Charidemus' actions revealed that he was the city's enemy. The man who saw fit to seize and turn over to your enemies, the Cardians, someone whom he knew to be always your most faithful ally among the Thracians, how

---

²⁰⁵The term "with full powers" (*autokrator*) indicates that Chares had the power to make tactical decisions in the field without consulting the Assembly.

²⁰⁶Fragments of this treaty are extant and are dated to 357/6 (*IG* ii² 126 = Tod 1947, no. 151). The treaty provided that if any of the cities owing tribute to the Thracian kings and to Athens does not pay the Athenians, the Thracian kings are to levy the sum (lines 4–9). If the cities do not pay the Thracian kings, the Athenians are to collect the money for them (lines 9–13). Those cities that pay the tribute are to be free and independent (lines 13–18). If any city revolts from Athens, the kings shall help the Athenians (lines 18–21).

did he not provide an example of his deep hostility toward you? Read the treaty that Cersebleptes made with the Thracians and with Athenodorus when he was afraid of war.

[TREATY]

[176] This was the treaty that he wrote and concluded after swearing the oath that you have heard. But when he saw the troops of Athenodorus dismissed and Chabrias arriving with only a single trireme, he did not surrender Iphiades' son to you nor did he fulfill any of the promises that he swore, but renounced the other clauses in the treaty.[207] This is the treaty he wrote. Take this one here for me and read it.

[TREATY]

[177] Observe that he claims the right to collect duties and tolls and negotiates as if the territory belonged to him by demanding that his toll collectors have control over these duties. As for Iphiades' son, whom he was holding as hostage for Sestos and promised to surrender to Athenodorus, he makes no such promise any more. Take the decree that you voted in response to these demands. Read.

[DECREE]

[178] After the ambassadors came to Thrace, Cersebleptes sent you this letter here and agreed to not a single fair condition. The others sent this letter here. Read them.

[LETTER]

Read the letter from the kings and see if you think that they have any complaints to make.

---

[207]Iphiades was the leader of a faction at Abydos, where he established a tyranny (Arist. *Politics* 5.1306a).

[LETTER]

Men of Athens, you see and understand his dishonesty and his treachery, how he turns everything upside down. At first he mistreated Cephisodotus, then from fear of Athenodorus turned around and stopped. Once more he mistreats Chabrias, then by contrast reached an agreement with Chares. He turned everything upside down and did nothing straightforward or honest.[208]

[179] After this, as long as your troops were in the Hellespont, he kept flattering and deceiving you. But as soon as he saw the Hellespont deserted by your troops, he immediately tried to dethrone and overthrow the two kings and place the entire kingdom under his own control. He has learned through experience that he could not break any of his agreements with you until he threw them out. [180] To accomplish this as easily as possible, he obtained a decree like this from you. Had it gone into effect—which it would have, had it not been for us and this case against it—the two kings would clearly have been treated unjustly, those serving as their generals, Bianor, Simon, and Athenodorus, would keep quiet from fear of malicious attacks prompted by the decree; he would have gained this freedom of action and placed the entire kingdom under his control; and you would have a powerful enemy.

[181] He has a base of operations, the city of Cardia, which he has always retained. In every treaty, he has reserved this city for himself and in the end openly took it away from you. Yet why should those who have foresworn any intention of doing you harm and chosen in all sincerity and without guile to take our side, keep for themselves a base of operations to use for a war against us? [182] You certainly know, some of you for certain by going there, others by hearing from them, that given the position of the city of Cardia, if the situation in Thrace remains in the hands of Cersebleptes, he can safely march in a day against the Chersonese. Just as Chalcis lies in the part of Euboea facing

---

[208]Euthycles portrays the actions of Charidemus from an Athenian perspective. Viewed from a Thracian perspective, his actions would appear in a different light.

Boeotia, the city of the Cardians lies in that part of the Chersonese facing Thrace. Those of you who know its location are not unaware of the reason why he has acquired it and why he has been eager to prevent you from taking it. [183] You should not help him to strengthen his position against you but prevent him as much as possible and make sure that this does not happen, since he has made it clear that he would not pass up even the smallest opportunity. When Philip came to Maroneia, Charidemus sent Apollonides to him and gave guarantees to him and Pammenes.[209] And if Amadocus had not been in control of the area and denied Philip the right to enter, nothing would have stood in the way of a war between us on one side and the Cardians and Cersebleptes on the other. To show that I am telling the truth, take the letter of Chares.[210]

[LETTER]

[184] This is what you must keep in mind: do not trust him; do not be foolish; and do not treat him as a benefactor. You do not owe him any thanks for the declaration of friendship he was forced to make in his effort to deceive you or for the trivial amount of his own money he spent on generals and politicians to get them to have his praises written up. Every time he has had the power to do as he wishes, he clearly tries to harm our interests, which is all the more reason to be angry with him. [185] Now, all the others who have ever received some benefit from you have been honored for the good they did for you. But this man alone of all the rest is being honored for the harm he tried to do you but could not. Indeed, to be released from the punishment that a man like this deserved to receive was a large reward for you to give him. Yet this is not the way the politicians see it: no, he receives citizenship, the

---

[209]Around the year 353/2 Pammenes brought mercenaries to the satrap Artabazus during his revolt from the Persian King (Diodorus 16.34). While in Macedonia, Pammenes was the guest of Philip, and Philip accompanied him on his journey through Thrace. For Apollonides as a friend of Philip, see Dem. 7.39.

[210]Chares was an Athenian general. For his activities, see Bianco 2002.

title of benefactor, crowns, and rewards as a result of the money he gives them in private. The rest of you sit there with the wool over your eyes, admiring his actions. [186] And finally they have now made you his protectors because of this preliminary motion. If we had not brought this charge, the city would be performing the job of mercenary and servant for Charidemus and acting as his bodyguard. Splendid, isn't it? By Zeus and the gods, the man who once took pay to serve as henchman for your enemies, this man is now clearly protected by your decree!

[187] Now perhaps someone might ask me: why did I, who knew in such detail about some of his crimes and was following them closely, not put a stop to them?[211] Why didn't I object when you made him a citizen or when you praised him? Why did I not say anything earlier before this decree was proposed? Men of Athens, I will tell you the whole truth. I knew that he did not deserve these rewards, and I was there and did not object when he asked for them. [188] For what reason? Because I thought, men of Athens, that even though speaking the truth, I would have less influence than the many people telling you lies about him. Next, it did not occur to me to feel any envy, by Zeus and all the gods, for the rewards he gained by deceiving you, since I did not see you suffering any unusual harm if you pardoned him for his many crimes and encouraged him to help you in the future. Both of these aims were implicit in granting him citizenship and awarding him a crown. [189] But now I see him scheming to obtain the kind of privilege that, if only he gets people here to help him deceive you about his actions, will prevent any of your friends abroad who want to help you and prevent him from opposing you—such as Athenodorus, Simon, Bianor, Archebius of Byzantium, the two Thracians, that is, the kings—from standing in his way and stopping him. This is why I am coming forward now and accusing him. [190] In my opinion, to speak against awarding privileges

---

[211] Euthycles alludes to his service a trierarch in the area at the time. See 5. Euthycles anticipates the objection that if Charidemus was acting against Athenian interests, he should have prosecuted him earlier. For such an argument, see Lys. 3.19.

that would not bring any extraordinary harm to the city were he
to receive them is the act of someone harmed by a personal enemy
or of a malicious accuser.²¹² But to oppose schemes that threaten
to damage the city's interests is the act of a good man and a patri-
ot.²¹³ These are the reasons why I said nothing at that time, but I
am speaking now.

[191] There is an argument with which they hope to distract
you: Cersebleptes and Charidemus may perhaps have acted
against the city's interests when they were enemies, but now they
are friendly and making themselves useful.²¹⁴ Indeed, one should
not hold a grudge against them. When we saved the Spartans,²¹⁵
we did not remember all the harm they did us when they were
our enemies, nor in the case of the Thebans,²¹⁶ nor most recently
in the case of the Euboeans.²¹⁷ [192] In my opinion, this argument would be justified if they were presenting this argument in
a situation where military support was being proposed for Cersebleptes and Charidemus, and we were opposing it. Yet if the situation is different and no such proposal has been made and if they
wish to make him more powerful than they should by having you
grant his generals immunity, then I think that what they are doing is dangerous. It is not right, men of Athens, to present the
kind of arguments used on behalf of those seeking protection for

²¹²Note that Euthycles considers bringing a public accusation without legal merit merely for revenge on some personal matter a dishonorable action.

²¹³For protecting the public interest as the correct reason for bringing a
public action, see Dem. 20.1; Lyc. *Against Leocrates* 5–6.

²¹⁴The section about Charidemus' character ends with a *prokatalepsis*
(anticipation of objections) in 191–195. See Papillon 1998: 37.

²¹⁵Demosthenes alludes to the Athenian decision to send help to the
Spartans during the Theban invasion of the Peloponnese in 369. See Xen.
*Hellenica* 6.5.33–49.

²¹⁶The Thebans had fought the Athenians in the Peloponnesian War but
joined them as allies in 378 to oppose Sparta. See *IG* ii² 43, lines 24–25, 79;
Diodorus 15.28.5.

²¹⁷The Athenians helped the Euboeans to gain their freedom from
Thebes in 357 (see 173n), even though they had revolted from Athens in 411
(Thuc. 8.91–95).

men who are trying to gain the power to do wrong. [193] Apart from this, if someone was an enemy and did us harm, then claims to be friendly and changed his attitude, one might perhaps listen to this argument. Yet when that is not the case, but from that moment when he pretends to be a friend, he has deceived you more than ever; one should certainly distrust him for the latter reason, if not hate him for the former.[218] Indeed, this is my opinion about not dredging up old grievances: the man who looks for reasons like this to do harm is dredging up old grievances, but the person who seeks to avoid suffering harm and to protect himself is acting prudently.

[194] Now, perhaps they will insinuate something like this: we will discourage a man inclined to be our friend and willing to do the city some good if we vote down the proposal, and we will cause him to suspect us. Men of Athens, consider my position. If he were truly and sincerely our friend and, by Zeus, were intending to do us all the good in the world, even in this case I would not think it necessary to listen to this argument. I do not think there would be anyone who could do so much good that you should betray your oath for his sake and cast a vote contrary to what is clearly just.[219] [195] Because he is proven to be deceiving you and doing nothing at all honest, one of two benefits will result if you vote down the proposal: either he will realize that he can no longer escape detection and will stop deceiving you, or, because he truly wishes to have close relations with you, he will try to do some good, knowing that he will no longer achieve what he wants by deceiving you. Thus, for this reason if for no other, it is in our interest to vote down the proposal.

[196] Now it is worth considering, men of Athens, how men in the past distributed honors and rewards to true benefactors and how many citizens and how many foreigners received them.[220]

---

[218]That is, distrust him for acting deceitfully, hate him for falsely pretending to be a friend.

[219]Euthycles again reminds the judges of their oath, which required them to vote only on the charges in the indictment and to disregard irrelevant issues.

[220]This section is very close to sections 21–24 in the speech *On Organization*, which, if genuine, was written about the same time. Volpis 1936: 18

If you see that their conduct is better than ours, it is good for you to imitate them.[221] If ours is better, you will do as you wish. Now, first of all, your ancestors did not set up bronze statues or show excessive admiration for Themistocles, who won the naval battle at Salamis; Miltiades, who was commander at Marathon; and many others whose achievements were greater than those of generals today. [197] Does this mean that they did not feel gratitude toward their benefactors? They certainly did, men of Athens, and paid them back in a way that was worthy both of themselves and of these men; because all of them were worthy men, they selected these men as their leaders. In the eyes of reasonable men with an eye on the truth, to be chosen first among honest and respectable men is a much greater honor than a bronze statue. [198] They did not deny themselves credit, men of Athens, for any of their achievements. There is no one who would say that the naval victory at Salamis belonged to Themistocles but not to the Athenians, that the battle at Marathon belonged to Miltiades but not to the city. But as it is now, men of Athens, many say that Timotheus captured Corcyra,[222] that Iphicrates destroyed the cohort,[223] that Chabrias won the naval battle at Naxos.[224] You seem to be yielding your credit for these achievements by the excessive honors you have granted to each of these men for these victories. [199] Men in the past used to grant awards to citizens in a way both noble and in their interest, but we do it in the wrong

---

believes that 196–214 form part of the epilogue, but see Papillon 1998: 38–39, who follows a scholion on this passage and calls it a *parekbasis* (digression). It serves to stress Charidemus' unworthiness by contrasting him with famous figures from the Athenian past.

[221]The Greeks admired their ancestors and thought that they should imitate their habits. See, in general, Jost 1936 and more briefly Hunt 2010: 123–132.

[222]Timotheus made Corcyra an ally of Athens in 375 (Diodorus 15.36.5; Xen. *Hellenica* 5.4.64; Isoc. 15.109; Nepos *Timotheus* 2.1; *IG* ii$^2$ 96; 97).

[223]Iphicrates destroyed a cohort of Spartan infantry at Lechaion in 390. See Xen. *Hellenica* 4.5.10–18. The victory is several times mentioned in the orators: Din. 1.75; Dem. 4.24; Aesch. 3.243.

[224]Chabrias defeated the Spartan fleet at Naxos in 376. See Xen. *Hellenica* 5.4.61; Diodorus 15.34–35. He is praised at length in Dem. 20.75–87.

way. How do we grant awards to foreigners? Menon of Pharsalus gave twelve silver talents for the war against Eion near Amphipolis and sent three hundred of his own *penestai* as cavalry to help you.[225] Those men did not vote that if someone killed him, he was subject to arrest but gave him citizenship and considered this honor sufficient.

[200] Another example: Perdiccas was king of Macedonia during the barbarians' invasion and destroyed them as they retreated from Plataea, bringing about the final defeat of the Persian King.[226] Yet they did not vote that if someone killed Perdiccas, who made the Persian King his enemy because of you, he was subject to arrest but gave him citizenship alone. In those days, the entire world considered the honor of receiving citizenship from you so prestigious that they were willing to perform great services like these to obtain it. But now they consider it so lacking in prestige that many of those who have obtained it have done you more harm than your declared enemies. [201] Not only has this reward of the city but all awards have been dragged though the mud and become worthless because of the depravity of the cursed and god-

---

[225]The Athenians captured Eion on the Strymon river from the Persians in 476/5 (Thuc. 1.98.1; Herod. 7.107). A Thessalian named Menon of Pharsalus brought a force to Athens during the Peloponnesian War (Thuc. 2.22.3). If Euthycles is not confusing the two events (see next note), this man may be the grandson of the Menon mentioned in this passage. The *penestai* were slaves whose condition was similar to that of the helots of Sparta. See Ducat 1994. Trevett 2011: 235, note 46, appears to be unaware of Ducat's work and mistakenly believes that the *penestai* were "nonchattel dependent workers" and the helots of Sparta had a similar status. On the helots, see Ducat 1990. On the use of slaves in warfare the best treatment remains Welwei 1974–1988. The study of Hunt 1998 should be used with caution.

[226]Euthycles is mistaken here. Perdiccas I was the first king of Macedonia and reigned around 640. See Herod. 8.138 with Hammond 1972–1988: 1.433–435. Perdiccas II reigned from around 454 to 413. On his reign, see Hammond 1972–1988: 2.115–137; Borza 1992: 132–160. Alexander I was king of Macedon during the Persian Wars and attacked the Persian army as it retreated through Northern Greece. On his reign, see Hammond 1972–1988: 1.98–104; Borza 1992: 98–131. Hammond does not think that Alexander was given citizenship, but see M. J. Osborne 1981–1983: 3.108–109.

forsaken politicians ready to propose decrees like this. Their greed has grown so excessive that they sell your honors and awards at bargain prices like men who auction off cheap trinkets, making whatever proposals they wish to many for the same markup.[227] [202] To start by mentioning the most recent case first, not only did they grant Ariobarzanes himself and his three sons all that they wanted, but they also added two men of Abydos, men who hate Athens and are utterly depraved, Philiscus and Agauos.[228] Next case: when you thought that Timotheus had performed some of his duties, in addition to the substantial rewards given to him, they added Phrasierides and Polysthenes, men not even free but wretches who have done the sort of things anyone in his right mind would shudder to mention.[229] [203] And finally now when they granted Cersebleptes what they thought he deserved and were enthusiastic about it, they added two men with him, the man who has done all the harm you have heard about and another whom no one in the world knows called Euderces.[230] This is why rewards that were previously large now appear small. The situation has already deteriorated even further. These honors are no longer enough, but if you do not provide protection for each of their supporters, it appears they feel no gratitude at all.

[204] The reason why the situation has deteriorated to this shameful point, if one should frankly speak the truth, men of Athens, lies with none more than you. You no longer wish to punish the guilty. No, the city has given up even this practice. Yet consider how your ancestors punished those who wronged them and whether you are like them.[231] [205] When they caught Themisto-

---

[227] For a similar view, see Dem. 51.22; 3.21; Aes. 3.177–188, with Liddel 2007: 239.

[228] On Philiscus, see 141. Agauos is not attested in any other source.

[229] Timotheus was a famous general who left Athens after being condemned to pay an enormous fine at his trial in 355, shortly before this speech was delivered. Din. 1.14, 3.17; Isoc. 15.129; Diodorus 16.21.4.

[230] Euderces is not attested in any other ancient sources.

[231] For the view that previous generations of Athenians punished criminals more harshly, see Lyc. *Against Leocrates* 64–66; Aes. 1.182. On the use of the ancestors as role models in Athenian oratory, see Jost 1936.

cles holding too high an opinion of himself, they drove him into exile and convicted him for collaborating with the Persians.[232] When Cimon altered the ancestral constitution for his own benefit, they failed by only three votes to punish him with death but inflicted a penalty of fifty talents.[233] That is how they used to behave toward men who performed such impressive deeds for them. They were right: they did not sell their freedom and pride in their achievements but honored them when they were helpful and did not tolerate their efforts to commit crimes. [206] But you, men of Athens, when men are guilty of the greatest crimes and clearly proven so, if they say one or two jokes and the advocates elected by the tribes make a plea for them, you acquit them.[234] If you vote to convict someone, you set the penalty at twenty-five drachmas. Yet certainly in the past the city was wealthy and famous in public, but no one in private rose above the many.

---

[232]Themistocles was ostracized around 470. See Thuc. 1.135.2–3; Plato *Gorgias* 516d; Plut. *Themistocles* 21.5 and Diodorus 11.55.1–3, with Brenne in Siewert 2002: 347–357.

[233]Cimon was ostracized around 362. See Plato *Gorgias* 516d with Brenne 2001: 193–195 and Scheidel in Siewert 2002: 350–357. There is no evidence for a trial and a conviction of Cimon on a charge of subverting the constitution. This was probably invented by Euthcyles to strengthen his contrast between past and present.

[234]This is a wild exaggeration. In this period the Athenians punished many officials with fines, exile, or death. Hansen 1975: 60 notes that out of 160 generals attested in the period 432–355, 33 were accused, and many convicted. At 167 Euthycles mentions the conviction of Cephisodotus around 359, and Timotheus was convicted around 355 and sentenced to a heavy fine (see 202n). In the *First Philippic* Demosthenes (4.47) complains about the large number of generals tried in this period. Worthington 2013: 113, note 54 claims that the points in 206–210 are repeated in Dem. 3.25–31, but the arguments in the two passages contain many different points. For instance, Dem. 3.31 mentions the need for citizens to go on campaign, a point missing in this speech. *Pace* Worthington, there is no reason to view this section of the speech as an attack on the policies of Eubulus. Neither Euthycles nor Demosthenes is known to have had any major political differences with Eubulus at this time. See E. M. Harris 2006: 121–40.

[207] Here is the proof: the house of Themistocles, that of Miltiades, and those belonging to famous men at that time, if any of you knows what they are like, he sees that there is nothing more arrogant than the average about them, but the buildings of the city and the adornments were so great and of such a type that no possibility was left for succeeding generations to surpass them, the Propylaea, the shipsheds, the stoas, the Piraeus, and all the others buildings that adorn the city.[235] [208] Now, however, in private life there is such an excessive amount of private wealth belonging to men who conduct public business that they have constructed private houses more impressive than many public buildings,[236] and some have bought up more land than all of you in the court possess. The public buildings that you construct and plaster, it is shame to say how small and shabby they are. Can you say what you will leave behind in public, just as they left behind the Chersonese, Amphipolis, the fame of noble deeds, which citizens like this who spend recklessly cannot erase, men of Athens? [209] Rightly so: when Aristides had the power to assess the amount of tribute,[237] his property did not increase by one drachma, but after he died, the city gave him a public burial. If you needed anything, there was more money in the public treasury than in all the rest of Greece. Thus, when you went on campaign, you had wages sufficient to last the whole time you decreed for the campaign. Now, the men who manage our public affairs go from poverty to riches and supply themselves with plentiful livelihood for a long time. But you do not have enough money in the public treasury to supply even a day's travel expenses. No, every time you need to do something, you do not have the resources to do it.[238] In the past, the people were the master of the politi-

---

[235]For the view that private dwellings in the past were modest and public buildings were grand, see Dem. 3.29, 13.29.

[236]For a similar criticism made about Meidias, see Dem. 21.158.

[237]Aristides assigned the amounts of tribute to be paid by the allies of Athens in 478/7. See Thuc. 5.18. He has a reputation for justice and incorruptibility. See Plut. *Aristides*.

[238]For the financial problems of this period, see the Introduction.

cians, but now they are their servants.[239] [210] The people who propose decrees like this one are responsible: they have gotten you into the habit of losing confidence in yourselves and admiring one or two men. Then these men have inherited your glory and success, but you derive no benefit from even the smallest thing. You are the witnesses to other people's success and without a share in anything but your own deception. Yet how would the men of the past mourn, men who died for glory and freedom and left behind memorials of many noble deeds, if they should see that the city has now fallen into the position and role of a servant and is debating whether to act as bodyguard for Charidemus? My god, Charidemus!

[211] But what is shocking is not that we make worse decisions than our ancestors did, whose virtue was unsurpassed, but that ours are worse than everyone else's in the world. Isn't it shameful that these Aeginetans over here,[240] who live on such a small island and have nothing to boast about, have not yet given citizenship to Lampis, who owns the largest fleet of ships in Greece and has built up their city and port, but have barely considered him worthy of an exemption from the metics' tax.[241] [212] And those accursed Megarians over there[242] are so pleased with them-

---

[239]For the image of the people as masters and politicians as their slaves, see Aristoph. *Knights*.

[240]Aegina is so close to Athens that it can be seen from the city. Pericles called it the "eyesore of the Piraeus."

[241]To encourage trade, many Greek cities gave honors to foreign merchants. For these honors at Athens, see Engen 2010. For the tax paid by metics at Athens, Oropos, and Megara, see Lys. 31.9; Dem. 29.3; Pollux 3.55, with Whitehead 1977: 77.

[242]Megara lies directly to the west of Attica. The Athenians considered them "accursed" in the late fifth century for encroaching on sacred land (Thuc. 1.139; cf. 1.67, 140, 144). Euthycles may call them "accursed" because of a dispute during this period about the Sacred Orgas ("meadow" or "field"). Philochorus (*FGrHist* 328 F 155) and Androtion (*FGrHist* 324 F 30) report that the Athenians and Megarians agreed to have two Eleusinian officials mark out the Sacred Orgas, that in accordance with the oracle at Delphi the marginal lands (*eschatiai*) were to remain uncultivated, and that

selves that when the Spartans sent Hermon the helmsman, who
with Lysander captured two hundred ships when we were defeated at Aegospotamoi and asked them to make him a citizen,
they answered that when they saw the Spartans making him a
citizen, then they too would make him a citizen of Megara.²⁴³
[213] What about those people of Oreus, who inhabit a quarter
of Euboea? Charidemus has a mother who is a citizen there, but I
will not say who his father is or where he is from (one should not
pry into these matters more than necessary).²⁴⁴ Yet although he
has half the qualification, they have not considered him worthy of
the other half but have registered him among the illegitimate just
as here the illegitimate are registered at Cynosarges.²⁴⁵ [214] You,
men of Athens, have given him a full share in the city and granted

---

Philocrates passed a decree to have this land marked out by marble stelai.
This account has much in common with a contemporary inscription, which
contains a decree about consulting Apollo of Delphi about the Orgas and
mentions an earlier decree of Philocrates (*IG* ii² 204). In the speech *On Organization* Demosthenes (13.32) says that the Athenians voted to defend this
land against the "accursed" Megarians but never followed through on their
decision. Didymus mistakenly dates this expedition to 350/49. See Rhodes
and Osborne 2003: 272–281; Gibson 2002: 40, 98–100, 132–134; and Harding 2006: 90–95, 246–255. On the other hand, Euthycles' reason for calling the Megarians "accursed" may have nothing to do with this incident
but with their foreign policy in this period. On the history of Megara, see
Legon 1981.

²⁴³The Spartans defeated the Athenians at Aegospotamoi in 405 and destroyed their fleet. See Xen. *Hellenica* 2.1.20–32; Diodorus 13.105–106. The
Spartans granted citizenship to very few foreigners. For one of the few exceptions, see Herod. 9.33–35. According to Pausanias (10.9.7), the Megarians
did make Hermon a citizen.

²⁴⁴Euthycles insinuates that Charidemus was a slave or had disreputa-
ble parents. For similar charges made by litigants about their opponents, see
Dem. 18.129–130, 21.149–150. Despite Euthycles' vague insinuations, other
sources identify his father as free and respectable. One should not take these
slanders seriously or infer from them that it was easy for slaves to become
citizens in Athens (*pace* Vlassopoulos 2009).

²⁴⁵There was a gymnasium of Heracles outside the gates at Cynosarges at
which illegitimate children were enrolled (Plut. *Themistocles* 2). On bastardy

him other honors; will you add this one too? For what reason? What ships has he captured that have caused those who lost them to plot against him? What city has he captured as prisoner and handed over to you? What dangers has he faced to protect you? What enemies has he chosen that are the same as yours? Not a single person can say.

[215] After speaking a few words to you about the laws that I have cited in my indictment, I wish to step down.[246] If you bear them in mind, I think that you will be more cautious if these men attempt to distract and deceive you. The first law explicitly states that if anyone kills, the Council judges the case. This man proposed that if anyone kills, he is immediately subject to arrest. Keep this in mind and remember that there is nothing more dissimilar to holding a trial than extraditing someone without trial.[247] [216] Next, the second law forbids the maiming of the convicted killer or extorting money from him.[248] This man, by making him subject to arrest, allows all of this. For those who catch them will have the power to do whatever they wish. The law provides for arrest to the *thesmothetai*, and this if someone catches him in the country of his victim. This man allows the person who has brought the charge to arrest him into his own custody even if he catches him somewhere in foreign territory. [217] There are certain crimes for which the law permits one to kill. The decree specifies none of these, and if someone kills in these cases, the decree orders the extradition of a man who is legally innocent.[249] If someone is the victim of such a crime, the law orders that a trial take place first; this man does the opposite and provides for no trial and does not require those who seize him to hold one, but he

in Greece in general, see Ogden 1996. On this gymnasium at Cynosarges, see Ogden 1996: 199–203.

[246] This phrase marks the transition to the *epilogos* (peroration) where Euthycles sums up his earlier arguments. For similar phrases introducing the *epilogos*, see Dem. 20.154; 21.184. On the function of the *epilogos*, see Papillon 1998: 39–41.

[247] Euthycles refers to his argument at 23–28.

[248] Euthycles refers to his argument at 29–36.

[249] Euthycles refers to his argument at 53–59.

has proposed that the killer be arrested right away and if someone releases him, they are to be banned from our alliance.[250] [218] As for taking hostages from the city where the offender is if he remains unpunished, the law permits there to be up to three. But this man proposes that if someone takes the offender from the person who arrests him and does not wish to hand him over before trial, he be banned from our alliance.[251] It is not allowed to introduce a law if one does not enact the same rule for everyone; this man proposes a private decree for one person.[252] The law does not allow a decree to prevail over a law. This man makes a decree prevail over all the laws in existence and destroys the laws.[253] [219] Keep this in mind and remember it as you sit here. Pay no attention to the attempts they will make to mislead you. Order them to show where he has written about a trial, or where he has written about the method of punishment if anyone is convicted of murder.[254] If he had written either that one should punish a man placed on trial somewhere else and convicted; if he had written about a trial to determine whether he was guilty or not or if he did it justly or unjustly, he would not be guilty. [220] But he wrote only the name of the charge: "if someone kills" and left out: "and if he is convicted of murder," and "is judged to have killed" and "let him suffer the punishment for murder" and "the punishment is to be the same as if he kills an Athenian" and leaves out all these rights, and has written "is subject to arrest," do not be deceived, but know that he has made the most illegal proposal in the world.[255]

---

[250] Euthycles refers to his argument at 61–81.

[251] Euthycles refers to his argument at 82–85.

[252] Euthycles refers to his argument at 86.

[253] Euthycles refers to his argument at 87.

[254] Euthcyles urges the judges to make Aristocrates reply to the charges in his plaint and to prevent him from distracting them with irrelevant issues.

[255] This final sentence indicates that the judges will vote not about the political advantages of the decree but about its legality (*pace* Yunis 1988).

# 24. AGAINST TIMOCRATES

## INTRODUCTION

In the Attic month Hekatombaion (roughly July) of the archon-year 353/2 a politician named Timocrates passed a law about those in debt to the public treasury. The law applied to any public debtor who had in the past been ordered to go to prison as an additional punishment or would be in the future.[1] If the debtor provided three sureties who promised to pay the debt if he defaulted, the debtor did not have to go to prison.[2] The Assembly was required to approve the sureties, and the *proedroi*, the officials who presided over the meetings of the Assembly, were required to present the sureties to the Assembly whenever a debtor wished.[3] This was obviously done to ensure that the sureties were creditworthy.[4] If the debtor or his sureties did not pay the debt by the ninth prytany, the debtor was to be placed in prison, and the property of the sureties was to be confiscated.[5] Those who were tax collectors, had rented public property, or were sureties for public debts were exempt from its provisions.[6]

Timocrates said that his law was humane and that it was aimed

---

[1] See sections 41, 44, 46, 55, 72, 77, 79.

[2] See 46, 64, 77, 79, 83, 87, 93, 103.

[3] See 84.

[4] For the requirement that sureties be creditworthy, see *IG* ii² 1678, line 18 (prior to 315 BCE).

[5] See 55, 87, 88–89.

[6] See 41, 59–60. Cf. 100 and Libanius' hypothesis to the speech.

at helping the poor.[7] This explanation certainly makes sense. Someone who was poor might not have the money to pay a fine and would have to work to make his payments to the Treasury. But if he were to be sentenced to prison, he would not be able to earn any money, and the fine would remain unpaid. The law was therefore not only humane but also in the public interest: it allowed poor men to stay out of prison and also enabled the state to collect fines imposed by the courts. If the debtor did not pay, the state could collect the debt from the surety by the ninth prytany or confiscate the surety's property. In this regard Timocrates' law is similar to many measures enacted after the Social War, which were aimed at improving financial administration and increasing public revenues.[8]

Sometime before the end of 353/2,[9] a politician named Dio-

---

[7] See 156, 170, 191–192. Sealey 1993: 119–120 thinks that the law may have been intended "as a permanent reform" but does not analyze its terms in detail.

[8] See, for example, the law of Leptines abolishing exemptions from liturgies (Dem. 20 passim), Periander's law about the naval symmories (Gabrielsen 1994: 182–199), the efforts to collect arrears of the *eisphora* (Dem. 22.47–58), Aristophon's decree setting up an inquiry into public property (11), and the reform of the Theoric Fund by Eubulus (Aes. 3.25). None of the previous commentators takes seriously Timocrates' motive for enacting the law or sees the law's benefits.

[9] On the date, see Dionysius of Halicarnassus *Ad Ammaeum* 1.4 with Sealey 1955: 74 and Rubinstein 2000, note 135, and 237–238 (353/2). Lewis 1954: 32 proposed dating the speech to 354/3. Lewis assumed that the documents about Timocrates' law inserted into the speech at 27, 39, and 71 are genuine. Because the prescript in these documents has the tribe Pandionis holding the first prytany, Lewis argued that they must belong to 354/3 when Pandionis might have held the first prytany and not to 353/2 when Pandionis did not hold the first prytany (*IG* ii² 140). This argument is not convincing: the document at 27 is a forgery, and prescripts in the documents at 39 and 71 contain several mistakes, which indicate that they are not genuine (even if the rest of these documents may be reliable). See Canevaro 2013a: 104–121. Rhodes in D. M. Lewis 1997: 230, note 1, claims that an inscription to be published by John Camp and Molly Richardson (Agora I 7495) sup-

dorus brought a public action against the law, claiming that it was "inexpedient."[10] In the previous year Demosthenes had written a speech for Diodorus when he spoke in support of Euctemon's prosecution of Androtion on a charge of proposing an illegal decree and wrote Diodorus' speech for this case.[11] Demosthenes may have had personal reasons for helping Diodorus: it is possible that Timocrates was the man of the same name who assisted Aphobus in his attempt to thwart Demosthenes in his attempt to recover the property embezzled by his guardians (Dem. 30). In his *Against Meidias* (21.139) Demosthenes names him and his son Polyeuctus as associates of his enemy Meidias.

The public action against an inexpedient law differed in substantive terms from the public action against illegal decrees (*graphē paranomōn*), the action that Euthycles brought against Aristocrates. A public action against an illegal decree could be brought only against a decree (*psēphisma*) that violated specific laws. The aim of the procedure was to maintain and enforce the superiority of laws, which were enacted through the special *nomothesia* (legislative) procedure. The public action against an inexpedient law could be brought in two circumstances.[12] First, it could be brought as part of the *nomothesia* procedure, for which our best evidence is found in the speeches *Against Leptines* and *Against Timocrates*.[13] The pro-

---

ports his proposed date. Richardson has kindly has allowed me to see her text of the unpublished inscription, which does not by any means support Rhodes' argument about the point made by Lewis. The inscription has Epicrates as the proposer of a law in 354/3, but this cannot be used as evidence to show that the Epicrates named in the document at 27 is the same person or that he must have proposed both measures in the same year.

[10] For the nature of the charge, see Hansen 1974: 44. Badian 2000: 41–42 mistakenly believed the case was a *graphē paranomōn*.

[11] For the date of the *Against Androtion*, see E. M. Harris 2008: 168. Cf. Dem. 22.24. For analysis of the political background, see Canevaro 2009.

[12] On the public action against inexpedient laws, see Canevaro 2016b, which decisively refutes Hansen 1979–1980.

[13] On the *nomothesia* procedure, Canevaro 2013b supersedes all previous treatments. The attempt of Hansen 2016a to defend the authenticity of the document at *Against Timocrates* 20–23 and to challenge Canevaro's analysis

cedure was started by a preliminary vote in the Assembly, which could take place at any time during the year, to permit proposals for new laws (25). All new proposals for laws had to be placed in front of the monument of the Eponymous Heroes so that everyone could read them (25; Dem. 20.94). The secretary was to read out all proposals submitted at every meeting of the Assembly until *nomothetai* ("legislators") were appointed (Dem. 20.94). During the third meeting of the Assembly after the preliminary vote, the people were to discuss the selection of *nomothetai* and pass a decree appointing them (25; Dem. 20.92). If there were any laws that were contrary to the proposed law, the proposer had to bring a public action against an inexpedient law to repeal these statutes (32, 34–35; Dem. 20.93). If such an action was brought, *synēgoroi* ("advocates") were to be elected to defend any laws to be repealed before the new laws could be enacted (36; Dem. 20.146). After any contrary laws were repealed by the court, the proposed law would be ratified by the *nomothetai* and placed in the Metroon. This is the way the action was used in the case *Against Leptines*: Leptines has passed a law removing all exemptions from liturgies; Apsephion wished to propose a law confirming all rewards for public service enacted by the Athenian people but to create a legal procedure to rescind all such rewards that had been made to people who did not deserve them.[14] The aim of the procedure was therefore to preserve the integrity and consistency of the system of laws as a whole (Dem. 20.93). This was one of the main features of the rule of law.[15]

Second, anyone could bring this public action against a law without proposing a new law. In this case, the accuser would

---

is not convincing. For a detailed refutation of all Hansen's points, see Canevaro forthcoming b.

[14]Kremmydas 2012 provides an introduction, text, translation, and commentary on the speech, but the analysis of legal issues contains several errors, which lead to a misunderstanding of the arguments presented by Demosthenes. For a more thorough commentary with improved analysis of the legal arguments, see Canevaro 2016.

[15]For Athenian concern with the consistency of the laws, see E. M. Harris 2013a: 246–273 and Canevaro forthcoming c.

bring either procedural or substantive charges against the law or both types of charges. On the one hand, the accuser might charge that the person who proposed the law had not followed the correct procedures for the *nomothesia*. On the other hand, the accuser might charge that the law was contrary to other laws that had been enacted. There is no reason however to believe that the accuser would bring political objections or deliberative arguments against the law he was indicting. In both the *Against Leptines* and the *Against Timocrates*, the accusers state that the law should be repealed because it clashes with other laws. Even when the accusers claim that the law they are trying to repeal is inconsistent with general Athenian values and beliefs, they show that these values and beliefs are contained in specific laws.

Diodorus begins his speech by describing the charge against Timocrates and claims that his law undermines democracy and the rule of law (1–5).[16] He next explains his personal motive for bringing the suit: Timocrates' associate Androtion had accused Diodorus of killing his own father (6–9).[17] In the rest of the speech, however, Diodorus says nothing about his desire for revenge and stresses instead the legal case against the law. A brief narrative follows and provides the motive for Timocrates' law (10–16; see below on the account of his motive). Diodorus then presents the main procedural arguments against the law. First he claims that Timocrates did not follow the correct procedures in enacting his law. He did not display his proposal at the monument of the Eponymous Heroes, he did not allow anyone to lodge an objection to his law, and he did not propose his law at the correct time (17–31).

In the next part of the speech Diodorus discusses the statutes that Timocrates' law violates and gives the substantive reasons for

---

[16]Wohl 2010: 292–300 attempts to argue that the public procedure against inexpedient laws could be used to dissolve the internal coherence of the laws and that the procedure was therefore just as illegitimate as Timocrates' law. For a convincing refutation of this far-fetched argument, see Canevaro 2012. For trenchant criticisms of the entire book, see Maffi 2009/2010: 332–337.

[17]Androtion had also attacked Diodorus' ally Euctemon. See Dem. 22.1, 48.

repealing the law (31–39). Diodorus argues that the Timocrates' law violates the principle that a statute should apply to actions committed only after it is passed, not before (41–44). It also violates the law that forbids the Assembly to restore civic rights to those who have lost them or to cancel debts to the gods or to the Treasury unless six thousand citizens vote by secret ballot (45–49). According to another law, it is illegal for public debtors to supplicate in the Council or Assembly, asking them to cancel a fine imposed by a court until after it has been paid, but Timocrates' law grants debtors the right to ask the *proedroi* to petition the Assembly (50–53). Timocrates' law allows the Assembly to set aside the verdict of the courts, but this goes against the laws requiring that one cannot reverse decisions made by the court (54–55) and that all decisions of the courts made under the democracy are binding (56–58).

The next section presents more substantive arguments (68–107). Diodorus argues that the law should be lenient not with those who have been convicted but with those who are awaiting trial (69). If it were wrong to put someone in prison, it would be better to take away the court's power to impose it rather than to enact a law allowing the court's decision to be overturned. This would make the Assembly superior to the courts (77–78). The law does not indicate what happens to the debtor between the moment when he is sentenced to prison and the day the Assembly approves his sureties (80–81; cf. 84–85). Normally, overdue payments are doubled in the ninth prytany or multiplied tenfold (for money owed to the gods), but Timocrates' law concerns only the original amount of the fine (82–83). His law also allows debtors to avoid prison completely (87). The law states that the sureties' property is to be confiscated if the debt is not paid by the ninth prytany, but there is no clause indicating what is to happen if the debtor who has not provided sureties does not pay (88–89). By delaying payment until the ninth prytany, the law reduces the amount of money coming into the Treasury (93–94) and deprives the city of the money needed to pay for the Council, the Assembly, and courts (96–101). Finally, his law will allow many types of criminals to avoid going to prison (102–107). He sums up these legal points at 108–109.

In the next part of the speech, Diodorus turns to Timocrates'

motives for enacting his law (110–112). He contrasts his law with
Solon's laws to punish theft (113–124). There is no reason to prevent Androtion, Melanopus, and Glaucetes from going to prison
when many other powerful politicians have received this punishment (125–138). The Athenians should imitate the people of
Locris, who make politicians propose laws with a noose around
their neck; if the measure fails, the noose is pulled tight (139–143).
In response to Timocrates' argument that the oath of the Council allows men to avoid going to prison if they provide sureties,
Diodorus observes that there is no such restriction in the Judicial Oath (144–148, 150–154). The final part of the speech delivers
a lengthy attack on Androtion, who will speak on Timocrates' behalf (170–186).[18] This section attempts to undermine Androtion's
statements and to blacken the character of Timocrates by association. Diodorus asks the judges to disregard the assertion that
Androtion, Glaucetes, and Melanopus have paid what they owed
because it is irrelevant to the legal issue (187–189). Timocrates
should not argue that the laws should be mild when they should
be harsh to those who harm the public interest (190–194). Androtion and Timocrates do not deserve pity because they showed
none to those in debt to the Treasury (195–199). After slander-
ing Timocrates and his family (200–203), Diodorus warns the
judges that the release of men from prison may be the prelude to
revolution and would undermine the rule of law (204–209). The
laws are the city's character, and to debase them is a more serious
crime than to debase the city's coinage (210–214). In the final section, Diodorus urges the judges to protect the laws by punishing
Timocrates (215–218).

Because Diodorus brought his charge within one year after the
law was passed, Timocrates was still subject to punishment.[19] As

---

[18] For Androtion as *synēgoros*, see 158–159, 187, with Rubinstein 2000: 165.
The attack on Androtion is largely taken from *Against Androtion* with a few
changes to make it relevant to the case against Timocrates. For the changes,
see the notes.

[19] For the rule that the proposer of a law was subject to punishment
within only a certain period, see Dem. 20.144. In contrast to *Against Leptines* there are many harsh attacks on motives and character in *Against*

in other public actions, the first part of the trial would determine whether the defendant was guilty, and the second part would decide what punishment to impose. If Diodorus wished to convince the court to vote for a harsh punishment, he had to prove that the defendant acted deliberately and with criminal intent.[20] On the other hand, if the defendant could convince the court that he had made a mistake or acted in ignorance, the court would repeal the law but not see any reason to punish him harshly. To supply a sinister motive for Timocrates' actions, Diodorus claims that he passed the law to enable Androtion, Glaucetes, and Melanopus from paying money they owed to the state. These three men had been sent as ambassadors to Mausolus, the ruler of Caria, in a ship commanded by two trierarchs, Archebius and Lysitheides. During their journey, they captured a ship from Naucratis in Egypt and took its cargo worth nine talents and thirty *mnas* as booty (11). The owners of the cargo appealed to the Athenian Assembly, which ruled that the cargo belonged to the state because Athens was at war with Egypt, and all booty seized from the enemy was public property (12).[21]

When Aristophon ordered an investigation into state property held by private individuals, Euctemon reported that the trierarchs still had the booty (11). When Euctemon gave this information to the Assembly, Androtion, Glaucetes, and Melanopus admit-

---

*Timocrates* because he had to prove the defendant's guilt. Cf. Rubinstein 2000: 138–40.

[20] At the very start of the speech Diodorus claims that Timocrates' enacted his law to deprive the city of stolen money (1–2) and that he received money to introduce it (3). For other allegations that he acted deliberately, see 14–16, 26, 48–49, 79, 81, 86, 99, 110, 122–123, 155, 159, 191, 195, 200, 206, 209.

[21] Roisman 2006: 109–110 claims that the Assembly "left the issue of the ownership of the cargo unresolved" at this point and that "Euctemon's subsequent proposal (*psēphisma*) officially made the status of the property public when it called on the people to demand it from the trierarchs." This misunderstands both the law and Euctemon's proposal. It was the law that made the merchants' cargo state property. Euctemon's proposal concerned only who was responsible for paying the money gained from the booty to the state.

ted that they held the nine talents. Euctemon then passed a decree instructing the trierarchs to pay the money and establishing a procedure to resolve the dispute between the trierarchs and the ambassadors (13). Androtion, Glaucetes, and Melanopus brought Euctemon to trial for enacting an illegal decree, but the court acquitted him. Diodorus claims that at this point Timocrates passed his law in great haste to allow Androtion and the others to avoid paying the money (14). Later in the speech he denounced the character of all three men to show that they did not deserve the lenient treatment they would receive from Timocrates' law (125–130). Other men who were better than they have spent time in prison (131–138).

Diodorus' explanation of Timocrates' motive for enacting the law is doubtful, and it is certainly suspicious that he brings forward no evidence to prove his allegations about Timocrates' motivations.[22] First, the procedure established by Euctemon ordered the trierarchs to pay the money to the state; if they wished to recover the money from Androtion and the others, there should have been a *diadikasia* (procedure to adjudicate two or more competing claims). Yet there is no evidence that the court in a *diadikasia* had the right to impose imprisonment as a punishment.[23] Nor does Diodorus provide any evidence to show that a court had sentenced Androtion and the others to prison until they paid or that Euctemon's decree provided for the imprisonment of those owing money to the Treasury. Moreover, if there had been a *diadikasia*, Androtion and the others would have owed the money to the trierarchs, not to the state. Second, the law of Timocrates

---

[22]For a method of evaluating the reliability of evidence in the orators, see E. M. Harris 1995: 1–16. All those who have written on the speech have not questioned Diodorus' account of Timocrates' motive for proposing the law (Wayte 1882; Jaeger 1938: 62–64; Navarre and Orsini 1954: 114–117; Sealey 1993: 119–120, 127–128; and MacDowell 2009: 181–196) and do not understand the role of these allegations in Diodorus' legal strategy. Roisman 2006: 107 mistakenly believes that the law would have benefited Androtion and the other ambassadors.

[23]On the *diadikasia*, see 13n.

would not have enabled Androtion and the others to avoid paying unless they provided sureties, but Diodorus never shows that they took advantage of the law to do so. Third, Diodorus reports that Timocrates will state that the money has already been paid.[24] Diodorus alleges that he could refute this claim, but he never does so, which strongly suggests that he could not.[25] There is thus no reason to believe Diodorus' repeated claims that illegal features of the law are the result of a deliberate plot to help his friends Androtion, Glaucetes, and Melanopus. He has clearly invented the connection between the actions of Androtion and the law to supply a criminal motive for Timocrates' legislation in hopes of convincing the court to inflict a harsh punishment.[26]

We do not know the outcome of the trial, but it does not appear to have damaged the reputation of Androtion, who was still politically active in 346 when he passed a decree honoring the sons of Leucon, the king of the Bosporus.[27]

---

[24]Wayte 1882: xlv claims that "in §§187–9 it is admitted by the prosecution that the claim has been satisfied (. . .)," whereas earlier in the speech Diodorus claims that Androtion and the others still owe the money. This led him to develop an elaborate theory about two stages of composition, the first written when the paid had not been paid and the second after it was paid. But Diodorus never admits that the money has been paid; he reports only that Timocrates will say that it has been paid but adds that he could disprove this. Yet after claiming that he could disprove it, he presents no evidence to show that they did not and tries to evade the issue by claiming it is not relevant to the main issue. MacDowell 2009: 195–196 makes a similar mistake and claims unconvincingly that the speech was unfinished. Roisman 2006: 112 accepts Timocrates' claim that the money was paid but does not analyze the issue in detail.

[25]The explanation for his refusal to do so is quite deceitful. See notes at 187–189.

[26]Note that the author of the second hypothesis to the speech says that Diodorus introduces the story about the ambassadors clearly for the purpose of slander (*diabolēs heneka*). Roisman 2006: 111–114 also finds the allegations of a conspiracy unconvincing.

[27]Rhodes and Osborne 2003, no. 64. Hunter 2000: 28, note 29, suggests on the basis of *Ath. Pol.* 63.3, Din. 2.13, and Dem. 56.18 that Timocrates' law

## 24. AGAINST TIMOCRATES

[1] The responsibility for the present trial, men of the court, not even Timocrates I think would deny, lies with no one other than himself. With the intention of stealing a large amount of money from the city, he introduced a law that violates all the laws and is neither expedient nor just, men of the court.[28] By listening to me, you will soon learn in detail all the other damage the law will inflict on the public interest and all the other disadvantages it will bring should it go into effect. But there is one type of harm (this is the most crucial and pressing point I have to make) that I will not put off discussing. [2] The law passed by this man here undermines and renders worthless your right to the vote that you cast on oath at all trials.[29] Its aim is not to benefit the city—how could it when it removes from the courts, which are recognized as the foundation for our constitution, the power to impose additional penalties for crimes, which has been established in the laws? No, its aim is to allow some men who have profited at your expense and seized a lot of your money to avoid paying even the amount they have clearly been caught stealing.[30] [3] Just consider how much easier it is to cater to the private interests of a few than to stand in defense of your rights: this man has already received money from them and did not introduce the law on their behalf before receiving it, yet I risk a fine of one thousand drachmas for

was rescinded either at this trial or later, but none of these passages is decisive (Dem. 56.18 refers to private actions, not public actions). I would like to thank Peter Long for help with this note.

[28]Demosthenes begins by stating the charge against Timocrates, which is to have enacted an inexpedient law. Because he is bringing his case against both the law and the man who proposed it, he also provides a motive for Timocrates' crime. Normally orators never say that a law is unjust and always equate law and justice: see E. M. Harris 2006: 168–70. The only exceptions are found in cases against inexpedient laws (cf. Dem. 20.2, 44, 87, 124).

[29]For the oath sworn by the judges, see E. M. Harris 2013a: 101–137, 353–357.

[30]The penalty for embezzling public funds was ten times the amount taken (*Ath. Pol.* 54.2).

defending you.³¹ That is how far I stand from gaining anything from you.

[4] Many who have chosen to address public issues are in the habit of saying that the topic that they happen to be discussing is extremely important for you and deserves your closest attention.³² If anyone has ever had a right to say this, I think that I too am justified in saying it now. [5] That there is nothing else more responsible for the advantages the city possesses and for our democratic constitution and freedom than the rule of law, I think no one would deny. Indeed, this is the very issue before you now: whether the rest of the laws you have enacted against men who harm the state are to be repealed while this one is to remain in force, or this one is to be repealed to allow the others to remain in place. To put it in a nutshell, this is the issue about which you must now decide.

[6] So that none of you wonder why after previously living what I personally am convinced has been a modest life, I am now involved in trials on public charges, I wish to speak a few words of explanation.³³ This point will not be irrelevant.³⁴ Men of Athens, I have clashed with a man who is malicious, quarrelsome, and god-forsaken, with whom ultimately the entire city has clashed.

---

³¹To win the sympathy of the court, the prosecutor often stresses the risk he runs in bringing a charge. The penalty for failing to gain one-fifth of the votes in a public case was a fine of one thousand drachmas and the loss of the right to bring any public actions in the future. See E. M. Harris 2006: 405–422.

³²Stressing the importance of one's topic was a standard rhetorical technique aimed at gaining the audience's attention. See, for example, Isoc. 3.1; Lyc. *Against Leocrates* 7.

³³To gain the sympathy of the judges, many litigants claim that they have never been in court before. See Lys. 1.3; Isoc. *Antidosis* 27; Is. 1.1; and Dem. 48.1, with E. M. Harris 2013a: 70–71.

³⁴All litigants swore an oath to "keep to the point" and tried to make all their arguments pertinent to the legal charge even when they appeared to stray from the main issue. The judges also swore to vote only about the charge made in the indictment. See Rhodes 2004 and E. M. Harris 2013a: 114–136.

I am talking about Androtion.³⁵ [7] The wrongs he has done me are far worse than what he did to Euctemon. Euctemon's losses were financial;³⁶ if Androtion had succeeded in his attack on me, I would not only have lost my property, but my life would have been finished. Even suicide, that solution available to all men, would not have provided an easy escape.³⁷ He charged me with a crime that any sane person would have shrunk from even mentioning, that I killed my own father,³⁸ then trumped up a charge of impiety³⁹ and brought the case to court. At this trial he did not even gain one-fifth of the votes and incurred a fine of a thousand drachmas.⁴⁰ I owe my safety, which I justly deserved, primarily to the gods, then also to those of you judging the case. [8] The person who unjustly placed me in such danger I now consider my implacable enemy. When I saw him doing injustice to the entire city both in the way he collected the property tax and in his manufacture of processional vessels and because he held a large amount of money belonging to the goddess,⁴¹ the Eponymous Heroes, and the city, I joined with Euctemon and pro-

---

³⁵This passage is very similar to *Against Androtion* 6–8, which was delivered two years before. On Androtion, see the Introduction to this speech. According to Dem. 22.48 Androtion prosecuted Euctemon for his activities collecting public funds. For Euctemon's position, see 159–160.

³⁶See 159–160 of this speech and Dem. 22.48–50.

³⁷Suicide would not have ended his troubles because he would have suffered the punishment for parricide in the underworld (Wayte).

³⁸To call someone a parricide was grounds for a private action for slander. See Lys. 10, with Loomis 2003.

³⁹The manuscripts add "against my uncle," but this is rightly deleted by modern editors. From *Against Androtion* (2–3) we learn that Androtion had charged Diodorus' uncle with impiety because he had associated with him after he killed his father. Anyone who associated with a murderer might incur pollution. For concern about pollution for homicide in the fourth century, see also 60 and E. M. Harris 2015.

⁴⁰Diodorus probably exaggerates the margin of Androtion's defeat. If he received fewer than one-fifth of the votes, he would have lost the right to bring other public suits, but Androtion may have brought a public case against Euctemon (14).

⁴¹I.e., Athena.

ceeded against him, thinking this was an opportune moment both to help the city and to inflict punishment for what I had suffered.[42] I would wish to gain what I want and that this man suffer what he deserves! [9] When the outcome of the case was no longer in doubt because the Council had already censured him, then the Assembly spent an entire day on the matter, and moreover two courts, each consisting of 1,001 judges, had voted,[43] and there was no longer any means of preventing you from taking the money, Timocrates here has so much contempt for these decisions that he introduces this law enabling him to rob the gods of sacred funds and the city of public funds,[44] to overturn the resolutions of the Council, the Assembly, and the courts, and to grant immunity to anyone wishing to plunder public funds. [10] We find this is the only solution to all these problems: to indict the law, to bring the case before you, and to repeal it if we can.

I will tell you what has happened from the beginning in a few words so that you can have a better understanding and follow all the injustices contained in this law.[45] [11] Aristophon[46] proposed

---

[42]Diodorus anticipates his discussion at 11–14. Even though Euctemon is a personal enemy, Diodorus still finds it necessary to justify his prosecution in legal terms. The Athenians did not approve of accusers bringing frivolous charges for the sole purpose of pursuing vendettas. See E. M. Harris 2013a: 61–71 and Kurihara 2003.

[43]In a public case there would normally be 501 judges, but there could be as many as several thousand.

[44]Diodorus makes a distinction between money that is *hiera* and money that is *hosia*. The meaning of the word *hosia* in this context has given rise to much debate because there appears to be a contrast between "sacred" and "secular" funds. But the term *hosios* has sacred associations in other contexts. Blok 2010 argues that the term *hosia chremata* should be translated "commonly owned money to be spent in a way pleasing to the gods." I have translated the term as "public" in the rest of this speech (11, 82, 96, 101, 111, 112, 120, 130, 137).

[45]Litigants often promise to speak briefly before starting the narrative of events. Cf. Dem. 21.21; 27.3, 12; 36.3; 37.3; 43.18; 45.2; 54.2; and [Dem.] 40.5.

[46]Aristophon had a long career in public life and was one of the most influential politicians at the time. He had recently convicted Timotheus of treason and forced him to go into exile. He later opposed the Peace of

a decree in your Assembly calling for the election of an investigating committee.[47] If anyone knew whether someone held sacred or public funds belonging to the city, he could report information to them. Next Euctemon denounced Archebius[48] and Lysitheides[49] for holding money from Naucratis[50] during their trierarchy and assessed the amount at nine talents and thirty *mnas*. He addressed the Council, and a preliminary motion was passed.[51] Next there was a meeting of the Assembly, and the people passed the motion without debate.[52] [12] Euctemon stood up and after saying many other things explained to you how the trireme carrying Melanopus,[53] Glaucetes,[54] and Androtion as ambassadors to

---

Philocrates with Philip (Theopompus *FGrHist* 328 F 166) and passed several decrees against Philip (Dem. 18.70, 75).

[47] The Assembly might appoint investigators (*zētētai*) on an ad hoc basis to collect information. See Lys. 21.16; And. 1.14.

[48] Archebius is probably to be identified with Archebius the son of Archebiades of Lamptrai, who was a trierarch in 373/2 (*IG* ii² 1607, line 10) and joint trierarch shortly before 356 (*IG* ii² 1622, line 188). His father Archebiades was a guest-friend of Lycon of Heracleia ([Dem.] 52.3–4, 21) and gave evidence for Apollodorus in 369 or 368 ([Dem.] 52.28). See Davies 1971: 68–69.

[49] Lysitheides, the son of Lysitheus of Kikkynna was a student of Isocrates (Isoc. 15.93) and is described as a "gentleman" by Apollodorus ([Dem.] 52.30: *kalos kagathos*). Sometime before 353 he was awarded a crown for his generosity to Athens (Isoc. 15.94) and was the leader of an *eisphora* symmory in 346 (Dem. 21.157). See Davies 1971: 356–357.

[50] Naucratis was a city in Egypt on the Nile delta where Greek merchants lived and conducted trade. For its status, see Bresson 2000: 13–84.

[51] All motions had to be submitted first to the Council for approval. The Council then submitted a preliminary motion (*probouleuma*) to the Assembly. See Rhodes 1972: 52–81. Euctemon's proposal was that the trierarchs turn over to the state the booty they had seized.

[52] At the beginning of a meeting of the Assembly it was possible to pass motions introduced by the Council without debate (*procheirotonia*). See Hansen 1983: 123–130. Diodorus includes this detail to show that there was virtually no opposition to the measure.

[53] On Melanopus, see below, 126 with note.

[54] On Glaucetes, see below, 128 with note.

Mausolus seized the ship,[55] how the owners of the cargo initiated a supplication for their money,[56] and how you voted that it was enemy property. He then reminded you about the laws that make the goods seized in this way the property of the city.[57] All of you thought that what he said was right. [13] Androtion, Glaucetes, and Melanopus jumped up (consider whether I am telling the truth here) and shouted, got angry, made insults, exonerated the trierarchs, admitted that they had the money, and asked the investigators to look to them for the money. When you heard this and after these men stopped shouting, Euctemon proposed a decree, which was the fairest solution possible, that you collect the money from the trierarchs and that they have the right to recover it from those who held it. If there were any dispute, there was to be a *diadikasia*,[58] and the losing party was to owe the money to the city.[59] [14] They indicted this decree.[60] The case came before you. To put it briefly, he was judged to have made his proposal according to the laws and was acquitted. What then should have happened? The city should have received the money, and the man who stole it should have been punished. There was certainly no

---

[55]According to one of the hypotheses to the speech, this embassy was sent to Mausolus, the ruler of Caria, to protest his support for the allies who revolted from Athens during the Social War (cf. Hornblower 1982: 215). But the embassy occurred after the end of the Social War and was more likely aimed at restoring relations between Athens and Mausolus. See Cawkwell 1962: 48–49; Harding 1976: 195–196; Moscati Castelnuovo 1980: 268–269; and Harding 1994: 21. A fragment of an inscription (*IG* ii² 150) may refer to this mission.

[56]On this formal type of supplication to the Assembly, see *IG* ii² 218 (364/3) with Naiden 2006: 173–183.

[57]In Athens and other Greek city-states booty captured in war became public property. See Pritchett 1971: 85–92.

[58]The *diadikasia* was a special procedure used in cases in which there was more than one claimant to property or a privilege and in which there was no accuser or defendant.

[59]Euctemon's proposal was an amendment to his decree about the trierarchs.

[60]This must have been an indictment for an illegal proposal (*graphē paranomōn*). See Hansen 1974: 32–33.

need at all for any law. Up to this point Timocrates here had done you no wrong. After this he became responsible for all the things previously mentioned. It will become clear that he has done you all sorts of injustice: he hired himself out to perform their tricks and their schemes, made himself their underling, and took complete responsibility for their crimes, as I will clearly show you.[61]

[15] First, I must remind you about the time and circumstances during which he proposed his law. This will make it obvious that he has insolently treated you with contempt. To be precise, it was the month of Skirophorion when they lost their case against Euctemon.[62] After they hired this man, since they were not prepared to respect your rights, they sent men to the Agora to start a rumor that they were ready to pay the money owed but would not be able to pay double.[63] [16] This was a ruse filled with contempt, a scheme to pass this law without attracting attention. Their actions testify that this was the case: in all that time they did not pay a drachma of the money,[64] but used one law to invalidate all the established laws. This was the most disgraceful and shocking of all the laws ever passed in your city.

[17] After briefly discussing the laws enacted to permit public accusations like this one, I wish to speak about the actual law that I have indicted. Once you have heard these laws, you will find it easier to understand my other arguments. Men of Athens, the laws now in effect in our city carefully and clearly define everything that must be done for laws to be enacted. [18] First of all, the period when it is permitted to make laws is specified. Second,

---

[61] Diodorus never provides any evidence to prove Timocrates' motive for introducing the law or that he was collaborating with Androtion, Glaucetes, and Melanopus.

[62] Skirophorion was the last month of the Athenian year and occurred in June/July.

[63] When debts to the Treasury were not paid before they were due, the amount was doubled. See *Ath. Pol.* 48.1; And. 1.73–74 with Rhodes 1972: 148–151. But there is no reason to think that the money owed by Androtion and the others would have been doubled as soon as the following month, Hekatombaion.

[64] This appears to contradict the statement later in the speech (187) that the ambassadors had already paid what they had taken.

it is not permitted even then for anyone to do this in whatever way he decides. No, the law orders a written copy to be placed in front of the Eponymous Heroes for anyone to see,[65] then orders that the same law apply to all citizens equally,[66] and also to repeal any laws contrary to it.[67] There are other provisions, but there is perhaps no pressing need for you to hear about them now. If anyone violates any of these rules, it is permitted for anyone who wishes to bring a public action. [19] Now if Timocrates were not subject to prosecution for breaking all these rules and had not proposed his law in violation of all of them, one would bring just one charge against him, whatever that might have been. As it is, however, it is necessary to divide them up and discuss each separately.

First, then, I will discuss his first offense, that he passed his law in violation of all the laws, then proceed in order through the remaining charges in order whatever ones you wish to hear. [*To the clerk*] Take these laws here for me and read them. It will be obvious that he has done none of these things. Pay attention, men of the court, as the laws are read out.

[APPROVAL OF THE LAWS[68]]

[20] During the first prytany on the eleventh day in the Assembly after the herald says the prayers,[69] there is to be an ap-

---

[65]This requirement is also mentioned at Dem. 20.94. Each of the ten Attic tribes had an eponymous hero. Statues of these ten heroes were placed in the Agora. Public notices such as legal indictments (Dem. 21.103), lists of men summoned for military duty (Aristoph. *Peace* 1183–1184), and proposals for laws (Aes. 3.38–39; Dem. 24.18, 23) were displayed here. See T. L. Shear 1970.

[66]For the requirement that the laws apply equally to all citizens, see And. 1.89; Dem. 23.86, with E. M. Harris 2013a: 5–7, 136–137.

[67]For this requirement, see 34–35 and Dem. 20.93, 95–97.

[68]Hansen 2016a attempts to defend the authenticity of this document, but see Canevaro 2013a: 80–102 and Canevaro forthcoming b.

[69]The standard phrase for an item to be placed first on the agenda is "after the sacrifices" (*meta ta hiera*). See, for example, *IG* ii² 107, line 16; 212, line 57; 238, line 13. The formula found in this document is unparalleled in

proval of the laws, first about those concerning the Council, second about the general ones, then about those enacted for the nine Archons, then about the other magistrates.[70] Let the first vote ask who thinks the laws about the Council are adequate, let the second ask who thinks they are not; next they shall vote about public affairs in the same manner.[71] The approval of the laws is to be in conformity with the laws.[72] [21] If there is a vote against some of the established laws, the *prytaneis*, during whose term of office the vote occurs, are to hold the last of the three meetings of the Assembly about the laws voted against.[73] The *proedroi* whoever happen to preside over this meeting of the Assembly are required to conduct busi-

---

Attic inscriptions of the fourth century BCE. Hansen 2016a claims that this formula refers to sacrifices, whereas *meta ta hiera* refers to sacred business, but if that were the case, the document would prescribe a vote before the sacrifices, which is unparalleled anywhere in the Greek world (see Canevaro forthcoming b). The law also lacks the name of a proposer, an archon date, and the standard enactment formula.

[70] The phrase "there is to be an approval of the laws" (*epicheirotonia poiein*) is unparalleled in Attic inscriptions and literary sources. The normal term is *epipsephizein* or *epicheirotonian didonai*. The sentence confuses two kinds of votes: one to approve laws, and the other to approve the conduct of officials.

[71] The summary of the law's contents at 25 calls for only one vote to determine whether the existing laws are sufficient or a new law must be introduced. The document provides for eight votes, two each about four categories of laws.

[72] This phrase makes no sense; if this is the law about legislation (*nomothesia*), a new law should be passed in accordance with this law, not other laws.

[73] According to the summary at 25, the third meeting of the Assembly after the initial vote was held to vote on the appointment of the *nomothetai*, not to discuss an existing law voted against. The document states that "the last of the three meetings of the Assembly" is dedicated to the laws rejected. Hansen and Mitchell 1984 use this evidence to argue that there were only three meetings of the Assembly each prytany, but the forger appears to have misinterpreted the summary, which can only be read to refer to the third meeting after the original one, perhaps on the basis of information found also in the scholion at Dem. 24.20. See Canevaro forthcoming b. On the number of meetings of the Assembly each prytany, see Harris 2006: 81–120, which is now accepted by most scholars.

ness first after the sacrifices about the way the *nomothetai* are
to meet and about the source of the money to be paid to the
*nomothetai*.[74] The *nomothetai* are to come from those who have
sworn the Judicial Oath. [22] If the *prytaneis* do not hold an
Assembly according to the above,[75] or the *proedroi* do not conduct business according to the above, each of the *prytaneis* is
to owe one thousand drachmas to be dedicated to Athena, and
each of the *proedroi* is to owe 40 drachmas to be dedicated to
Athena. Let them be denounced to the *thesmothetai* as in the
case of anyone who holds office while in debt to the public
treasury. Let the *thesmothetai* bring those who have been denounced into court according to the law, or do not let them go
up to the Areopagus[76] on the grounds of obstructing the rectification of the laws.[77] [23] Before the meeting of the Assembly, let any Athenian who wishes write the laws that he is proposing and display them in front of the Eponymous Heroes,
so that the Assembly may vote to set the length of the meeting
for the *nomothetai* according to the number of laws passed.[78]
Let the person who has proposed a new law write it on a white
board[79] and display it in front of the Eponymous Heroes as
many days as remain before the Assembly meets. Let the people elect five men from all the Athenians to defend the laws
that are to be rescinded at the meeting of the *nomothetai* on
the 11th day of Hekatombaion.[80]

---

[74] Payments for magistrates were fixed by law, not set by the Assembly by
an ad hoc decree.

[75] This phrase makes little sense. It was the *prytaneis* who drew up the
agenda (*programma*) for meetings of the Assembly (see *Ath. Pol.* 43.4),
which instructed the *proedroi* how to conduct business.

[76] The *thesmothetai* and the other archons normally became members of
the Areopagus after their term of office.

[77] According to the summary of its contents at 25, the law concerns new
legislation, not the "rectification" of the laws.

[78] There is no parallel for a vote by the Assembly setting the length of a
meeting for another official body.

[79] For the use of white boards (*leukomata*) to display temporary items, see
Sickinger 1999: 4.40, 41, 65, 66, 68–70, 72, 79, 82, 97, 138.

[80] Five men (*syndikoi*) were elected to defend a law indicted on a charge
of enacting an inexpedient law (see Dem. 20.146–153). This trial, however,

[24] All these laws have already been in effect for a long time, men of the court, and have often proved themselves beneficial for you.[81] No one has ever denied that they are good, and rightly so. They do not order anything harsh, violent, or oligarchic, but quite the opposite: they command us to act in a generous and democratic way. [25] First, they place in your hands the power to vote whether a new law should be introduced or the existing laws seem adequate. Next, if you vote to introduce a new law, they order you not to enact it straightaway but assign the third meeting of the Assembly[82] and do not allow you to pass it even then, but to consider on what terms you will appoint *nomothetai*. During the intervening period they order those wishing to introduce laws to display them before the Eponymous Heroes so that whoever wishes may examine them, and, if someone notices anything contrary to your interests, he may point it out and make an objection at his convenience. [26] Yet although there were so many requirements, Timocrates here did not meet any of them: he did not display the law, did not allow anyone who read it and wished to lodge an objection to do so, and did not wait for the time appointed by law. The meeting of the Assembly during which you voted about the laws took place on 11 Hekatombaion. He immediately proposed his law on the next day, the 12th, though that was during the Kronia and when the Council was in recess.[83] He

took place in a regular court, not before the *nomothetai*. According to the inserted document, the defenders of the law are elected at the same meeting during which the initial vote about the laws was held. But how could the Athenians have elected *syndikoi* to defend indicted laws when the new proposals had not yet been made and posted, and no one could have known what old laws would have to be repealed?

[81] For the idea that old laws have proven their worth, see Ant. 5.14 = 6.2.

[82] This is unquestionably the third meeting after the original one, and, *pace* Hansen 2016a, cannot be read inclusively. See Canevaro forthcoming b.

[83] For the festival of the Kronia, see Parker 2005: 202–203. Even though the Council did not meet during festivals, the law courts (and presumably the *nomothetai*) could still meet. Diodorus gives the false impression that all public business was suspended during this festival. Mikalson 1975: 28 thinks that Diodorus is referring to a meeting of the Assembly, but see Hansen 1982: 332, note 5.

was acting in concert with men plotting against you to have the *nomothetai* sit by decree on the pretext of the Panathenaea. [27] I wish to read to you the actual decree that they passed so that you know how craftily they arranged everything and left none of these things to chance.[84] Get the decree for them and read it.

[DECREE[85]]

During the first prytany, that of the tribe Pandionis, on the eleventh of the prytany, Epicrates proposed:[86] in order that the sacrifices may be offered, the budget[87] for them may be sufficient, and if anything is needed for the Panathenaea, funds may be provided, the *prytaneis* from Pandionis should have the *nomothetai* meet tomorrow, there should be 1,001 *nomothetai* from the men from those who have sworn the oath and they should pass laws in conjunction with the Council.[88]

---

[84]Note how Diodorus stresses the deliberate intent of Timocrates and his associates.

[85]This decree is a forgery. See Wayte 1882: 108–110; Piérart 2000; and Canevaro 2013a: 104–113.

[86]The prescript departs from the standard form in this period and is without parallel. The normal form and sequence of elements is: archon, prytanizing tribes, name of secretary with patronymic and demotic, day of the prytany, name of the chairman of the *proedroi*, an enactment formula, and the name of the proposer. See, for example, *IG* ii² 130, lines 2–7, with Henry 1977: 27. This prescript is missing the archon, the name of the secretary, and the enactment formula. Some contemporary prescripts lack one or more elements of the standard form, but no prescript from this period has this form. There are 159 men of the same name in Attica (*Lexicon of Greek Personal Names*).

[87]The word *dioikesis* ("funds") in this period denotes the entire budget of the *polis*, not a specific fund. See Rhodes 2007: 349–355 (*dioikesis* "refers to regular administration in general, particularly to the funding of that regular administration . . ."), who does not discuss this passage. In the adjoining text (28), the word is used in the correct sense.

[88]In all the epigraphic *nomoi* of the fourth century, laws are enacted by the *nomothetai* alone, not acting in conjunction with the Council. See the prescripts of laws collected by Rhodes 1972: 276, to which should be added Rhodes and Osborne 2003, no. 25, line 1; *SEG* 35.83; Themelis 2002: 112,

[28] You noticed as the decree was being read out[89] how craftily its author held out the excuse of the budget and the pressing needs of the festival in order to eliminate the time appointed by law when he proposed that the legislation be passed on the next day. His aim, by Zeus, was not to ensure that the festival be as splendid as possible,[90] for there was nothing left to be done, and no funds had to be provided, but that this law now on trial be enacted and go into effect for their benefit without anyone noticing in advance and lodging an objection. [29] Here is the proof: when the *nomothetai* hold a meeting about these matters, the budget and the Panathenaea, no one has ever introduced any law, be it better or worse. Yet Timocrates here was casually passing laws concerning matters that the decree did not order and the laws do not allow: he believed that the time appointed by the decree had more authority than the time stated in the laws. He was not afraid at all if—when you were all celebrating the holy month when the law prohibits men from doing wrong, whether public or private, to each other either and does not allow any business to be transacted except about the festival[91]—he will clearly be harming not just one individual but the entire city. [30] And yet isn't it shocking for someone who knows the laws that you heard just a moment ago are in force and who knows that another law does not allow a decree, even if it is legitimate, to prevail over a law,[92] to propose and enact for you a law in accordance with a decree that he knew was proposed illegally? [31] When the city has granted us immunity from suffering anything painful or ter-

---

lines 8–9. Moreover, Diodorus has just stated that the Council was not in session on 12 Hekatombaion, the day when the *nomothetai* met.

[89]I have followed the text of Wayte and Orsinsi/Navarre (*enethymēthēt' anagignōskomenou tou psēphismatos*) rather than that of Dilts (*enthumēthēte tou psēphismatos*).

[90]For a similar phrase in contemporary documents, see *Agora* 16.55 (= Meritt and Traill 1974), lines 5–6; *IG* ii² 712, lines 9–11; *SEG* 28.103, lines 5–6; *IG* ii² 1186, lines 10–11.

[91]For these laws, see Dem. 21.11–12, 175, with E. M. Harris in Canevaro 2013a: 216–223.

[92]For the rule that no decree has precedence over a law, see And. 1.89.

rible at this time by instituting the sacred month, how is it not intolerable for the city itself not to receive this protection against Timocrates but to suffer the greatest injustices during this sacred month? For what greater injustice could a private citizen do than to destroy the laws that regulate its affairs?

[32] He has done none of the things that he should and that the laws prescribe. Anyone could understand this by examining what has been said so far. His refusal to observe the time set by law and his efforts to take away your opportunity to deliberate and reflect before he passed his law during the holy truce are not his only crimes. He also committed another crime, which was to introduce a law that violates all the established laws.[93] You will clearly understand this in a minute. [*To the clerk*] Take and read for me first this law here, which explicitly forbids the enactment of any law contrary to the existing laws, and if someone enacts it, provides for a public action against him. Read it. [33]

[LAW[94]]

It is not permitted to rescind any of the existing laws except at a meeting of the *nomothetai*.[95] At that time it is permitted for any Athenian who wishes to repeal it and propose another in place of whichever law he repeals. The *proedroi* are to take

---

[93]Having shown that Timocrates committed procedural violations in proposing his law, Diodorus moves on to show how the law violates existing statutes.

[94]This document is another forgery. See Canevaro 2013a: 102–104. Anyone who wished to introduce a new law contrary to an existing law was required to repeal the existing law by bringing an action for enacting an inexpedient law against it before a regular court, not before the *nomothetai*. The summary clearly states that this statute ordered that those proposing new laws according to the prescribed procedure had to repeal any contradictory law. Yet this document provides a procedure for repealing existing laws and requires that those who do so must propose a law to replace any laws that are repealed. This reverses the logical order of the procedure.

[95]This statement is contradicted by the provision later in the document that one can repeal a law by the public action against an inexpedient law.

a vote by show of hands about these laws,⁹⁶ first about the existing one if it is thought to be advantageous for the Athenian people or not, then about the proposed one. Whichever law the *nomothetai* approve by a vote, this law is to be valid. It is not permitted for any law to be contrary to any of the existing laws.⁹⁷ If anyone repeals any of the existing laws and proposes in its place a law inexpedient to the interests of the Athenian people or contrary to any existing law, there is to be a public action against him in accordance with the law in effect against the person who enacts an inexpedient law.⁹⁸

[34] You have heard the law. The city has enacted many excellent laws, but there is none better or more deserving of praise than this one. Look at how just it is and how well it protects the people's interests. It prohibits proposing a law contrary to the existing ones unless one rescinds the one already in effect. What is the aim? First, to give you the power to cast a just vote with respect for the gods.⁹⁹ [35] Imagine if there should be two laws contradicting each other, and two litigants should appear before you in court about some private or public matter, with each one demanding to win his case without citing the same law. It would certainly be impossible for the judges to vote for both litigants. How could they? Nor could they vote for either litigant and abide by their oath, for their verdict would go against the opposing law, which was equally valid. [36] To protect you against this, the lawgiver established these rules. It was also his aim to make you guard-

---

⁹⁶The expression *poiein diacheirotonia* ("to hold a preliminary vote") is unparalleled in inscriptions and in literary sources. See Canevaro 2013a: 104.

⁹⁷This should strictly speaking be "to any other of the existing laws." See Wayte 1882: 115.

⁹⁸According to the summary, this should be the law that created the public action against an inexpedient law, but the text of the document implies that such an action was created in another law.

⁹⁹In the Judicial Oath the judges swore by the gods to follow the laws. If there were two contradictory laws, they could not abide by their oath. For Athenian concern for consistency in their laws, see Dem. 20.93 and Sickinger 2008.

ians of the laws.[100] He knew that there are many ways to evade the many other measures enacted to protect the laws. Someone might persuade the advocates whom you elect to remain silent.[101] He provides that proposals be placed on display so that all can read them. But possibly someone who might have objected if he knew about it might not notice[102] or those who read it might not pay close attention.[103] [37] But, by Zeus, every citizen can bring a public charge, as I have in fact done now. But in case the person who objects decides to relent, the city loses out. What is the only just and sure protection for the laws? You, the people. For no one could deprive you of your ability to understand and approve what is best. No one could make you stand aside or bribe you to pass a worse law instead of a better one. [38] For all these reasons, the lawgiver places obstacles in the path of each crime by stopping and not allowing those plotting against you to advance. All these safeguards, which have been so well and justly established, Timocrates has to the best of his ability destroyed and eliminated. He has introduced a law contrary to virtually all those now in effect. He did not read out anything, repeal anything, give you any choice, or follow any of the correct procedures.

[39] That he is subject to a public charge of having introduced an inexpedient law contrary to those now in effect, I think you all know this. For you to understand what kind of laws he has violated and what kind of law he has introduced, the clerk will first read to you this man's law, then the others that it contravenes. Read.

---

[100] For the judges as the guardians of the laws, see also Din. 3.16.

[101] For the advocates elected to defend the law indicted by a public action against an inexpedient law, see Dem. 20.146.

[102] The manuscripts have *mē* before *proaisthointo*, which would change the meaning of the phrase to "It may possibly happen that persons who, with previous notice, would have opposed the law, without such notice may fail to detect its bearing" (Wayte). Most editors however delete *mē*.

[103] I have accepted the reading *anagnoien* here. Most manuscripts read *agnooien*, which would change the meaning of the phrase to "others through inattention may be ignorant of the whole matter" (Wayte).

[LAW[104]]

During the prytany of Pandionis, the first, on the 12th day of the prytany, Timocrates proposed that even if anyone owing money to the Treasury has been assessed an additional penalty of imprisonment by law or decree or is assessed this additional penalty in the future, it is permitted for him or anyone on his behalf to provide sureties for the debt, whom the Assembly approves by vote, to guarantee that he will pay the money that he owed. The *proedroi* must hold a vote when someone wishes to provide sureties. [40] If the one who provides sureties pays back to the city the money for which he provided sureties, he is to be released from prison. If he does not pay the money, either he himself or the sureties, in the ninth prytany, the one who provided sureties shall be put in prison, and the property of the sureties confiscated. But for those who have bought the right to collect taxes and their sureties and those who collect taxes and for those who have leased rentals and their sureties, the state has the right to collect from them according to the established laws. If he owes in the ninth or tenth prytany, he must pay by the ninth prytany of the next year.[105]

[41] You have heard the law. Recall first the phrase "if any debtor has been given the additional penalty of imprisonment or is given it in the future," next that except in the case of tax collectors, lessees, and those who act as sureties for them, it requires the law to be followed. The entire law violates existing statutes, especially these. You will realize this by hearing the laws themselves. Read it. [42]

---

[104]The text of this document is consistent with the summary in the adjoining text and does not contain any phrases without parallel in Athenian laws and decrees. See Canevaro 2013a: 113–120.

[105]The text of the manuscripts reads, "If he owes in the ninth prytany, he must pay by the ninth prytany or the tenth prytany of the next year." Dilts follows Dobree and emends the text to read, "If he owes in the ninth or tenth prytany, he can pay in the next year." I have adopted the text of Westermann, whose solution is more economical. This clause was added because the Athenian fiscal year ended at the end of the eighth prytany.

[LAW[106]]

Diocles proposed: The laws enacted before the archonship of Eucleides[107] during the democracy and as many as were enacted after the archonship of Eucleides and are written up are to be in force. Those enacted after the archonship of Eucleides and enacted in the future shall be in effect from the day each is enacted except if a date has also been specified on which the law is to take effect.[108] The secretary of the Council is to add this clause to the established laws within thirty days. In the future, let whoever happens to be serving as secretary add that the law is valid from the date on which it has been enacted.

[43] The existing laws are excellent, but this one that was read just now has, as it were, made them more precise and secure. It provides that each law be valid from the day on which it is enacted unless a period of time is added on which the proposed law is to go into effect. For what reason? Because in many laws it has also been written that "this law is valid during the archonship that follows the present one." Writing later than these laws, the man who enacted this law that has been read out did not think it right to make laws written up take effect on the day on which they were enacted or to make them retroactive to a period before the legislator requested. [44] Consider, then, how much the law that this man enacted violates this law.[109] On the one hand, this

---

[106]The text of this document is consistent with the summary in the adjoining text and does not contain any phrases without parallel in Athenian laws and decrees. See Canevaro 2013a: 121–127.

[107]The archonship of Euclides was in 403/2 and marked the restoration of the democracy.

[108]On this rule, see Sickinger 1999: 150.

[109]The objection to Timocrates' law is that it violates the principle that a law should not apply to events occurring before it was passed. The argument is invalid because this rule applies only to offenses committed before the law was passed, not to the penalties imposed for these offenses. As Wayte observes, the laws of Athens did allow for "a mitigation of statutory penalties." See also MacDowell 2009: 187–188.

law provides that a law be valid either from a specified time or on whatever day it is enacted.[110] Yet this man writes "if there has been an additional penalty for someone" and is speaking about the past. He does not limit this by adding the name of an archon from which it is valid, but has made it valid not only before the day on which it was enacted but also before any of us was born. He has included the entire past without any limit. And yet, Timocrates, you should either have not proposed your law or repealed that one instead of throwing everything into confusion just to suit your wishes. [*To the clerk*] Read another law.[111] [45]

[LAW]

[. . .] neither about the disenfranchised that they must regain their rights, nor about those who owe money to the gods or the Treasury of the Athenians about a release or partial payment of the debt unless no fewer than six thousand Athenians vote for the immunity who decide in a secret ballot. Then it is permitted to hold a discussion on terms set by the Council and Assembly.

[46] There is this other law, which does not allow any proposal or discussion about a release from debts or partial payment for the disenfranchised and debtors unless immunity is granted, and only when not fewer than six thousand have voted. This man has written explicitly "and if imprisonment has been given to a debtor as an additional punishment, there is a release granted to anyone who provides sureties" although no proposal was added about this matter, and no immunity was granted for him to speak about

---

[110]Laws often indicated that their provisions were to apply "in the future" (*to loipon*). See E. M. Harris 2006a: 425–428.

[111]There are no decisive grounds against authenticity, but there seems to be a verb missing at the beginning of the document, and it cannot be a complete text of the law. The phrase "so that they must regain their rights" is also odd (the verb *chrē* seems out of place). On the other hand, the contents are similar to the paraphrase, and there are no phrases or expressions without parallel in contemporary laws and decrees. See Canevaro 2013a: 127–132.

it.[112] [47] Not even when someone obtains immunity does the law allow him to act as he wishes, but as the Council and Assembly decide. It was not enough for him to commit only the crime of speaking without having received immunity and introducing a law on this topic. No, he also went further. Without making any proposal in the Council or Assembly about this,[113] he surreptitiously introduced his law when the Council was in recess and the rest were observing the sacred truce because of the festival.[114] [48] Yet, Timocrates, you know this law that I have read. If you wished to act justly, you should have first proposed approaching the Council, then a discussion in the Assembly, and, if the Athenians approved, made a proposal and passed a law about this matter, waiting for the times appointed by law, so if anyone attempts to show that the law is inexpedient for the city, you do not seem to have plotted, but to have failed because of an error in judgment.[115] [49] But, as it is, by slipping your statute into the lawcode stealthily, hastily, and illegally and not properly enacting it, you have lost any right to lenience. One shows lenience to those who do wrong against their will, not to those who act deliberately.[116] That is what you have been caught doing. I will return to this subject in a few moments. Now read the next law. [50]

---

[112]The objection is specious: Timocrates did not propose that debtors be released from their obligations, only that they could leave prison if they provided sureties. Even after their release, they would still owe money to the Treasury. Moreover, Timocrates did not propose that any particular debtor be released.

[113]"Without making any proposal in the Council or Assembly about this": This refers to the 12th of Hekatombaion, the day of the Kronia, when the Council was adjourned. *Pace* Hansen 2016a, it is not evidence that the preliminary vote (which, in this case, was held on the 11th of Hekatombaion), could be held without a *probouleuma* (see Canevaro forthcoming b). It just shows that Timocrates had proposed his law about public debtors without having it first discussed in the Council.

[114]I have followed Dobree, who deletes *lathra* as an intrusive gloss on the phrase *en parabysto*.

[115]Once more Diodorus stresses that Timocrates acted deliberately to justify a more severe penalty at the *timesis* phase.

[116]For the idea that those who plot deliberately are not entitled to forgiveness, see Thuc. 3.40.1.

[LAW¹¹⁷]

If anyone supplicates in the Council or Assembly about those whom a court, the Council, or the Assembly convicted, if the debtor himself supplicates before paying, let him be denounced in the same way as when someone in debt to the Treasury sits as a judge.¹¹⁸ If anyone else supplicates on behalf of a debtor before he has paid, let all of his property be confiscated. If any of the *proedroi* put to the vote such a request by a debtor or by someone on his behalf before the debt is paid, let him lose his rights.

[51] It would be quite a task, men of the court, for me to discuss all the laws this man has violated by introducing his law. But if any of these deserves analysis, it is the law that I have just now read. The man who enacted this law, men of Athens, understood your generosity and mild nature. He also saw that many times you had willingly caused yourselves serious harm because of these qualities.¹¹⁹ [52] Because he wished to leave behind no excuse for harming the public good, he thought those who have been judged guilty by the court's decision rendered according to the laws should not benefit from your good nature by having an opportunity to beg and to supplicate in their misfortune.¹²⁰ No, he completely forbade the guilty man or anyone else to supplicate or speak on behalf of such people but to do what he should in silence.¹²¹ [53] If someone should ask you to whom you would

---

¹¹⁷The text of this document is consistent with the summary in the adjoining text and does not contain any phrases without parallel in Athenian laws and decrees. See Canevaro 2013a: 132–138. The provisions in the document probably formed part of a general law about public debtors because the first clause contains the particle *de*.

¹¹⁸Sometimes Athenian laws prescribe a penalty taken from another legal procedure. See, for example, Dem. 20.156. The public debtor who sat as a judge could be punished with a fine and remain in prison until he paid (*Ath. Pol.* 63.3). Alternatively he could be sentenced to death (Dem. 21.182).

¹¹⁹For the idea that the Athenian people are mild and generous, cf. Dem. 21.184, 22.51 and Hyp. *Dem.* 25, with Whitehead 2000: 437–438.

¹²⁰See the note on 12.

¹²¹This argument is not compelling. Timocrates might have countered that this law did not apply to punishments (such as imprisonment) imposed

more likely do some favor, to those who make a request or to those who give a command, I know that you would say, "To those who make a request." That is the way honest men act; the other is the way cowards behave. Certainly the laws order what must be done, whereas those who place suppliant branches make a request.[122] If, then, supplication is illegal in this case, can it be possible to introduce a law containing an order? I myself do not think so. Indeed in cases where you have decided that requests must not be granted, it would be shameful for you to allow requests made by some men to be carried out against your will. [*To the clerk*] Read the next law in order after this one. [**54**]

[LAW[123]]

Concerning those who have undergone a trial, an audit[124] or a *diadikasia*[125] about something in court or whose property the state has sold, whether in a public or a private trial, it is not

---

by the court but only to fines and that his law did not cancel the fines imposed by the court.

[122]Suppliants might make their request by placing a bough on an altar. See Naiden 2006: 36.

[123]This law is also quoted or discussed at Dem. 20.147; 36.24; 37.1, 19–20; 38.16; but this document is a clumsy attempt at reconstruction. "From all these allusions it is possible to draw a quite accurate account of the law: it forbids to hold *dikai, euthynai, diadikasiai* on matters already decided with similar procedures, or settled with a release or a discharge, or that have been the object of a public sale. No magistrate shall put such a matter to the vote. If anyone does bring such a charge, the defendant has the right to bring a *paragraphe* against him. (. . .) the document lacks two elements that were, according to the other sources, mentioned in the law: it does not list releases and discharges, and it does not name *paragraphe*, the procedure available against charges brought against its provisions." Furthermore, its contents do not conform to Demosthenes' summary (Canevaro 2013a: 138–142 at 140 and 142).

[124]The word for audit in the document is *euthyna* in the singular but the word always occurs in the plural in documents and literary texts (including the paraphrase at 55).

[125]The expression *diadikasia peri tou* is never found in contemporary documents or literary works. For this procedure, see 13 with the note there.

permitted for any of the archons to introduce their case to the court or to hold a vote,[126] nor should they allow any accusations that the laws do not allow.[127]

[55] Well, now, Timocrates immediately begins his law by violating this rule as if to provide testimony for his own crimes. The law does not allow discussion of any matter about which a court has made a final decision, yet he has written that if an additional penalty is imposed on someone by law or decree, the people are to discuss his case so that the court's decision will be overturned, and the debtor will provide sureties. Moreover, the law states that no magistrate is to put a proposal to the vote in violation of this rule. But he has written that the *proedroi* must present the sureties if anyone provides them and has added "whenever someone wishes."[128]

[56] Read another law.

[LAW[129]]

All verdicts and decisions of arbitrators that were made according to the laws during the democracy are to be binding.

This is certainly not what Timocrates says, at least not for those who have received imprisonment as an additional penalty.

---

[126] The verb *epipsephizein* is used only for the *proedroi* who submit proposals in the Assembly, but the document assigns this function to the archons. Moreover, the law only forbids the courts to overturn a verdict and does not concern procedure in the Assembly.

[127] This clause makes no sense: it refers to other laws that forbid accusations, but this is the law that forbids them.

[128] Diodorus appears to assume that the law applied both to the courts and to the Assembly, but it applied only to the courts. As the law cited at 45 and the decree of Patrocleides (And. 1.73–76) indicate, the Assembly had the power to overturn the verdicts of the courts. See Pecorella Longo 2004, overlooked by MacDowell 2009: 188.

[129] This law is also mentioned at And. 1.87, but this document is probably a forgery. The document contains the phrase *epi tois nomois*, but the normal phrase is *kata tous nomous*. For other evidence against authenticity and analysis, see Canevaro 2013a: 142–145.

[LAW[130]]

All measures voted during the Thirty, or legal judgments rendered, either public or private, are invalid.

[57] Stop. Tell me, what would all of you say is the most terrible event you have heard about and would pray not to happen again? Wouldn't it be that what happened under the Thirty never happen again? I certainly think so. In my opinion, this last law protects against this danger by rendering all acts of their regime invalid. Now this man here has attributed the same illegality to acts of the democracy that you attributed to those of their regime. He therefore makes them invalid in the very same way. [58] So what are we to say, men of Athens, if we allow this law to stand? That the courts under the democracy, manned by those who swear the oath, have committed the same crimes as those committed under the Thirty? Wouldn't that be shocking? Or that the votes they cast were just? Then how are we to explain the reason for enacting the law that invalidates these verdicts? Only if someone says that we were mad. For there is no other answer.[131]

[59] Read another law.

[LAW[132]]

It is not permitted to enact a law about an individual unless one enacts the same law for all Athenians when no fewer than six thousand vote and decide by secret ballot.

---

[130] This document is likely to be a forgery. See Wayte 1882: 135 and Canevaro 2013a: 142–145. The Thirty were a group of oligarchs who seized control of Athens in 404 and were driven out by democratic forces in 403. See Krentz 1982.

[131] This argument is not as strong as it might at first appear (*pace* MacDowell 2009: 189). The intent of the law was to rescind legal judgments rendered under the Thirty and to affirm that judgments rendered under the democracy were binding. It did not, however, remove the power of the Assembly to annul or modify verdicts.

[132] This law is a forgery. Dilts adds *ean mē* ("if not") before *psephisamenōn* ("of those voting") to bring the text into conformity with And. 1.87, but this text is also a forgery. For the correct form of the law, see Dem. 23.86 and the summary in the following sentence. For discussion, see Canevaro and E. M. Harris 2012: 116–119 and Canevaro 2103a: 145–150.

This forbids the enactment of any law that is not the same for all citizens; its provisions are good and democratic. Just as each man has an equal share in other rights of citizenship, this law commands that in the same way each man has an equal share of these rights. You know as well as I do for whose benefit this man introduced his law. But apart from these men, he himself has admitted that he did not enact the same rule for all by adding a special clause excluding tax collectors, lessees, and their sureties. Whenever there are some people whom you set apart, you do not enact the same rule for everyone.[133] [60] Indeed, you would not argue that of all those who are given imprisonment as an additional penalty, tax-farmers commit the most serious crimes so that they alone should not share the protections of the law. Much more serious criminals are certainly those who betray the public interest, those who harm their parents, or those have unclean hands and enter the Agora.[134] The existing laws impose imprisonment for all these criminals, but your law grants them a release. Here again you reveal for whose benefit you were enacting the law. It was not for those who owed money because they were collecting taxes but because they had stolen—or rather looted—public funds. This is the reason you have paid no attention to tax collectors.

[61] Anyone could cite many excellent laws, all of which the law enacted by this man violates. Yet if I discuss them all, I might lose the chance to discuss how this law is completely against your interests. Moreover, you will see how it is liable to the charge even if it violates just one of the existing laws. What, then, do I think I should do? Pass over the other laws but discuss the law this man earlier enacted and move on now to that part of the charge that

---

[133]Diodorus claims that Timocrates' law violates the rule against passing a law for an individual. First, he claims it was introduced for Melanopus, Glaucetes, and Androtion; second, he claims that Timocrates makes exceptions for certain groups. Neither objection is cogent: the law does not name these three individuals, and despite the exceptions, the law still applies to all Athenians. For an exception made in a law for a group of individuals, see Dem. 20.29, 128, 160.

[134]Murderers incurred pollution and were barred from the Agora because they were unclean. Those who violated this ban could be arrested and placed in prison (Dem. 23.80).

if this law should go into effect, it would cause the city an enormous amount of harm.[135] [62] To have introduced a law contrary to those passed by others is terrible, but it requires another person to make the charge. But for someone to enact a law in violation of a law he himself enacted earlier places him in the position of being one's own accuser. For you to understand what is happening, the clerk will read to you the law that this man has enacted. I will remain silent. Read it. [63]

[LAW[136]]

Timocrates proposed that as many Athenians as are now or will in the future be put in prison as the result of an impeachment (*eisangelia*) before the Council and whose preliminary verdicts of guilty have not yet been delivered by the secretary for the prytany to the *thesmothetai* according to the impeachment law, it shall be resolved by the *nomothetai* that the Eleven bring them before the court within thirty days from the date of their arrest unless some public business prevent them, but if not, as soon as possible. Any Athenian who wishes from among those qualified may bring a charge. If he is convicted, let the Heliaea assess whatever punishment or fine it sees fit. If he is assessed to pay a fine, let him be placed in prison until he pays whatever he is sentenced to pay.

[64] Do you hear this, men of the court? Read this part to them again.

If he is assessed to pay a fine, let him be placed in prison until he pays.

Stop. Could anyone enact two laws more opposed to each other? In one, those convicted are placed in prison until they pay;

---

[135]This section marks a transition between the procedural violations of the law and the substantive issues.

[136]The text of this document is consistent with the summary in the adjoining text and does not contain any phrases without parallel in Athenian laws and decrees. See Canevaro 2013a: 151–157. For more on the Eleven, see *Against Aristogeiton* 1 n. 88.

in the other, those same people can put up sureties but are not put in prison.[137] This is the charge brought against Timocrates by Timocrates, not by Diodorus, or any of the rest of you even though there are so many of you. [65] Yet what sort of gain do you think he would refrain from, what would he shrink from doing for profit, when he thought it right to pass laws contradicting each other when the laws do not allow one to enact laws contradicting other laws? A man like this I think would be ready to do anything through lack of shame. Just as the laws order punishment without trial for criminals who confess to committing other offenses,[138] so too it is right to condemn a person when he is caught vandalizing the laws without letting him speak or wishing to listen. By enacting this law contradicting his earlier laws, he has confessed his guilt.

[66] I think that it is obvious to all of you that he has enacted his law in violation of these laws and those mentioned earlier, in fact, I could almost say in violation of all the laws in the city. I wonder what he will dare to say about this. He will not be able to show that his law is not contrary to the other laws. Nor would he be able to convince you that he did not notice because he is a private citizen and lacks experience,[139] since he has been seen proposing and introducing laws for pay for a long time. [67] Nor indeed could he confess that his action was wrong but that he deserves to receive sympathy. He clearly has not passed his law against his will or to help the unfortunate or his family and associates. No, he did this willingly to help those who have committed serious crimes against you and are not in any way related

---

[137]MacDowell 2009: 189–190 considers this the strongest argument against Timocrates' law.

[138]Diodorus exaggerates here. It was illegal to put an Athenian to death without a trial. See Carawan 1984. The only exception was for certain categories of criminals who confessed their guilt: see *Ath. Pol.* 52.1, with E. M. Harris 2006a: 373–390.

[139]Diodorus anticipates the argument that Timocrates made an error through ignorance. For this type of argument from *epieikeia* (fairness), see Dem. 59.78–84, with E. M. Harris 2013a: 274–301.

to him—unless of course he claims that he considers those who hired him his blood relations.[140]

[68] I will now try to show that the law he passed is neither expedient nor to your advantage. I think that all of you would agree that a law that is correct and intended to serve the people's interests should be written simply and in terms comprehensible to everyone, not in a way that allows one person to interpret it in one way, another in another way.[141] Next, the actions that must occur because of the law must be feasible. If the law is good, but gives an order impossible to obey, it would be doing the work of a prayer, not a law. [69] Moreover, it should be clear that the law grants lenient treatment to none of the guilty. If anyone thought it was democratic for laws to be mild, let him ask himself, to whom? If he wishes to address the issue correctly, he will find it is toward those about to go on trial, not those convicted. It is not clear whether the former have been unjustly slandered, but there is no room for argument about the latters' bad character. [70] It will be obvious that this law contains none of these features found in the laws I have discussed, but the opposite on every point. Indeed, one would be able to show this in many ways, above all by going through the actual law that he has enacted. It is not the case that one part of the law is well drafted, and another part in error; the entire law from the start, from the first syllable down to the last, was enacted to harm your interests. [71] [*To the clerk*] Take the indictment itself, and read the law to the end of the first part. This will be the easiest way for me to show and for you to understand what I mean.

---

[140]Diodorus argues that Timocrates had no excuses for his actions; he cannot plead inexperience or the desire to help friends and family. On the accuser's need to show that the defendant has no excuses, see Anaximenes *Rhetorica ad Alexandrum* 4.6.1427a18–20.

[141]For the idea that the law should be clear and easy for everyone to understand, see Dem. 20.93. This was of course an ideal; in reality laws might contain ambiguous terms or clauses that might give rise to disputes about their meaning. On the problems of "open texture" and legal interpretation, see E. M. Harris 2013a: 175–245. The term "open texture" is misunderstood by R. G. Osborne 1985 and Ober 1989: 144–145.

[LAW[142]]

During the prytany of Pandionis, the first, on the 12th day of the prytany, Aristocles of Myrrhinous, one of the *proedroi*, put the motion to a vote. Timocrates proposed that even if anyone owing money to the Treasury has been assessed an additional penalty of imprisonment by law or decree or is assessed this additional penalty in the future, it is permitted for him or anyone on his behalf to provide sureties.

[72] Stop. Soon you will read each clause. This clause here, men of the court, is just about the most shocking one in the entire law. Not one other person so far, I think, has dared to introduce a law for citizens to follow that attempts to overturn verdicts reached according to laws previously in effect. This man here, Timocrates, has shamelessly done this without any attempt to conceal it. He has explicitly written: "And if anyone owing money to the Treasury has been assessed an additional penalty of imprisonment by law or decree or is assessed this additional penalty in the future." [73] If what he persuaded you to do about future cases were correct, he would not be guilty. Yet when a court has reached a verdict, and its decision is final, isn't it shocking for him to introduce a law that will overturn these verdicts? Imagine if someone were to allow this law to go into effect, then propose another law such as this: "And if some who are in debt and have been imprisoned as an additional penalty have provided sureties in accordance with the law, they have no right to be released on bail, and no one is to obtain such a release in the future." [74] No one in his right mind would do this, I think, yet you were guilty

---

[142]This document may be a forgery. At this time the *proedroi* could not be members of the tribe that held the prytany. See Rhodes 1972: 25–28. The *proedros* in this prescript, however, comes from the deme of Myrrhinous, which was in the tribe of Pandionis. For discussion, see Wayte 1882: 147. MacDowell 1975: 63 believed that this document showed that the *proedroi* of the *nomothetai* were different from the *proedroi* of the Assembly, but see Canevaro 2013a: 107–108, 113–117. The prescript suspiciously lacks the name of the archon and the enactment formula found in prescripts of decrees from this period. See, for example, *IG* ii² 128.

of overturning those verdicts.[143] If he thought the measure just, he should have enacted a law for future cases and not have thrown together under the same clause future offenses with past offenses, unknown with known, and should then have proposed the same rule for all. Isn't it shocking to consider those who have earlier been convicted of crimes against the community worthy of the same legal treatment as those for whom it is not yet clear whether they will commit an offense worth bringing to court?

[75] Indeed, anyone could see from this too that Timocrates has committed a terrible crime in passing a law about the past. Let him consider the difference between the rule of law and oligarchy, why those who are willing to be ruled by law are considered virtuous and good, while those ruled by oligarchies are cowardly and slavish.[144] [76] For he would discover that this is truly the most salient difference: each man in an oligarchy has the power to overturn previous decisions and to give whatever orders he decides about the future, but the laws indicate what should happen in the future and are enacted on the conviction that they will benefit those who obey them. Now Timocrates, who is legislating in a democratic city, has imported oligarchy's injustice into his own law: he has demanded that he have more authority about past cases than the judges who decided them.[145] [77] This is not his only act of insolence. He also inserted a clause that "in the future if anyone is imprisoned as an additional punishment, it is permitted for him to be released after appointing sureties to guarantee payment." Yet, if he thought it was terrible to be put in prison, he should have enacted a law abolishing imprisonment as an additional punishment for those who provided sureties in-

[143]This sentence and the next refer to Timocrates but shift abruptly from the second person to the third person. Note that one papyrus of the passage reads *ēdikei* ("he was guilty").

[144]Diodorus implicitly equates democracy with the rule of law. Cf. Aes. 1.4–5, 3.6.

[145]The Athenian legal system recognized the principle of *res iudicata*. For the rule that cases once decided cannot be brought to court again, see Dem. 20.147, 38.16, and 40.39–43. For the implications of this rule for the Athenian legal system, see E. M. Harris 2013a: 72–73.

stead of allowing sureties only after you have imposed the penalty of imprisonment and the defendant is already hostile to you. As it is now, he is declaring that even if you decide to put someone in prison, he will release him. This is the way he has enacted his law. [78] Does anyone then think that a law like this will benefit the city, one that will take precedence over a court's decision and will also order those who have not sworn an oath to overturn the verdicts rendered by those who have?[146] I do not think so. And yet Timocrates' law clearly contains both these features. Therefore, because you all have some regard for the constitution and think that your verdicts in cases in which you have voted on oath should remain binding, a law like this must be repealed and not be allowed to take effect.

[79] It was not enough for him to remove the court's power to impose additional punishments. No, even the rules that he has rightly laid down in his law and imposed on debtors have clearly not been written in a clear and honest manner, but rather by a man whose overriding objective is to trick and deceive you. Look at how he has written it. "Timocrates proposed," it states, "that even if anyone owing money to the Treasury has been assessed an additional penalty of imprisonment by law or decree or is assessed this additional penalty in the future, it is permitted for him or anyone on his behalf to provide sureties for the debt, whom the Assembly approves by vote, to pay the money which he owed." [80] Notice how far he has jumped from the court and its judgment to the Assembly and has stolen away the defendant and the requirement to surrender him to the Eleven. Which official will hand over the debtor? Who will take him from the Eleven? This law allows sureties to be appointed in the Assembly, but it is impossible to hold a meeting of the Assembly on the same day as the court meets, and the law nowhere requires that the defendant be held in custody until he provides sureties. [81] Yet why did he refrain from clearly adding "the official is to keep the debtor in custody until he provides sureties"? Wouldn't that be right? I am cer-

---

[146]While the judges who tried cases swore an oath, those who voted in the Assembly did not.

tain that all of you would agree. Would this clause violate any law? No; it would be the only lawful provision in his law. What, then, was his motive? One would discover that his aim was nothing other than to prevent to have those whom you condemn from paying the penalty and to ensure this would not happen.[147] [82] What, then, is the next clause? "Provide sureties to pay the money he owed." Here again he has stolen away the tenfold payment of sacred debts and reduced by half the amount of public debts, which are doubled in the law. How does he do this? By writing "the money" instead of "assessed penalty" in one place and "the amount he owed" instead of "the total amount" in another.[148] [83] What is the difference? If he had written "provide sureties promising to pay the total assessed amount," he would have also taken account of the laws that impose tenfold fines in some cases, double fines in others.[149] The result would have been to force debtors to pay the prescribed amount and the additional penalties imposed by law. As it is, by writing, "It is possible to provide sureties promising to pay the money owed," he sets the amount to be paid at the figure recorded in the plaint and other documents that formed the grounds for the case against each defendant. In all these documents the money owed is given as the simple amount.[150]

---

[147]Diodorus notes that the law does not specify what is to happen to the man sentenced to pay a fine and to be imprisoned until it is paid between the time the court makes its decision and the moment when the Assembly approves his sureties. The criticism appears justified, but there is no reason to accept Diodorus' claim that the omission was designed to benefit Androtion, Melanopus, and Glaucetes. It may have been an oversight on Timocrates' part.

[148]Dilts places quotation marks around the phrase *to gignomenon ho ōphlen*, which makes no sense.

[149]For an explanation of these figures, see III.

[150]Diodorus draws attention to a potential ambiguity in one phrase of the law: the words "the money he owed" may refer to the amount of the original debt or the sum that was to be paid after the original debt was multiplied. Timocrates might have argued that the ambiguity arose by error and that he intended the second meaning.

[84] Next, after eliminating such an important matter by altering the words, he added: "The *proedroi* are required to put this matter to the vote whenever someone wishes to provide sureties." Throughout his entire law he thinks it necessary to protect the guilty man convicted in your courts. By permitting him to provide sureties "whenever he wishes," he made it possible for him to avoid payment and imprisonment. [85] Who, then, will not bring forward some worthless people? When you vote to reject them, he will still remain free. If someone demands that he be put in prison for not providing sureties, he will say that he is finding some or intends to do so and cite this man's law, which permits him to provide sureties "whenever he wishes" but does not require him to be placed in custody until then nor orders that he go to prison if you should vote to reject his sureties.[151] No, this law truly functions as a lucky charm for would-be criminals.

[86] "For the man who provides sureties," it states, "if he pays the money." Here again he continues with the ruse that I discussed a little while ago. He does not miss a chance: for the debtor to avoid prison, he does not write that he must pay off "the total fine assessed" but "the money owed."

[87] "If he does not pay the money, either himself or his sureties, during the ninth prytany, the debtor who provided sureties is to be placed in prison and the property of his sureties confiscated." In this last clause he clearly charges himself with committing a crime. He did not consider putting a citizen in prison shameful or shocking and forbid imprisonment but snatched away the moment when it was possible to arrest the guilty man when he is here; he left you who are wronged only the semblance of punishing those who commit crimes but took away the reality. Against your wishes he granted a release to those who see fit to keep your property by force and all but added a clause permitting them to bring an action against judges who imposed the additional punishment of imprisonment![152]

[88] There are many shocking features that he placed in his

---

[151] This argument is similar to the one presented at 80–81.

[152] This argument is similar to the ones at 54 and 56.

law, but I want to tell you about the one that most deserves your anger. Everywhere throughout the entire law he mentions the man who provides sureties. As for the man who provides none, whether better or worse, or pays no attention to you at all, he has not added any legal procedure or punishment but has granted him the greatest possible immunity there could be. The deadline that he has specified, the ninth prytany, he mentions for the man who provides sureties. [89] Anyone could understand this. He added that the property of the sureties is to be confiscated if he does not pay. But if the debtor provides none, there certainly cannot be any sureties. He has required that the *proedroi*, who are selected by lot from among you and preside over meetings, must accept them whenever anyone provides them. Yet there is no requirement for those who wrong the city. In fact, he treats them like benefactors and gives them a choice whether to pay the penalty or not.[153]

[90] How could there exist a law that was more against your interests or more evil? First, about cases decided in the past it gives orders that overturn your decisions. Second, about cases to be decided in the future, it allows the judges who have sworn an oath to impose additional penalties but makes those penalties null and void. Next, it restores rights to debtors who have not paid the correct amount. In general, it reveals that the oath you swear, the penalties you assess, the sentences you decide, and the indignation you feel, indeed all that you do is pointless. If Critias,[154] who was a member of the Thirty, passed this law, I think that he would have written and proposed it in the very same way this man has.

[91] I think you will easily understand that the law subverts the entire constitution, destroys political activity, and deprives

---

[153]This argument is not persuasive. As MacDowell 2009: 191 notes, Timocrates "might retort that such a debtor will remain in prison until he pays the debt."

[154]Critias was the most ruthless member of the Thirty who seized power in 404 after the defeat of Athens. For his activities, see Xen. *Hellenica* 2.3.2–56; 4.8, 9, 19; Lys. 12.43, with Bultrighini 1999. Aes. 1.172–73 claims that the Athenians executed Socrates because he taught Critias. On Demosthenes' use of history, see Nouhaud 1982: 362–364.

the city of many incentives for patriotism. Of course, you know that the city owes its security to the campaigns of our army and navy and that you have often accomplished many fine deeds and have protected some communities, punished others and brought about peace. [92] What must be done to achieve these goals? You must pass decrees and laws and order some to pay the war tax, others to serve as trierarchs, others to enroll as rowers, and others to perform their duty. To bring this about, you set up courts and sentence those lawbreakers to prison. Just consider how the law passed by this fine gentleman undermines and destroys these institutions.

[93] As you know, it has been written in his law: "And if anyone has been put in prison as an additional punishment or will be in the future, he can provide sureties to pay the money in the ninth prytany and be released from prison." What revenue will there be? How will an expedition be sent? How will we collect money if every person who owes money provides sureties according to this man's law and does not perform his duty?[155] [94] By Zeus, will we say to the Greeks, "Our city has a law of Timocrates; wait until the ninth prytany, and then we will march out"?[156] That is all we can say. If you need to defend yourselves against attack, do you actually think that your enemies will wait for the scoundrels among us to stop their evasions and dishonesties? Or that your city, after enacting laws that hinder its efforts and order actions contrary to its interests, will be able to perform any of its duties? [95] We must consider ourselves fortunate, men of Athens, if when everything goes our way and there is no law like this one, we defeat the enemy and are able to respond to sudden events and crises of war and not miss any of them. But if you

---

[155]Diodorus gives the false impression that money from fines provided the main source of funding for military expeditions. In this period money to pay for military campaigns came from the Military Fund. Diodorus also overlooks that putting the debtor in prison would not ensure that he paid his fine.

[156]For the idea that the court's verdict will affect Athens' reputation among the Greeks, cf. Lys. 14.13, 28.15; [Lys.] 6.5, 7, 18; Lyc. *Against Leocrates* 14, 110; Hyp. 5.22.

have clearly enacted a law like this, which impairs advantages like these that have made our city proud and famous in the world, is there any misfortune you would not deserve?

[96] Men of Athens, the law also destroys our finances, both sacred and public. I will tell you how. You have a law now in effect as fine as any other, that orders those who hold sacred and secular money to make payments in the Council-chamber, and if not, the Council should collect the money following the laws about tax-collection.[157] [97] Through this law public finances are administered, for this is the law that makes sure funds are fully provided for meetings of the Assembly,[158] sacrifices,[159] the Council,[160] the cavalry,[161] and other items. When there is not enough money from taxes in the budget, the so-called extra levies are paid through fear of the law.[162] [98] Won't all the city's finances inevitably be destroyed when the payments of taxes are not sufficient for the budget, but much more money is needed, and when it is not possible to collect these funds until the end of the year, and the Council and the courts do not have the authority to put those who do not make the extra payments into prison, since they provide sureties until the ninth prytany? [99] What, then, will we do during the eight other prytanies? Tell me, Timocrates! Will we not meet and deliberate if something is needed? Will we still live in a democracy? Will the courts not judge private and public cases? What protection will there be for the victims of injustice? Will the Council not hold meetings and transact its legal busi-

---

[157] In Classical Athens, the right to collect taxes was often sold at auction to private individuals. See, for example, And. 1.133–34. See Langdon 1994.

[158] In the fourth century, Athenians received money to attend meetings of the Assembly (*Ath. Pol.* 41.3).

[159] The city conducted many public sacrifices at which meat and other food might be distributed to citizens. See Rosivach 1994.

[160] Members of the Council received payment and a budget. See Rhodes 1972: 13–14.

[161] The cavalry received money to pay for fodder and maintenance. See *Ath Pol.* 49.1, with Bugh 1988: 60–62, 131–133, 154–156.

[162] Wayte 1882: 167, following Schaefer, believes "extra levies" are a euphemism for fines and confiscations.

ness? What other fate remains for us except disaster? Or, by Zeus, will we do these things without pay?[163] Isn't it shocking that you took pay to pass this law, but the Assembly and the Council and the courts go without pay? [100] You should have added this, Timocrates, to your law, in the same way you did against tax collectors and sureties: "And if it has been stated in another law or decree that there is to be the same right of execution in regard to debtors as there is in regard to tax collectors, there is also to be the same right to collect against these in accordance with the existing laws." [101] Now he goes out of his way to avoid the laws about customs duties that the decree of Euctemon has stated must be followed when collecting money from public debtors.[164] This is why he omitted this clause. In this way he repealed the existing punishment against those who hold state property, and by not adding another penalty he ruins our entire political system, the Assembly, the cavalry, the Council, sacred and public business. In response, if you are sensible, men of Athens, he will be punished, pay the appropriate penalty, and serve as an example to discourage others from enacting laws like this one.[165]

[102] It is not enough for Timocrates to remove the court's authority to impose additional penalties, to grant immunity to those who harm the public good, to weaken the armed forces protecting the city, and to destroy our finances. No, he has also enacted a law helping common criminals, father-beaters, and deserters because it destroys the existing penalties in the laws now in effect. [103] The laws established by Solon, a lawgiver completely different from this man, state: "If anyone is convicted of theft and not sentenced to death, he will be imprisoned as an additional punishment; if anyone is convicted of mistreating his parents and

---

[163] For the payment of Athenian officials in the fourth century, see Gabrielsen 1981 and Pritchard 2014. Hansen 1979, 1980, and 2014 argue that officials did not receive payment after 400 BCE, but his arguments have generally been rejected.

[164] This is the decree passed by Euctemon about the enemy property seized by Androtion, Melanopus, and Glaucippus. See 13.

[165] For the deterrent view of punishment, cf. Thuc. 3.40.7; Dem. 19.343, 21.227, 22.68; Lyc. *Against Leocrates* 150.

entering the Agora, he will be put in prison; and if anyone owes a fine for not reporting for military duty and continues to exercise the rights of citizenship,[166] he too will be put in prison." Timocrates grants all these people immunity when he allows them to avoid imprisonment by providing sureties. [104] As a result, in my opinion—what I am about to say may appear rather coarse, but I will say it and not change my mind—for this reason alone he deserves death as a punishment so that he can pass this law in Hades for the sacrilegious and allow us, the living, to follow our sacred and just laws from now on. [*To the clerk*] Read these laws too. [105]

[LAW[167]]

Whatever one should lose, if he recovers[168] it, the penalty to be imposed is double;[169] if not, ten times the amount claimed [. . .].[170] Let his foot be chained in the stocks for five days and as many nights if the Heliaea imposes this additional penalty.[171]

---

[166]The person who was convicted on a charge of cowardice, which might include failure to report for duty, lost his rights as citizen. Dem. 15.32; cf. [Dem.] 59.27 and Dem. 21.103.

[167]This document is a forgery. To begin with, the summary says that the law also covers *apagoge* for theft, but the document does not include this procedure. For general discussion, see Canevaro 2013a: 157–173.

[168]The normal verb for "getting back" is *apolabēi*, not *labēi*, which is found in the manuscripts. Dilts follows Bernard and emends to *apolabēi*.

[169]The document states that the penalty is twice the value of the stolen item in addition to the recovery of the stolen item, whereas the summary indicates that the penalty is only twice the value of the stolen object.

[170]There is no evidence for a penalty of ten times the value of the stolen item in the *dike klopēs*. The expression *pros tois epaitiois*, which I have not translated, has no parallel and makes no sense in this context. On theft in Athenian law, see Pelloso 2008. The study of the topic by D. Cohen 1983 is not reliable and should be used with caution. See E. M. Harris 2006: 373–390.

[171]A similar phrase is found at Lys. 10.16, but as Carey notes, there is no reason to believe that this is from the same law. Canevaro (2013a: 164–165) suggests that this speech may be the source of this phrase.

He who wishes may propose an additional penalty when there is a vote about the penalty.[172] If anyone is arrested after being convicted for mistreating parents, for not reporting for duty, or if he enters after proclamation has been made barring him from entering where the laws say he must not go, let the Eleven put him in prison and introduce his case to the Heliaea[173] and let anyone who wishes among those who have the right make an accusation.[174] If he is convicted, let the Heliaea assess what he must suffer or pay. If he is assessed a fine, let him remain in prison until he pays.

[106] Men of Athens, aren't this man and Solon the lawgiver rather similar? The former makes men better both now and in the future. The latter shows those who have committed crimes in the past the way to avoid punishment, discovers how those in the present can commit crimes with impunity, and provides that those in the future, in short, criminals at all times, can remain safe and suffer no harm. [107] What penalty do you deserve? What punishment would suit your crimes? Leaving aside the rest, you weaken the laws protecting old age, which compel children to look after their parents when they are alive and, after they die, ensure that they receive what is prescribed by law.[175] How would it not be right to consider you the worst person in the world, you

---

[172]The term *ton boulomenon* ("he who wishes") is used only for the accuser in public cases, but this law concerns the private suit for theft.

[173]This clause contains several errors. First, *apagoge* is never used against *atimoi*. The correct procedure was *endeixis*. See Hansen 1976: 94–95. Second, the expression "after proclamation has been made barring him from entering where the laws say he must not go" *vel sim.* is always used for those accused of homicide, never for other kinds of offenders. Yet homicide is not mentioned in the summary of the law's contents. Third, the expression "where he must not go" (*eision hopoi mē chrê*) is never found in the Attic document; the correct expression is *hopoi mē exeinai* (*IG* ii² 28, line 11; 43, line 36; 97, line 12).

[174]This phrase appears to have been taken from the document at 63 but is out of place in this context.

[175]On the duties of children toward their parents, see Rubinstein 1993: 62–76.

damned criminal, who clearly care more about thieves, criminals, and men who have deserted our country and for their sake have passed a law that harms us?

[108] Now I wish to show you that I have done what I promised at the beginning of my speech. I said that I would prove that he is guilty of all the charges in the indictment, first, legislating illegally; second, proposing a law contrary to the existing laws; and, third, enacting measures harmful to the state.[176] You have certainly heard which procedures the laws require someone enacting a law to follow. By contrast, I demonstrated to you that this man has followed not a single one of these procedures.

[109] Then you heard those laws that this man's law clearly violates; you know that he enacted his law before repealing these laws. Finally you heard that it is inexpedient. I just finished talking about this. Thus, he is clearly guilty on all counts: it is obvious that he paid no attention and took no precaution about any of this. No, I think that if besides these there were some other rule written in the existing laws forbidding something, he would have violated that too.

[110] Everything shows that Timocrates made this proposal as part of a plot and not by some mistake in judgment. The greatest proof of his intent is that the law is framed in such terms right down to the last syllable. He did not include one correct provision even unwillingly nor one that is going to bring you any benefits. Could it possibly be wrong to despise and punish this man, who did not care about the injustices suffered by the people and passed laws to protect criminals past and future? [111] I am amazed, men of the court, at his impudence: when he was in office with Androtion, he had no pity for the large number of you who were worn out by paying taxes, but when Androtion had to return the money, both sacred and public, he stole from the city long ago, he then passed a law designed to rob twice this amount from the

---

[176]Diodorus summarizes his arguments in the first half of the speech: Timocrates has not followed correct legislative procedure (24–32), did not repeal opposing laws (33–67), and enacted a law detrimental to the public interest (68–107).

city and ten times this amount from the gods.[177] This is the way this man, who in just a moment will claim to have passed this law for your benefit, has conducted himself toward you, the people. [112] I think that any punishment would be just for someone who thinks that if there is a market-official (*agoranomos*),[178] a policeman (*astynomos*), or a judge appointed for the demes[179] convicted for embezzlement at his review (*euthynai*), a poor man, a private citizen without much experience, assigned to office by lot, that this man must pay a tenfold penalty but does not propose a law to help people like them, yet when some envoys, who have been elected by the people and are wealthy, steal a large sum of money, part belonging to the gods, part to the city, and keep it for a long time, he has found a way precisely to allow them to avoid the punishment imposed by both laws and decrees.[180]

[113] Indeed, Solon, men of the court, a lawgiver whom not even Timocrates himself would claim to resemble, instead of clearly providing safety for future criminals like this, but rather with the aim of either stopping their crimes or else inflicting the punishment they deserve, passed this law: if anyone should steal more than fifty drachmas by day, he can be arrested and handed to the Eleven; if anyone steals any amount at all at night, he may be killed or wounded during pursuit or led to the Eleven if one should wish.[181] The person convicted of a crime for which he

---

[177]Diodorus considers the amount held by the ambassadors similar to an unpaid debt to the state, which would double in the ninth prytany. Because one-tenth of all booty was paid as a tithe to Athena and two percent to the others, the ambassadors would have owed ten times this amount if it remained unpaid.

[178]On the powers of market-officials in Athens and other Greek cities, see Migeotte 2005 and Capdetrey and Hasenohr 2012.

[179]On the judges for the demes, see *Ath. Pol.* 53.1–2.

[180]Note that Diodorus makes a contrast between officials chosen by lot, who were often poor, and those elected by the Assembly, who were rich. For the use of the lot as a way to make public office accessible to the poor, see Thuc. 2.37.1, with E. M. Harris 2006: 38.

[181]For the procedure of arrest to the Eleven and the death penalty for theft, see *Ath. Pol.* 52.1.

can be summarily arrested is not allowed to provide sureties and pay back the amount stolen; the penalty is death. [114] Next, if anyone steals a cloak, flask, or some other cheap item from the Lykeion, the Academy, or Cynosarges,[182] or some equipment from the gymnasium or harbors worth more than ten drachmas, he passed a law providing for the death penalty. If anyone is convicted in a private action for theft, he must pay double the value, but the court may also put the thief in prison for five days and as many nights in addition to the payment so that everyone may see him in chains.[183] You heard these laws a few minutes ago. [115] He thought that when a person did something shameful, he should not be released after merely returning what he stole. He thought there would be many thieves if those who escaped detection kept what they stole, but those who did not had only to return it. No, he thought the thief should pay double and be placed in prison in addition to this penalty so that he lives the rest of his life in shame. But not Timocrates! No, he has arranged that they will pay only the simple amount, which should be double, and that there will be not the slightest additional penalty beside that. [116] It was not enough for him to help future criminals; no, if anyone committed a crime and was punished, he set him free. Yet I thought the lawgiver should legislate about the future, the kind of things one should do and how they should be done, and the sort of punishments appropriate for each offense. This is what it means to enact laws that are the same for all citizens. To propose laws about the past is not legislating, but protecting criminals. [117] To show that I am telling the truth, consider the following point. If Euctemon had been convicted on a charge of proposing an illegal decree, Timocrates would not have passed this law,[184] nor would the city have needed this law, but they would have

---

[182]The Lykeion, the Academy, and Cynosarges were three gymnasia located near the city of Athens. The Lykeion later became the location of the school of Aristotle; the Academy, the site of the school of Plato. For discussion of their locations and remains, see Wycherley 1978: 219–335.

[183]On the private action for theft and the way it differed from the arrest of thieves to the Eleven, see E. M. Harris 2006: 373–390.

[184]Diodorus refers to the trial of Euctemon mentioned at 14.

been content after stealing money from the city to forget about the rest. But now that Euctemon has been acquitted, Timocrates thinks that he must annul your decision, the court's verdict, and the rest of the laws. In their place he and his own law should have authority. [118] In fact, Timocrates, the laws that have authority in our city give these judges here power over everything[185] and grant them the right to hear the case and feel as much anger toward the guilty man as they think his offense deserves, much anger for a great offense, less anger for a small offense. When it is time to determine what punishment or fine should be imposed, the assessment lies in the hands of these men.[186] [119] You, on the other hand, remove the punishment by abolishing imprisonment.[187] For whose benefit is this? For thieves, looters of shrines, father-beaters, murderers, draft dodgers, and deserters.[188] You protect all these men with your law. Yet when a lawgiver in a democracy does not legislate for the good of religion or the people but for those I just mentioned, how does he not deserve to receive the ultimate punishment?[189] [120] Timocrates will certainly not deny that justice and the laws require that such men be subject to the greatest punishments nor that these men for whose benefit he invented the law are thieves and looters of sacred property when they have seized and still retain tithes of the goddess[190] and the

---

[185]Diodorus exaggerates the power of the judges. M. H. Hansen has used this passage and other similar ones to argue that the courts enjoyed sovereignty in Athens during the fourth century BCE, but the Assembly could overrule the verdicts of the courts. See Pecorella Longo 2004, esp. 110, with the bibliography cited in note 134 and E. M. Harris 2016a.

[186]If a defendant was convicted on a public charge, the accuser and the defendant each proposed a penalty at the *timesis* phase, and the court decided which one to impose.

[187]By removing the power to imprison a defendant, Timocrates' law limits the court's power to impose punishment.

[188]Diodorus uses the same argument at 102–103.

[189]I.e., the death penalty.

[190]Greek normally dedicated one-tenth of all booty captured in war to the gods. See Pritchett 1971: 93–100. At Athens the share was dedicated to Athena. On *dekatai* in general, see Jim 2014.

fiftieths of the other gods instead of returning them and that they have stolen public property that belongs to you. Their sacrilege is greater than that of others because they never brought money to the Acropolis at all when they were required. [121] By Olympian Zeus, I think, men of the court, that insolence and arrogance did not come upon Androtion by accident, but were sent by the goddess so that just like those who hacked the wings from the statue of Victory and brought destruction on themselves,[191] these men too will in the same way bring about their own destruction by accusing each other and paying a tenfold penalty according to the law or be put in prison.[192]

[122] I want to tell you something about the law he enacted that occurred to me while I was speaking, something strange and amazing.[193] Judges, this man has written that there are to be penalties for those who purchase the right to collect taxes and do not make their payments according to the earlier laws, in which both imprisonment and a fine for a double amount have been prescribed. This is for men who as a result of losses on their contracts were going to be guilty of a public offense committed against their will.[194] But for those who embezzle public funds or steal

---

[191] Nothing is known about this incident. The statue of Athena in the Parthenon held a winged Victory in her hand. See Pausanias 1.24.5–7. For a photograph of the Varvakeion Athena, a Roman miniature copy of this statue, see Hurwit 2004: 149. Diodorus probably refers to this statue rather than the cult statue of Athena in the temple of Athena Nike as the author of one of the scholia on this passage believes. For a similar charge, see Isoc. 18.57.

[192] For the idea that the gods influence men's actions so that they will be punished, see Lyc. *Against Leocrates* 90–93; And. 1.113.

[193] Diodorus pretends to speak extemporaneously here to appear more sincere. For suspicions about speakers who use a written speech, see Dem. 21.191.

[194] The *poletai* held an auction each year for those who wished to purchase the right to collect certain taxes (*Ath. Pol.* 47.2–3). They awarded the contract to the highest bidder, who was required to make payments in ten installments: the first two when he received the contract, the rest once each prytany. Any amount not paid by the ninth prytany was doubled, and the delinquent contractor was placed in prison until he paid. Those who pur-

the goddess' property he has removed the penalty of imprisonment. Yet if you are going to claim that the crime committed by the latter is less serious than that of the former, you have to admit that you are out of your mind. But if you consider it more serious (as it in fact is) and yet you are releasing the latter but not the former, isn't it obvious that you have sold your services for these men? [123] Now, men of the court, it is certainly worth telling you also how much more magnanimous you are than your politicians. There are some harsh measures in your laws directed at the common people. If anyone receives pay for two positions,[195] attends the Assembly, or serves as a judge when in debt to the Treasury,[196] or does anything that the laws forbid, you do not repeal these penalties, although you know that the person who commits any of these offenses does it because of poverty. Nor do you enact laws like this to grant the right to commit crimes, but rather to prevent them. But the aim of these men is to stop men who commit the most shameful and shocking crimes from being punished. [124] In their speeches they are dragging your private lives through the mud, as if they were fine, upstanding men, when they are acting like vile and ungrateful slaves. Indeed, those of them who have gained their freedom feel no gratitude toward their masters for their freedom but hate them more than all men[197] in the world because they know that they were their former slaves.[198] In the very same way, these politicians are also not satisfied with rising from poverty to wealth at public expense. No,

---

chased the contracts might make a mistake and bid too much. If they lost money, they would not be able to make their payments. On bidding for public contracts, see Langdon 1994.

[195] It was illegal to hold two offices at once and receive pay from both.

[196] For the death penalty imposed on a public debtor who served as a judge, see Dem. 21.182.

[197] Dindorf and Dilts omit *pantōn* ("all") found in some manuscripts.

[198] Freedmen were required to show gratitude to their former masters by performing certain duties. If they did not, their masters could bring a private action (*dikē apostasiou*) against them. See Zelnick-Abramowitz 2005: 274–292.

they drag the common people through the mud because each of them knows the kind of life they led when they were poor and young.

[125] But by Zeus, would it perhaps have been shameful to put Androtion, Melanopus, or Glaucetes in prison? No, by Zeus, it is far more shameful, judges, for the city, which has been wronged and insulted, not to impose punishments for the sake of the goddess and its own interests. As for Androtion, doesn't spending time in prison run in his family? You know for yourselves that his father spent many periods in prison and escaped before he was released.[199] [126] Was it for his activities in his youth?[200] He deserved to be put in prison for this no less than for the money he stole.[201] Or because he entered the Agora when he was not allowed[202] and dragged from there into prison men who had led virtuous lives.[203] But it would be shocking, by Zeus, if Melanopus were about to be led off to prison. I would not say anything derogatory about his father even though I have much to say about the money he stole. As far as I am concerned, let him be the sort of person that Timocrates praises to the skies.[204] [127] But after having a respectable father, he has become a low-down thief, has

---

[199]Diodorus uses the term *pentērides*, which means four-year periods. It is unlikely that Androtion's father spent this long in prison. For the charge that he escaped from prison, see Dem. 22.68.

[200]Diodorus alludes to slanders mentioned in Dem. 22.21, 29, 73 that he has been a male prostitute in his youth. Those who had been male prostitutes were not allowed to speak in the Assembly, hold office, or bring public charges. See Aes. 1.18–20.

[201]Diodorus alludes to the charges of embezzlement made against Androtion.

[202]Diodorus claims that Androtion's crimes made him polluted and therefore banned from the Agora. Cf. Dem. 22.78.

[203]Diodorus refers to charges about Androtion's abuse of power when elected to collect arrears of the *eisphora* in Dem. 22.52, 56.

[204]Little is known about Melanopus beyond the information supplied in this passage. He may have been associated by marriage with Diophantus, an ally of Eubulus: Diophantus had a son named Melanopus (Dem. 35.6). For his family and political activity, see the following notes.

been convicted of treason, and paid a fine of three talents, then, after becoming a delegate to the congress has been condemned by a court for embezzlement and paid a fine of ten times the amount,[205] then betrayed his duty as an ambassador to Egypt,[206] and wronged his own brothers. Is there not all the more reason to put him in prison when he has turned out like this after his father was an honorable man? I think so. If Laches had been an honorable man and a patriot, he would have personally put his son in prison for acting like this and causing him such terrible disgrace.[207] But enough about him; let us take a look at Glaucetes. [128] Wasn't this man the first to desert to Deceleia and, using this as a base, to raid and plunder your property?[208] But all of you know this. From the money he gained by seizing your children, wives, and other property, he paid precisely a tithe to the

---

[205]Melanopus was a member of the congress of the Second Athenian League, which was formed in 378/7 and included representatives from Athens' allies.

[206]This is a different embassy from the one mentioned at 12, which was sent to Mausolus. It may have been associated with the Greek support for King Tachos of Egypt in 362/1 (Diodorus 15.92–93; Xen. *Agesilaus* 2.28–31; Plut. *Agesilaus* 36–37).

[207]The father of Melanopus may have been the famous general Laches, who was sent to Sicily in 427 (Thuc. 3.86; Diodorus 12.54.4); served in Messenia, Locris, and Rhegion in 426 (Thuc. 3.90.2, 3.103.3, 3.115.2), proposed the truce of 423 (Thuc. 4.118); swore the oaths for the peace of 421 with Sparta (Thuc. 5.19, 24); and died at the battle of Mantinea in 418/7 (Thuc. 5.61, 74.3; Diodorus 12.79.1). In Plato's dialogue named after him he is said to have sons who were too young to be taught by Sophists (Plato *Laches* 200c). Alternatively the general Laches may have been the grandfather of Melanopus, and Laches, the taxiarch who fought at the battle of Coronea in 394 BCE, his father (Lys. 3.45).

[208]In 413 the Spartans seized Deceleia and used the town as a base to raid Attica (Thuc. 7.19). According to Lycurgus (*Against Leocrates* 120–121), severe penalties were imposed on Athenians who went to Deceleia at this time. It is unlikely that Glaucetes was old enough to have deserted to the Spartans over sixty years before; the charge is probably just slander. For the phrase *pherōn kai agōn*, see Dover 1968a: 129.

harmost;[209] [129] then, after being granted the honor of serving as your ambassador, he stole from the goddess from the tithes for the spoils taken from the enemy. Next as Treasurer[210] he stole from the Acropolis the trophies that the city had taken from the barbarians, the throne with golden feet, and the sword of Mardonius, which weighed three hundred darics.[211] These crimes are so notorious that everyone knows about them. But in other regards, is he not violent? No man in the world is more violent! [130] So, then, does any of them deserve to be pardoned? Should we therefore for their sake pay no attention to the tithes of the goddess or the double penalty for public money? Should we not punish the man who tries to protect them? What will prevent all men from becoming evil, men of the court, if they will profit from these crimes? As far as I see, nothing.

[131] Don't preach to him but punish him! Don't let them grumble about being put in prison for keeping your money, but bring them under the power of the laws! Those who are convicted on charges of falsely claiming citizenship do not complain about being put in that place until cases for false testimony are heard.[212] No, they stay there and do not think they ought to wander

---

[209]A harmost was a Spartan military governor who was placed in occupied cities after the fall of Athens in 404. See Thuc. 8.5.2; Xen. *Hellenica* 3.1.4, 4.2; 5.2.18, 37.

[210]He was one of the Treasurers of Athena who oversaw the goddess' treasures. The manuscripts add "on the Acropolis," but this is probably an intrusive gloss.

[211]The *akinakes* was a type of short sword. The inventories of the Parthenon record six such swords dedicated in 434/3 and one in 428/7. They may have been "among war relics captured or left behind in the Persian wars" (D. Harris 1995: 109). Pausanias (1.27) was shown this sword when he visited the Acropolis in the second century CE but doubted that it belonged to Mardonius, because the Persian general was killed by the Spartans, not the Athenians (Herod. 9.63). On Persian objects in Classical and Hellenistic inventories, see the useful study of Kosmetatou 2004 (148–149 discuss this passage).

[212]If a defendant who was convicted in court was able to prove that a witness who testified for the accuser had given false testimony, his conviction would be overturned. See Harrison 1971: 193–196. "That place" is a common euphemism for prison.

around at liberty after providing sureties. [132] The city has decided not to trust them and believes that it should not be cheated of its chance to punish them because sureties are named, but that they should remain in the same place as many other citizens. Indeed, several have been put in prison for debts and as a result of convictions, but still they put up with it. Although it is perhaps unpleasant to mention some by name, it is necessary to compare them with these men. [133] To start with, I will leave aside those before the archonship of Eucleides and those long before that.[213] Yet during each of those generations, men considered very deserving at an earlier point have incurred the people's anger for crimes committed later in their careers. The city did not think that they should remain honest for a certain period, then become thieves, but always remain honest, especially in public life.[214] For they thought that such a man had been honest at an earlier point not by nature but as a plot to gain your trust. [134] After the archonship of Eucleides, as you all remember, judges, first Thrasybulus of Kollytos was twice placed in prison and put on trial both times in the Assembly.[215] Yet this man was one of the men of Phyle and the Piraeus.[216] Next Philepsius of Lamptrai,[217] then Agyrrhius of Kollytos,[218] a fine man and a democrat who had many

---

[213]The archonship of Eucleides (403/2) was the year the democracy was restored and marked a watershed in Athenian history.

[214]These examples show that the Athenian courts did not take social status and public service into account (*pace* Lanni 2006: 46–64). For other examples and discussion, see E. M. Harris 2013a: 127–129.

[215]Thrasybulus of Kollytos was an enemy of Alcibiades and attacked him after the battle of Notion (Plut. *Alcibiades* 36.1). He was defeated by Antalcidas in a naval battle at Abydus in 387 (Xen. *Hellenica* 5.1.26–27) and accused of bribery after his return to Athens (Lys. 26.24). He was one of the ambassadors sent to conclude the alliance with Thebes in 378 (*IG* ii² 43, line 77; Aes. 3.138).

[216]I.e., he was one of the democrats who overthrew the Thirty.

[217]Aside from this passage, Philepsius is mentioned only at Aristoph. *Wealth* 176.

[218]Agyrrhius was a politician whose political career began late in the Peloponnesian War (Aristoph. *Frogs* 367–368). After the war he introduced

times demonstrated his loyalty to you the people. [135] Yet this man still thought that the laws must apply equally to him just as to the weak. He spent many years in that place until he paid the money belonging to the city he was judged to have taken.[219] After him, his nephew Callistratus, who was powerful, never enacted laws for his benefit.[220] So too Myronides, the son of Archinus, the man who captured Phyle and next to the gods was the person most responsible for the return of the democracy and who had many other fine achievements in politics and served as general many times.[221] [136] All these men still accepted the laws.

---

payment for attending the Assembly, at first one obol, then three obols before 393–390 (Aristoph. *Women at the Assembly* 186–188, 289–311; *Ath. Pol.* 41.3). In 389 BCE he was sent to replace Thrasybulus after the latter's death (Xen. *Hellenica* 4.8.30–31; Lys. 28.5–12, 29; Diodorus 14.9.4–5). Harpocration (s.v. *theorika*) states that he created the Theoric Fund. There is no reason to doubt this evidence (*pace* Cawkwell 1963; Ruschenbusch 1979: 303–308; Rhodes 1981: 492, 514; Sealey 1993: 256) and attribute the creation of the fund to Eubulus. As Aeschines (3.3.25) makes clear, Eubulus changed only the rules about the fund, which was already in existence. See Stroud 1998: 21. In 374/3 he passed a law about taxes on grain. See Stroud 1998; E. M. Harris 1999; and Rubel 2009: 340–341. See Stroud 1998: 17–25 on the career of Agyrrhius.

[219] Diodorus may be exaggerating here.

[220] Callistratus was the nephew of Agyrrhius and began his career by prosecuting the ambassadors sent to Sparta about the Peace of Antalcidas in 389/8 (Philochorus *FGrHist* 328 F 149a, with Badian 1991). He was a general in 378/7 (Diodorus 15.29.7) and convinced the Athenians to send help to Sparta in 369 (Dem. 59.27). In 362/1 he fled into exile and was condemned to death *in absentia*. Around 355 he returned to Athens and was put to death (Hyp. 4.1; Dem. 50.48). On his career, see Sealey 1956.

[221] This man may be identified with the Myronides who made a dedication to Demeter and Kore (*SEG* 24.224). He may have been the grandson of the general Myronides who won the battle of Oenophyta in 456 BCE (Thuc. 1.105, 4.95). His father Archinus was one of the democrats who seized Phyle during the tyranny of the Thirty and helped to restore the democracy in 403 (Aes. 2.176). He proposed honors for the men of Phyle (Aes. 3.187; cf. *SEG* 28.45, line 55) and passed a law introducing the *paragraphe* procedure for those who violated the amnesty (Isoc. 18.2).

Then the treasurers who were in office when the Opisthodomus was burned, both those of Athena and those of the Other Gods, remained in this place until their trial took place.[222] So too those found guilty of offenses regarding the grain trade and many others, men of the court, who were all better men than Androtion. [137] The long-established laws had to be enforced in their case, and they had to pay the penalty according to the existing laws. Must there then be a new law because of Androtion, Glaucetes, and Melanopus, men who have been convicted and tried by vote according to laws established long ago for retaining sacred and public funds? Won't the city be judged a laughingstock if it becomes obvious that a law was passed to save some temple robbers? I, for one, think so. [138] Do not allow either yourselves or the city endure this insult. No, remember that you put Eudemus of Cydathenai to death for enacting an inexpedient law, not a long time ago but when Evander was archon.[223] You almost executed Philip, the son of the ship captain Philip, but instead accepted by a few votes his counterproposal of a large fine.[224] You should feel the same anger also for this man here. Beside all the other reasons, remember what this man would have done to you had he gone alone as ambassador.[225] I think that he is the sort of man

---

[222]According to the scholia on this passage, some said that the treasurers stole money from the Opisthodomus, while others said that the treasurers lent money from the Treasury of Athena and the other gods to some bankers in the hope of making a profit. When the bank failed, they burned down the Opisthodomus to hide the loss of the money. Bogaert 1974 believed that the latter story was evidence for a banking crisis in Athens in 377/6, but see E. E. Cohen 1992: 221–224. For the Treasurers of the Other Gods, see Linders 1975. On the controversy about the location of the Opisthodomus, see Hopper 1971: 110–115.

[223]In 382/1. Nothing else is known about Eudemus.

[224]After Philip was convicted, his accuser proposed the death penalty at the penalty phase, and he proposed a heavy fine. The court accepted Philip's proposal by a narrow margin. The majority of manuscripts read *ētimōsate* ("you deprived of his rights"), but the reading of A *etimēsate* ("you assessed") should be preferred. See Wayte 1882: 203.

[225]Diodorus refers to the embassy mentioned at 12.

who would stop at nothing. You see his intent because the law he dared to enact reveals his character.

[139] I wish to explain to you, men of the court, how the Locrians enact laws.[226] It will do you no harm to hear about their example, especially one followed in a well-governed community.[227] There they are so committed to the idea that it is necessary to follow the long-established laws, to preserve the ancestral ways, and not to legislate on a whim nor to provide guilty men with a means of escape[228] that if anyone wishes to pass a new law, he proposes his law with a noose around his neck; if the law is judged good and beneficial, the proposer lives and walks away, but if not, he dies when the noose is drawn tight. [140] In fact, they do not dare to pass new laws, but strictly adhere to the long-established laws. Men of the court, it is said that for very many years only one new law has been enacted in their community. There was a law that if someone gouged an eye, he was to have his own eye knocked out in return, and no monetary penalty was permitted. The story goes that a man threatened to gouge the eye of his enemy who had just one eye. [141] The one-eyed man, alarmed by this threat and thinking that life would not be worth living were it carried out, is said to have worked up the courage to introduce a law ordering that if anyone gouged the eye of a person with just one eye, he was to have both his eyes gouged in return so that both men would suffer an equal misfortune. It is reported that

---

[226] The city of Locri in southern Italy was renowned for its good government (Pindar *Olympian Odes* 10.17; Plato *Timaeus* 20a).

[227] The following story reflects the Greek view that the laws should remain stable. According to Thucydides (1.18), the Spartans kept the same laws for over four hundred years. After Solon finished his legislation, he made the Athenians swear an oath that they would not change them for one hundred years. Athens and other Greek states often added entrenchment clauses to laws providing harsh penalties for those who tried to alter the laws: see E. M. Harris 2006: 23–25. In the fourth century the new procedures for legislation were aimed in part at making it harder to introduce new laws. See Canevaro 2013b.

[228] I have accepted the reading *diaduseis*. Some manuscripts have *dialuseis* ("settlements"). See Wayte 1882: 204.

this is the only law the Locrians have passed in more than two hundred years. [142] By contrast, men of the court, the politicians in our city, first pass laws for their own advantage almost every month,[229] then, when they are in office, they drag private citizens off to prison, but they do not believe that the same rule of justice should be applied to them. Finally, even as they are abolishing the laws of Solon, which your ancestors enacted and which have passed the test of time, they claim that you should obey their laws, which they are enacting to the city's detriment. [143] If, then, you do not punish them, it will not be long before the majority of you become the slaves of these beasts. Men of the court, you know for sure that if you firmly show your anger, they will be less arrogant, but if not, you will find more arrogant people insulting you while pretending to be patriots.[230]

[144] I also have to speak to you, judges, about the law that I hear he will use as a precedent and claim that his law follows from it.[231] This law contains the clause: "I will not put any Athenian in prison who provides three sureties paying the same tax-rate except if he has been caught in an act of treason against the city, meeting for the purpose of overthrowing the democracy, or if he has bought the right to collect a tax or promised to be a surety or is collecting taxes and does not make payments." Listen to what I have to say about this. [145] I will not mention that Androtion dragged men with his own hands to prison and placed them in chains despite this law being in effect.[232] Rather I am going to show you the reasons why this law was passed. This law was

---

[229] For a similar complaint, see Dem. 20.92.

[230] I have translated the term *philotimia* as "patriotism," but a more literal translation would be "love of honor." On this term, see Whitehead 1983.

[231] Some scholars have claimed that the Athenians did not aim to maintain consistency in their legal system and paid little attention to decisions made in earlier cases, but see E. M. Harris 2013a: 274–301. For records kept of prior decisions, see E. M. Harris 2013b, which also shows that the view of Gagarin 2008: 195 that the Athenians did not maintain records of trials is untenable.

[232] For the allegation that Androtion had people put in prison, see Dem. 22.54–56.

passed, judges, not for men who had been judged and whose trials were over, but for those awaiting trial. This way they would not be completely unprepared or have to plead their cases at a disadvantage from being in prison. This man here is about to tell you that this law, which was enacted for those awaiting trial, was enacted to apply to all cases.[233] [146] I will tell you so that you will clearly know that I am speaking the truth. You would not have the power, men of the court, to assess a punishment or a fine (and since imprisonment is a form of punishment, you would not have the power to impose imprisonment as a punishment), nor would it have been written in the laws in cases involving denunciation or arrest "let the Eleven place the person who has been denounced or arrested in the stocks," if you did not have the power to place in prison others besides those conspiring to betray the city or to overthrow the democracy or those who have bought the right to collect taxes but have not made payments. [147] Let this serve as evidence that you do in fact have the authority to put men in prison. Otherwise the sentences you pass would be completely null and void. Next, men of the court, this phrase "I will not place in prison any Athenian citizens" is not by itself a law, but has been written in the Oath of the Council.[234] Its aim is to prevent politicians in the Council from joining forces to propose that any citizen be put in prison. [148] Solon took away the power of the Council to imprison anyone by adding this clause in the Oath of the Council but not in your oath.[235] He thought

---

[233]For the anticipation of arguments to be made by the defendant, see Dorjahn 1935.

[234]For the Oath of the Council, see Rhodes 1972: 194–195. Other clauses in the oath were a promise to follow the laws (Xen. *Memorabilia* 1.1.18), to recommend what is best for the people of Athens (Lys. 31.1–2; [Dem.] 59.4), to report anyone ineligible to serve in the Council (Lys. 31.2), and not to accept any denunciation (*endeixis*) or arrest (*apagoge*) made in violation of the Amnesty of 403 (And. 1.91). A much damaged inscription appears to contain a copy of the oath (*IG* i³ 105, lines 8–10) and may have contained the clause quoted in this passage.

[235]The Oath of the Council was not created by Solon but was probably enacted after the reforms of Cleisthenes. See Rhodes 1972: 192. The Athe-

that the court must be the highest authority and that the man found guilty must suffer whatever punishment it should decide. To demonstrate this point, the clerk will read the Judicial Oath. Read it.

[THE JUDICIAL OATH²³⁶]

[149] I will vote in accordance with the laws and decrees of the Athenians and the Council of the Five Hundred. I will not vote that there be a tyrant or oligarchy. If anyone overthrows the democracy of the Athenians, makes a proposal, or puts one to the vote contrary to these laws and decrees, I will not obey. I will not vote for a cancellation of private debts or a redistribution of land or houses belonging to Athenians. I will not bring back exiles or those condemned to death. Those residing here I will not myself send into exile contrary to the established laws and decrees of the Athenian people and the Council, nor shall I allow anyone else to do so. [150] I will not confirm any official to serve in office while he is subject to review for another office, whether he be one of the nine *archons* or a *hieromnemon* or one of the officials selected by lot with the nine archons on that day, or herald, or ambassador, or delegate to the *synedrion*.²³⁷ I will not allow the same man

---

nians attributed to Solon many laws that were passed long after his death. Cf. Dem. 20.90.

²³⁶This document is another forgery. See Canevaro 2013a: 173–180. The document contains some of the clauses of the Judicial Oath but lacks two key clauses attested in several sources: the pledge to use one's most just judgment in cases where there are no laws (Dem. 20.118, 39.40; Pollux 8.122, with E. M. Harris 2013a: 109–114, refuting Mirhady 2007) and the pledge not to recall past wrongs (And. 1.91, with Joyce 2014 on the meaning of *mnēsikakein*). For quotations or allusions to the Judicial Oath in the Attic Orators, see E. M. Harris 2013a: 353–357. Despite the overwhelming case against the document's authenticity, some scholars still consider it genuine. See, for example, Johnstone 1999; Thür 2007; and Phillips 2013: 26–27.

²³⁷The term used here *synedros* refers to a member of the Council of Allies established in 378/7 for the Second Athenian League. These officials

to serve twice in the same office or the same many to hold two offices in the same year. I shall not accept gifts for my service in court, neither I myself nor any man or woman on my behalf with my knowledge by any means or device.[238] [151] I am not younger than thirty years old. I will listen to the accuser and to the defendant both in like manner.[239] I will give my judgment about the issue contained in the accusation.[240] [The judge] is to swear by Zeus, Poseidon, and Demeter[241] and to call down destruction on himself and his household if he violates any of these pledges, but if he is true to his oath, he is to have many blessings.

In this oath, men of the court, there is no pledge "I will not put any Athenian in prison." The courts decide all cases and have the power to imprison and to impose whatever other punishments they wish.

[152] That you have the power to put men in prison I have now shown. I think that you would all agree that to annul court decisions would be shocking, impious, and tantamount to overthrowing the democracy. After all, men of the court, our city manages its affairs by laws and decrees. If, then, someone is going to use a law to annul verdicts reached by vote, where will it end? How would it be right to call this a law rather than illegality? How does a legislator like this not deserve the fullest extent of your anger?

---

were appointed by the member states; it is unlikely that they would have undergone a *dokimasia* before an Athenian court. This list also omits many officials who would have been subject to *dokimasia*: see Canevaro 2013a: 178–179. On the *dokimasia*, see Feyel 2009.

[238] This phrase is found in no passage about the Judicial Oath.

[239] For this clause, see, for example, Dem. 18.1; Aes. 2.1; Lyc. *Against Leocrates* 1.

[240] For this clause of the oath, see Aes. 1.170, 175–176, 179; Dem. 18.56. For the meaning and significance of the clause, see E. M. Harris 2013a: 114–137.

[241] According to Pollux (8.122), the gods by whom the judges swore were Apollo Patroos, Demeter, and Zeus Basileus. This information is confirmed by a scholion on Aes. 1.114 9 (Dilts), which is based on a passage from Dinarchus. Cf. [Dem.] 52.9.

[153] In my opinion, he deserves the ultimate penalties, not only because he has enacted this law but also for showing to others the way to destroy the courts, bring back men from exile and commit other very terrible crimes. If this man enacts a law like this and gleefully escapes conviction, men of the court, what prevents another man from openly undermining another of the foundations of the city with a new law? Nothing, I think. [154] I hear that this is the way the democracy was overthrown in the past when public actions against illegal decrees were abolished and the courts lost their powers.²⁴² When I mention the overthrow of the democracy, someone might object that the situations now and then are not similar. On the contrary, not even the seed of such activities should be sown in the city, even if it might not yet have taken root; anyone who attempts to say or do such a thing must be punished.

[155] It is worth also hearing about his clever attempt to harm your interests. Because he sees that on every occasion everyone, politician and private citizen alike, considers the laws responsible for what is good in our city, he searched for a way to destroy them without attracting attention, and if he was caught doing this, to make it appear that he was doing nothing shocking or impudent. [156] This is the means he found to destroy the laws by means of a law so that his crimes would bear the name "public safety." Indeed, the laws are responsible for the city's safety, and the measure that this man enacted, although it has nothing in common with them, is still a law. He perceived that nothing pleases you more than the humane quality of this word. He overlooked in practice his law will clearly have the opposite effect. [157] By Zeus, is there any *proedros* or *prytanis* who would ever

---

²⁴²In 411 the Athenians voted to allow anyone to make proposals about reforming the constitution and temporarily abolished the public action against illegal decrees (Thuc. 8.67; *Ath. Pol.* 29.2–5). This was followed by an attempt to overthrow the democracy. On the events of 411, see E. M. Harris 1990. Nouhaud 1982: 283 suggests that Demosthenes' source was an Atthidographer, the local historians of Athens, but his words suggest that he was relying on oral tradition.

put any clause written in the law to a vote?²⁴³ No, I don't think so. How, then, did he slip this through? He has given his crimes the name of "law." These men do not do harm you innocently or by accident. No, they actually do this deliberately. Not only this man but many politicians who will soon come forward to join in his defense, not, by Zeus, out of desire to do Timocrates a favor. For what reason, then? Because each of them thinks he will derive some benefit from his law. So just as they defend their own interests against yours, you too must defend your own interests. [158] Indeed, when someone asked him what his aim was in proposing the law and pointed out how difficult this trial would be for him, Timocrates replied that this man was a fool: Androtion would be at his side and at his leisure had thought up arguments to meet every objection such that he was certain nothing serious would happen to him as a result of the indictment. [159] Really, I am quite amazed at both men's shameless behavior, the former for asking for his help, the latter for coming forward and joining in his defense. This will of course provide clear testimony for all of you that he passed his law for this man's sake and did not pass one that was the same for all. Even so, it is better for you to hear a few words about Androtion's political activity and in particular those in which Timocrates participated and the reasons why you should hate the latter no less than the former. I will tell you nothing you have already heard unless some of you were present at the trials of Euctemon.²⁴⁴

[160] First, let us examine his proudest achievement, how he

---

²⁴³The *proedroi* were responsible for putting motions to a vote in the Assembly (*Ath. Pol.* 44.2–3). The *prytaneis* were responsible for drawing up the agenda for the Assembly (*Ath. Pol.* 43.4).

²⁴⁴The two trials are the prosecution of Euctemon by Androtion and his friends for passing an illegal decree (14) and the prosecution of Androtion by Euctemon on the same charge (Dem. 22.1) at which Diodorus gave a supporting speech. Much of the following sections (160–186) are taken from the speech *Against Androtion*, with slight changes. Sections 160–168 are taken from Dem. 22.47–56, sections 167–171 are an abbreviated version of Dem. 22.57–64, and sections 172–186 reproduce almost all of Dem. 22.65–78.

collected money from all of you with this good man's help. This man accused Euctemon of withholding your tax revenues and promised to prove it or pay the money out of his own pocket. On this pretext he abolished by decree an office filled by lot and wormed his way into the job of collecting taxes. On the grounds of bad health he put this man forward, claiming that "I need his help." [161] He made a speech in the Assembly on this topic, claiming that there was a choice among three options: melt down the sacred vessels into coins, levy another property tax, or collect money from those who owe it. When you reasonably chose to collect the money from those who owed it, once he had you bound by his promises, he took advantage of the unusual situation at the time to gain power for himself. He did not think he was bound to follow the laws established for these activities, nor enact new ones if he considered these inadequate, but right in front of you proposed terrible illegal decrees,[245] which allowed him to make a profit, using this man as his agent to collect his gains. [162] With his help he stole much of your money, having proposed a decree ordering the Eleven, the Receivers, and their assistants to follow him around.[246] With them at his side, he entered into your houses, and you, Timocrates, were following along, the only one of his ten colleagues. Let no one think that I am saying it was not necessary to collect from those who owed the money. It was.

---

[245]The Athenians drew a strict distinction between laws (*nomoi*), which were general rules and valid for all time, and decrees (*psephismata*), which were orders dealing with particular situations. For the distinction, see Plato *Definitions* 415b and Hansen 1991: 171–174. Diodorus claims that Andronion should have proposed a law when he changed the way of collecting the arrears from the property tax and that his decrees were therefore illegal. But it may have been possible to create ad hoc appointments by decree. See Aes. 3.13.

[246]The Eleven functioned as a police force and supervised the prison (*Ath. Pol.* 52.1), but they were not the only officials who enforced the law. The Receivers collected all public revenues. See *Ath. Pol.* 48.1, with Rhodes 1981: 557–559.

But how? In the way the law commands[247] and for the benefit of other citizens. This is the democratic way.[248] The advantage you gained, Athenians, from the five talents they collected and gave to you did not outweigh the damage you suffered when such practices were introduced into our political life.[249] [163] If you would wish to examine why someone would choose to live in a democracy rather than an oligarchy, you would find this the most salient reason: all things are kinder and gentler in a democracy. Now, I pass over the fact that these men acted more abusively and terribly than any oligarchy you choose. But look at our city; when did the worst atrocities occur in our city? I know you would all say "under the Thirty." [164] But at that time, so one hears, there was no one who lost hope of survival as long as he kept himself hidden inside his house.[250] Rather they criticize the Thirty for arresting men unjustly in the Agora. Yet these men's brutality so far surpassed theirs that they made each man's own home his prison by bringing the Eleven into private houses—even though they were conducting public business in a democracy.[251]

[165] And yet, men of Athens, what do you think when a poor man—or even a rich man who has spent a lot and is perhaps

---

[247]The nine archons and the members of the Council were required to swear an oath that they would act in accordance with the laws (*Ath. Pol.* 55.5: archons; Rhodes 1972: 194: Council). This requirement probably extended to other officials.

[248]The Athenians often claimed that democracy was the only form of government that lived up to the ideal of the rule of law. See Aes. 1.4–6 and 3.6; Thuc. 2.37.

[249]At Dem. 22.44 the amount collected is seven talents.

[250]To put Androtion's actions in the worst possible light, Diodorus makes the crimes of the Thirty appear less serious than they actually were. According to Lys. 12.8, 30, the Thirty did break into the houses of metics and citizens and arrest them there. Diodorus also compares Timocrates to Critias, one of the leaders of the Thirty at 90. The Thirty are rarely mentioned in the Attic orators after 390. See Nouhaud 1982: 307–320.

[251]Normally an official could not enter a private house without a decree authorizing him to do so. See Dem. 18.132, with E. M. Harris 1995: 172.

likely to be short of money in some way—not only is afraid to enter the Agora but doesn't think it safe to remain at home, and Androtion is responsible for this situation, a man whose conduct and life do not allow him to bring an accusation for his own sake, let alone for the city?[252]

[166] And yet if someone were to ask him or you, Timocrates, you who praised these actions and collaborated with him, whether one owes one's property or one's person as the property tax, you would say "one's property" if you were willing to speak the truth. It is from this that we pay our property tax. Then, why did you not take the opportunity to confiscate land or houses and report them[253] and instead insulted and imprisoned citizens and unfortunate metics, whom you have treated in a more insulting way than your own slaves?[254] [167] Indeed, if you wish to examine the difference between a free man and a slave, you will find this the greatest distinction: the bodies of slaves are subject to punishment for all their crimes, but for free men corporal punishment is a last resort.[255] In general, it is right to punish the latter by taking their property. But they did the opposite: they inflicted punishment on their bodies as if they were slaves. [168] Androtion treated you in such an unequal and greedy way that he thought it was all right for his own father, in prison for a public debt, to escape without either paying the money or submitting to trial and winning acquittal, yet other citizens who are unable to pay their taxes are dragged from their houses into prison thanks to him. [169] And

---

[252] The speaker alludes to his charge that Androtion was a prostitute and thus did not have the right to bring public charges. For the law, see Aes. 1.19. The manuscripts add the phrase "collect property taxes" (*eisprattein eisphoras*), but van Herwerden, followed by Dilts, notes the absence of the phrase at Dem. 22.54 and deletes.

[253] If someone owed money to the Treasury, anyone could report his property, which was then confiscated and sold by the Poletai to pay the debt; see Harrison 1971: 211–217.

[254] In some circumstances men in debt to the Treasury could be put in prison; see Harrison 1971: 241–244. Androtion's decree seems to have made failure to pay the *eisphora* such a circumstance.

[255] For this distinction between slaves and free, see Hunter 1994: 154–184.

at the time when Timocrates was collecting double the amount, he wouldn't accept sureties from even one of us common citizens, but not even for one day, let alone until the ninth prytany. No, we had to pay double the amount or immediately be put in prison. He would turn over to the Eleven even men who had not been fined by a court. Now, to allow men whom you have convicted to wander around free without going to prison, he has dared to introduce a law and to make himself responsible for it.

[170] Still, they will say they have acted both then and now for your benefit.[256] Will you admit that these things have been done for your benefit? Will you view indulgently their acts of arrogance and dishonesty? No, men of Athens, you ought to hate men like them rather than protect them. The man who acts to help the city and earn your indulgence should clearly possess the city's character. [171] What is this? To pity the weak, not allow the strong and powerful to become abusive, and not to treat the many harshly and flatter the man who at any time has power. This is what you do, Timocrates: these judges would therefore be more justified in refusing to listen and condemning you to death than in acquitting you because of Androtion.

[172] They have never done anything for your benefit, not even collecting taxes, as I will immediately make clear to you. Take two kinds of people: men who farm and are frugal but fall behind in paying taxes because they spend money on raising children or household expenses or other liturgies, and men who steal money from those who wish to pay the tax and from our allies, then waste it. Despite their complete lack of shame, if someone asked them which group they think commits the greater crime against the city, they would certainly not be so bold as to claim that those who do not pay their own taxes commit a greater crime than men who steal public funds. [173] Why, then, Timocrates and Androtion, in the more than thirty years each of you has been in politics, when during this time many generals and many politicians have committed crimes against the state and been tried in this

---

[256]I.e., they collected money owed for the property tax and passed this law for the people's benefit.

court, and some have been executed for their crimes and others have admitted their guilt by going into exile,[257] neither of you has ever stepped forward to prosecute any of them nor expressed any anger about the harm done to the city, but only in this case did you clearly show any concern, one in which you had to mistreat so many people? [174] Men of Athens, do you want me to tell you the reason for this? It is because they share in the crimes some have committed against you and steal from those whose money they collect. They thus reap a profit from the city to satisfy their greedy habits in two ways. For it is not easier to incur the wrath of the many who commit small injustices than of the few who do great wrongs. Nor indeed is it more democratic to pay attention to the injustices of the many rather than those of the few. But this I tell you is the reason. [175] You must take these things into account and, bearing in mind each man's crimes, punish him when you catch him; consider only whether he committed the crime and not how long ago it occurred. If you now show leniency toward crimes that stirred your anger in the past, people will think you fined them out of anger, not because they did you wrong. Those who act out of anger inflict immediate harm on the person who has caused them pain, but those who suffer an injustice inflict punishment whenever they catch the guilty man. You must not now be weak, thereby appearing to neglect your sworn oaths, and indulge your feelings contrary to what is right. No, you should hate them and not allow politicians who act like this even to open their mouths, neither this one nor that one.

[176] Yet, by Zeus, you might say, they have acted this way only during their political career, but there are other tasks they have managed well. Far from it: in all the rest of their careers they have treated you in such a way that the things you have heard about are the least reason to hate them. What do you want me to discuss? How they repaired processional vessels and melted down

---

[257]This statement is not an exaggeration. Hansen 1975: 60 has shown that in the period 432–355, out of 160 Athenian generals attested in our sources, 33 were brought to trial, and many were convicted.

crowns, and their splendid production of plates?[258] [177] For these actions by themselves, even if they committed no other crime against the city, I think they deserve to die three times, not once; indeed they are guilty of temple robbery, impiety, theft, and all the most serious crimes. I will not mention the many things that Androtion said to deceive you. But he claimed the leaves on the crowns had fallen off and persuaded you to melt them down, alleging that they became rotten over time, as if they fell off violets or roses, not objects made of gold.[259] When he was elected to this office, he chose this man here as an accomplice in all his crimes. [178] Then for the property tax, as if indeed he were an honest citizen, he added a clause that the public slave be present—even though everyone who paid the tax was going to act as an auditor of his accounts.[260] But for the crowns that he melted down, he did not add this same honest provision, but he acted alone as politician, goldsmith, treasurer, and auditor.[261] [179] And indeed if you asked that all the things you do for the city be placed in your hands, it would just make your embezzlement less conspicuous. As it is, in regard to the property tax, you stipulated that the city entrust its affairs not to you but to its slaves, which is the correct procedure. Yet when you were involved in some other task and handled sacred objects, some of which were dedicated even be-

---

[258]Androtion's decree about these dedications may be referred to at *IG* ii² 216, line 13 and 217, line 13.

[259]As D. Harris 1995: 33 notes, "Demosthenes makes the claim sound ridiculous; but there is one entry in the inventories which shows that wreaths did lose leaves from time to time." See *IG* ii² 1377, lines 22–24.

[260]Some public slaves acted as clerks. On public slaves, see Ismard 2015, with the critical review of Pébarthe 2015. When Androtion drew up the decree granting him the power to collect arrears, he added a clause instructing one of these slaves to check his accounts. He did this as a way of assuring the Assembly of his honesty, but Diodorus dismisses the precaution as unnecessary because everyone who paid the tax could determine if his accounts were trustworthy.

[261]The Athenians generally did not allow someone to hold more than one position at once; Diodorus accuses Androtion of violating this rule.

fore our lifetime, you clearly did not include this safeguard that you included for the property tax. Isn't the reason for doing this already obvious? I think it is. [180] Consider, then, men of Athens, how noble and admirable were the inscriptions he has forever destroyed and how impious and shocking what he has written in their place. I think all of you have seen written on the mounting underneath the crowns: "The allies have given a crown to the people because of their nobility and justice," or "A prize of valor from the allies for Athena," and from individual cities, "Such and such have given the people a crown for saving them," such as, "The Euboeans gave the people a crown for restoring their liberty," and again, "Conon from the naval battle against the Spartans,"[262] "Chabrias from the naval battle at Naxos."[263] Such were the phrases written on the crowns. [181] These phrases, which brought the city much admiration and honor, vanished when the crowns were melted down.[264] On the bowls that this whore had made for you in their place has been written, "Under the supervision of Androtion." The man whom the laws prohibit from entering temples for having prostituted his body has his name written on the bowls in our temples! It's just the same, isn't it, as the earlier inscriptions? And conferring on you all the same amount of honor? [182] Anyone could see from this that they have committed three of the worst offenses: they robbed the goddess of her crowns; they destroyed the admiration won by the city for its accomplishments, which these crowns served to commemorate while they existed; and they deprived the dedicants of their not inconsiderable fame and their reputation for being willing to re-

---

[262]Conon commanded the Persian fleet during their naval victory over the Spartans at Cnidus in 394. See Dem. 20.68.

[263]Chabrias defeated the Spartan fleet at Naxos in 376 (Diodorus 15.34.3–35.2).

[264]Demosthenes makes the melting down of these dedications sound like a terrible crime, but it appears to have been a routine matter. See D. Harris 1995: 31–36. Even though the names inscribed on the dedications would have disappeared, it was still possible to record the names of those who made dedications on lists preserved by officials. See *IG* ii³ 1154 (220/19 BCE), lines 37–40.

member the favors they received. Having committed such a great number of misdeeds like this, they have come to this point where they are so arrogant and so obtuse that one thinks you will acquit him because of the other, and the other sits down next to him and does not slink away for what he has done. [183] He is not only so shameless about money but also so uncouth that he does not realize that crowns are a mark of valor, whereas bowls and the like are a sign of wealth. Every crown, no matter how small, brings as much honor as a large one; chalices, censers, and similar objects, if their number is excessive, rub off on their owners a reputation for wealth. But if a man takes pride in trifles, far from gaining honor through them, he also appears lacking in taste. By destroying the objects that gave you your fame, he has cheapened the objects that constituted your wealth and made them unworthy of you. [184] He did not understand that the people have never been eager to gain wealth but rather to acquire fame above anything else. Here is a proof: when the people had the most money of the Greeks, they spent it all on the pursuit of honor. They paid the tax from their private property and shunned no danger in pursuit of fame. What they acquired from this effort is everlasting, both the memory of their deeds and the beauty of the dedications set up to commemorate them: the Propylaea, the Parthenon, the stoas, the shipsheds. Not two little jars, or even three or four gold ones, each weighing a few pounds. [185] Not by imposing a tithe on themselves nor by doubling the property tax (that is a curse we reserve for our enemies) did they make these dedications. They did not conduct their public business using advisors like you but by defeating their enemies and bringing unity to the city, a goal that every sensible man would pray for, they have left behind their immortal fame—and they banned from the Agora people who lead the sort of life you do! [186] You have progressed, men of Athens, to the point where you are so simple-minded and heedless that even with these examples in front of you, you do not follow them. Instead, you have Androtion repairing sacred vessels, Androtion, Earth and gods! What impiety do you think is greater than this? In my opinion, the man who enters temples to dip his hands in lustral water and in sacred baskets and to take responsibility for religious administration should not only keep himself pure for a prescribed number of days but keep his entire life pure from the kind of activities that this man has practiced during his life.[265]

[187] I will say more about these matters when I have time. As for the arguments he will present in support of Timocrates, although I have much still to say, I will stop.[266] I know this: he will not be able to deny that the law is contrary to your interests, was introduced in violation of all the laws, and is completely unjust. I hear that he says that Androtion, Glaucetes, and Melanopus have paid the money and that he would suffer the most terrible treatment in the world if, when the men for whose benefit he is charged with passing the law have acted most justly, he himself is nonetheless judged guilty. [188] I do not think that he is in a position to make even one of these points. If you agree that you enacted the law for the benefit of men who you allege have acted correctly, for this very reason you clearly should be convicted because you should not have enacted a law unless it was the same for all citizens; this is stated explicitly by the laws in effect, in accordance with which these men have sworn to give judgment.[267] [189] If you will claim that you passed the law for the public in-

---

[265]For the need to be morally pure when performing religious rites, see Parker 1983: 96–97.

[266]This section marks a transition between Diodorus' invective against Androtion and his concluding arguments against Timocrates. Diodorus makes a distinction between Androtion's actions, which he promises to discuss again on another occasion ("when I have time"), and the arguments he will make in support of Timocrates at this trial, which he will not discuss further in this speech, although he has much more to say (cf. 158–159). I follow the majority of the manuscripts in reading *toutōn*, which must refer to Androtion's actions discussed in the previous sections. Wayte 1882: 236 and most editors adopt the reading *toutou*, which is found in only one manuscript. The manuscripts also read *Timokratei sunerei*, which I have retained. Dobree, followed by Dilts, emended this phrase to *Timokratēs nûn erei* ("Timocrates will now say"), but the emendation is unnecessary, as the above explanation should make clear. Moreover, the emendation makes no sense because in the next passage Diodorus addresses the arguments he believes Timocrates will make (*pace* MacDowell 2009: 195).

[267]Another allusion to the Judicial Oath.

terest, do not discuss the payment made by these men, for this has nothing to do with the law. Show instead that the law is expedient and good. This is the reason why you claim to have introduced it while I have asserted the opposite in my indictment. This is the question these men have to decide.²⁶⁸ Yet I would also have no trouble proving that these men did everything but make their payment in the legally prescribed way. Since, however, you are not going to cast your vote about this issue, why should I bother you by discussing it?²⁶⁹

[190] I think he will not refrain from using the following arguments: it would be terrible for him if after proposing that no Athenian be put in prison, he himself were to suffer ill-treatment and that the laws should be as mild and restrained as possible toward the weak. It would be better for you to hear a few words of warning against this argument so that you will be less deceived. [191] When he says that his aim was that no Athenian be put in prison, do not let him get away with this lie. That was not his aim in enacting the law, but to deprive you of the power to inflict additional punishments. His law overturns your reasoned decision taken on oath. Do not let him pick out words from the law that sound very humane. No, let him present the entire law in order and allow you to examine what will result from it. You will discover that it contains the defects I am discussing, and not what this man says it contains. [192] As for the argument that it is in the majority's interest for the laws to be gentle and moderate, one should consider the following. There are two categories, men of Athens, into which the laws in all cities fall. One of these cate-

---

²⁶⁸The Judicial Oath bound the judges to decide only about the charges contained in the written indictment brought by the accuser. Because the accuser has charged that the law is inexpedient, the payments made by Androtion, Melanopus, and Glaucetes are irrelevant and should not affect the judges' decision.

²⁶⁹This is a rhetorical bluff. Even though the payment was not relevant to the charge about the law, it was directly relevant to the issue of Timocrates' motive for proposing the law. Diodorus' dishonest attempt to evade this evidence strongly suggests that the money was paid. For discussion, see the Introduction.

gories regulates the way we interact and do business with one another, the rules we lay down about what must be done in the private sphere, in short, the way we live with one another. The other regulates the way each of us should conduct the city's public affairs if he wishes to participate in public affairs and to declare his concern for the city. [193] The former laws regulating private life are mild and generous in the interests of the majority. Those regulating public affairs take the opposite approach; they are firm and harsh to protect your interests. In this way those in politics would do the least harm to you, the common people. When he presents this argument, reply that he is not enacting the former type of law, which is less harsh, to protect you, but the latter, which are designed to intimidate politicians. [194] There would be much to say if someone should wish to show that every argument he is going to make is designed to trick and deceive you. But I will leave aside most of them and will discuss a key point for you to bear in mind. Pay attention to all the points he makes to see if he can make an argument to demonstrate that it is right for a legislator to lay down the same rules about actions in the past that are completed and those in the future. Of all the disgraceful and shocking things written in his law, this is the most shocking and illegal thing he has written. [195] If neither he nor anyone else can show this, you must realize that you are being deceived, then consider for yourselves what inspired him to enact a law like this one. You did not enact this law without receiving anything in return, Timocrates—how could you? Far from it.[270] There is no other reason you could give that encouraged you to introduce the law than your own god-forsaken greed, for none of these men is your relative, friend, or associate. [196] Nor could you claim that you took pity on men who suffered terribly and choose to help them for this reason. For them to return these people's property after a long time, grudgingly and against their will, after convictions in three trials, do you think that this is terrible suffering? That is a

---

[270]Translators differ about the meaning of the Greek phrase *oud' oligou dei*, which could either mean "not for a small payment" (Budé) or "far from it" (Loeb).

shocking way to act and should stir someone to hate you rather than move someone to pity. Beyond that, you are hardly exceptional for your mildness and generosity when you feel pity for them. [197] You feel pity for Androtion, Melanopus, and Glaucetes if they pay the money they have stolen and kept. Yet you did not have the same attitude toward any of the great number of those present here or the other citizens, whose houses you invaded with the Eleven, the Receivers, and their assistants; you never felt any pity for them.[271] No, you tear their doors down, drag out their bedding, and seize their female slave if they have one.[272] All that is what you and Androtion did for one entire year. [198] You people have certainly suffered far worse treatment! These men are far more deserving of pity, since they do not stop paying even a bit of their taxes, thanks to you speakers, you cursed man! Even this is not enough, but they are forced to pay double, all because of you and Androtion, who have never once paid the war tax. [199] This man indeed had such a high opinion of himself, thinking he would never be brought to justice for this, that he alone of his ten colleagues dared to present his accounts with Androtion.[273] Without getting anything in return, for no benefit, Timocrates earns your hatred and introduces laws contrary to all your legislation, then, the final straw, contrary to his own earlier law! By Athena, I do not think that this has escaped your notice.

[200] I will now tell you one thing that certainly deserves your anger most of all: I do not hesitate to say that he did this for money, men of Athens, and deliberately chose—this is the truth—to take payment. He is not spending the money on anything that would cause someone hearing about it to have sympathy for him. What would this be? His father, men of the court, owes money to the Treasury (I say this not to insult him, but because I have to), and this fine man pays no attention. [201] The

---

[271] In forensic oratory, pity is reserved only for those who have suffered unjustly. See Konstan 2000.

[272] Because slaves were considered the property of the master, they could be confiscated if the master had any debts to the state.

[273] At 162 Diodorus says that Timocrates was one of the Eleven who accompanied Androtion when he was collecting taxes.

man who is about to inherit his disenfranchisement,[274] should anything happen to his father, does not think that he has to pay the debt; rather, he counts the time his father continues to live as profit for himself. Where do you think he would stop? Don't you pity your father and think he suffers terribly? While you do business and make money from the war tax you were collecting, from the decrees you propose, from the laws you introduce, because of a tiny sum your father has no rights, and you claim that you pity others? [202] But, by Zeus, he has done a good job managing his sister's affairs. Indeed, if he had committed no other crime, he would deserve to die for this: he sold her, not gave her away in marriage.[275] It was to one of your enemies, a man from Corcyra, someone belonging to the party now in control,[276] who used to stay with him during his trips here as ambassador. He wanted to have her (in what way I will not mention), and Timocrates took some money and gave her to him. Now she is in Corcyra. [203] In fact, he sold her for export, though he claims to have given her in marriage. He looks after his father in old age by playing the flatterer, by writing decrees and conducting politics for a fee. Now that you have caught him, will you not put him to death? Otherwise, men of Athens, people will think you enjoy holding trials and causing yourselves trouble but do not wish to get rid of scoundrels.

---

[274]Athenian law, like Roman law, recognized the principle of universal succession, that is, the doctrine that the heir took on all the rights and duties of the deceased whose property he inherited. This meant that son might become liable for his father's debts and any loss of rights incurred for failure to pay public debts.

[275]That is, sold her into slavery. It was illegal to enslave an Athenian citizen.

[276]Corcyra became an ally of Athens in 374 (Xen. *Hellenica* 6.2.9–38), but according to Diodorus (15.93.5) the general Chares stirred up a civil war there in 361/0. Aeneas Tacticus (11.13–15) gives a more detailed account and says that Chares helped the oligarchs to seize power. Cargill 1981: 172–176 argues that the incident belongs earlier in the 360s, but see Bianco 2002 1983: 7–9. This passage indicates that Corcyra had become hostile to Athens before 354. For discussion, see Pritchett 1974–1991: 1.56–8.

[204] Now indeed if someone should ask, "Is it right to punish all guilty men?" I know that you would all answer, "Yes!" How much more important it is to punish this man, who introduced a law to harm the people's interest, I will attempt to explain.[277] Let us take thieves, robbers, and other criminals like this. First, each one of them actually harms just his victim. He could not rob everyone or steal their property. Second, he brings shame only on his own reputation and life. [205] Yet if someone introduces a law that grants all those wishing to wrong you complete power and immunity, he wrongs the entire city and brings shame on everyone. When a shameful law goes into effect, it is a reproach for the city that enacted it and harms everyone who would follow it. This man attempts to harm you and cover the city with a bad reputation;[278] won't you punish him now that you have caught him? What are you going to say? [206] The best way to understand his aims in plotting to write the law and how far opposed they are to the established constitution is to bear in mind that when people attack the democracy and attempt to start a revolution, they do this first of all: they release those who lawfully are undergoing this punishment for some crime. [207] Why, then, does this man not deserve to die three times, not just once? By himself he was certainly not about to overthrow your government; on the contrary, it is in your power, if you do what is just and appropriate, to end his life. Just the same, he followed the example of this crime and decided by this law to release those whom the courts put in prison by writing this disgraceful clause that if anyone has received a prison sentence as an additional punishment or is given this punishment in the future, he is to be released. [208] Look, now, imagine that right now you should hear shouting in front of the court, and someone should say that the prison has been opened and prisoners are escaping. There would be no one so old or so disaffected that he would not rush to help as much as he could. But if someone were to come up and say

---

[277] Having proven Timocrates' guilt, Diodorus now attempts to justify a harsh penalty for his crimes.

[278] For a similar expression, see Dem. 20.28.

that this man here is releasing them, he would not get a chance to speak but be hauled off immediately and punished with death.[279] [209] You have him now, men of Athens; he did not do this in secret but by tricking and deceiving you he enacted this law openly; it does not open the prison but destroys it and demolishes the courts along with it! What need is there for either courts or prisons when those sentenced to prison are released and any penalty you impose on someone in the future will do no good?

[210] Well, now, another matter you should consider is that many of the Greeks have often voted to follow your laws; this is a source of pride for you and rightly so.[280] The statement attributed to one of your orators I think is true: "All those who are wise understand that the laws are the city's character."[281] You must therefore take seriously the task of making the laws seem as good as possible and punishing those who damage and distort them. If you neglect this task, you will lose this source of pride and give the city a bad reputation. [211] Indeed, if you are right to praise Solon and Draco, whose public contribution you could not describe as anything other than making useful and good laws, it would certainly be right for you to make clear that you are angry with those who enact the opposite sort and to punish them. I know that when Timocrates passed this law he did it mostly for his own benefit: he was aware that much of his political activity deserved a prison sentence.

[212] Well, now, I wish also to discuss the following statement that is attributed to Solon when he was prosecuting a man for an inexpedient law.[282] It is said that he told the judges after finishing the rest of his speech that there is a law in virtually all cities that if someone counterfeits money, the penalty is death.[283] He then

---

[279] This passage is praised by [Longinus] *On the Sublime* 15.9 for its vividness.

[280] For Athens as an example followed by other Greeks see Thuc. 2.37.1.

[281] For the idea that the laws reveal the city's character see also Isoc. 4.39–40, 7.14.

[282] The story is implausible; the public action against an inexpedient law was not established until after 400 BCE.

[283] The penalty in Athens for counterfeiting coins was death. See Dem. 20.167.

asked whether they found this law just and good. [213] After they said yes, he said that coinage (*nomisma*) was invented for private individuals to carry out their private transactions,[284] but the laws (*nomoi*) serve as the city's currency (*nomisma*).[285] Thus if someone debases the city's currency and introduces a counterfeit coin, the judges ought to despise and punish him much more than someone did this to coins for private citizens. [214] To prove that corrupting the laws is a worse crime than counterfeiting money he added the point that although many cities openly using coins mixed with bronze and lead have survived and suffered no harm at all,[286] none of those following bad laws and allowing the destruction of existing laws has ever survived. Timocrates is right now subject to this charge; it would be just for him to suffer the appropriate penalty.

[215] Although you should be angry with everyone who establishes shameful and wicked laws, you should be most angry with those who corrupt the laws that make our city weak or great. Which laws are these? Those that punish wrongdoers and grant honors to honest men. [216] If all men were eager to do good for the community and ambitious to gain honors and awards for this, and if all were to refrain from criminal acts out of fear for the harm and penalties imposed for these, would anything prevent our city from being great? Does Athens not have more triremes than any Greek city? More hoplites? More cavalry? More revenue? More possessions? More harbors? What protects and preserves all these things? The laws. When the city obeys them, all these resources serve the common good.[287] [217] If, on the other hand, just the opposite happens, and the virtuous gain no advantage, and criminals gain all the immunity Timocrates has proposed for them, how much chaos would be likely to result? You

---

[284]For the idea that coinage was invented to facilitate commercial exchange, see Plato *Republic* 371b and Arist. *Politics* 1.3.13.1257a.

[285]In the Greek there is a play on the words law (*nomos*) and currency (*nomisma*), both formed from the same root.

[286]On bronze coins at Athens, see Philochorus *FGrHist* 328 F 141b. On Athenian coinage in the final years of the Peloponnesian War, see Kraay 1976: 63–77. For the image of counterfeiting, see Brock 2013: 165.

[287]For a similar argument, see Dem. 20.154.

are well aware that even if there were twice as many of the resources I have just described, they would do us no good. This man is clearly trying to harm you by attacking this law that provides penalties for those attempting to commit crimes. [218] For all the reasons stated, therefore, you should show your anger and punish this man as an example for others.[288] To show indulgence to men like this by finding them guilty but assessing a small penalty is a way of teaching as many of you as possible the habit of committing crimes.

---

[288]Toward the end of their speeches accusers often ask the court to make an example of the defendant. See Lys. 30.24; Lyc. *Against Leocrates* 150; Dem. 19.343, 21.227, 22.68 with E. M. Harris 2013a: 331–332. Cf. Thuc. 3.40.7. These should not be confused with precedents (*pace* Rubinstein 2007, with the criticisms of E. M. Harris 2013a: 251, notes 14–16).

# 25–26. AGAINST ARISTOGEITON I
# AND II

## INTRODUCTION

The speeches of Demosthenes and the other Attic orators remained popular not only in Athens but in the rest of the Greek world after the Classical period.[1] In the first century BCE Dionysius of Halicarnassus wrote an appreciation of Demosthenes' style and a treatise about the relationship between his speeches and Aristotle's *Rhetoric.* Cicero (*Brutus* 35) thought that Demosthenes was the perfect orator. Cicero admired him so much that he drew on Demosthenes' speeches against Philip when writing his own *Philippics* against Mark Antony in 44 and 43 BCE.[2] Quintilian (*Institutio Oratoria* 10.1.76) considered him the best of the ten Attic orators. Plutarch wrote a life of Demosthenes in his *Parallel Lives* and paired him with Cicero. There was so much interest in the Attic orators during the Roman Empire that the scholar Harpocration wrote a dictionary of terms found in their speeches to help contemporary readers.[3]

Demosthenes' speeches were also studied in the rhetorical schools during the Hellenistic period and Roman periods. Students in these schools were taught how to write declamations (*meletai* in Greek) by imitating the orations of the Attic orators. The grammarian Theon (137.18–21) recommended that students copy

---

[1]On Demosthenes' reputation in antiquity, see Drerup 1923 and Pernot 2006.

[2]On Demosthenes' influence on these speeches, see Wooten 1983.

[3]There is no reliable modern edition of Harpocration. On the edition of Keaney 1991, see Slater 1994.

passages from speeches and make an anthology of selections to memorize.[4] Students would then compose speeches on themes drawn from Greek history, especially the Classical period.[5] An interesting example is found on a papyrus from the Hellenistic period, which purports to be the speech that Leptines delivered to defend his law against the attacks of Demosthenes in his speech *Against Leptines*.[6] The author of the speech shows a good knowledge of Demosthenes' speech and imitates several of his stylistic features but commits errors about Athenian legal procedure and history, which show that the composition is not a genuine work of fourth-century oratory.

The demand for Demosthenes' speeches and those of other Attic orators gradually exceeded the limited supply, and this led to the production of imitations, which are very similar to the exercises produced in the schools.[7] For instance, the corpus of speeches attributed to Andocides contains the speech *On the Peace*, which Dionysius of Halicarnassus declared a forgery and about whose authenticity Harpocration several times expressed doubts.[8] The speech contains many errors about Athenian history and political institutions that reveal it to be a forgery.[9]

---

[4]Pack 1965: no. 290 may provide a portion of such an anthology.

[5]On these *meletai*, see Cribiore 2001: 231–238.

[6]For the text of the speech and commentary, see Kremmydas 2007.

[7]On forgeries in antiquity, see Grafton 1990.

[8]For the evidence against the authenticity of the *On the Peace*, see E. M. Harris 2000. The conclusions of this essay have been endorsed by several scholars. See Conwell 2008; Martin 2009: 102; Couvenhes 2012.

[9]Hansen 1976: 145 claims that there are no examples of forged speeches in the corpus of the Attic orators ("if the speech is [i.e., a Hellenistic forgery] it is unique among the forensic speeches") and claims that the second speech *Against Aristogeiton* was a genuine speech of the fourth century BCE, though not written by Demosthenes. This statement does not take into account Andocides' speeches *On the Peace* and *Against Alcibiades* and the speech preserved in papyrus fragments recently edited by Kremmydas 2007. For the grounds against authenticity of Andocides *On the Peace*, see E. M. Harris, previous note. On *Against Alcibiades*, see Edwards 1995: 133–136.

The two speeches entitled *Against Aristogeiton* fall into the category of speeches composed during the Hellenistic period.[10] The evidence of stichometry shows that the two speeches were not part of the earliest editions of the Demosthenic corpus and were inserted into the Demosthenic corpus after the Classical period (for an explanation of stichometry, see the Introduction to this volume).[11] For the public speeches preceding these two speeches in the manuscripts (18, 19, 20, 21, 22, 23, 24) and the two private speeches coming after these speeches in the manuscripts (27 and 28) there are both partial and total stichometries, which indicate that they belonged to the earliest stages of the transmission; the two speeches against Aristogeiton, however, have neither partial nor total stichometry, an indication that they were added to the corpus at a later stage.[12] The literary critic Dionysius also denies that the speeches were the work of Demosthenes probably on stylistic grounds,[13] and Harpocration (s.v. *theoris* and *neales*) ex-

---

[10]Among the scholars who have accepted the authenticity of the first speech *Against Aristogeiton*, see Braun 1873; Weil 1882; Weil 1887; Blass 1897–1898: 3.1: 408–417; Schläfke 1913; Kramer 1930; Mathieu 1947: 134–138; Hansen 1976: 144–152; Carmigiato 1999; Rubinstein 2000: 30–32; MacDowell 2009: 298–313; Martin 2009: 182–202; Faraguna 2011: 75–77; Worthington 2013: 286. Among those who have rejected authenticity, see Boeckh 1840: 538–540; Stier 1883; Lipsius 1883; Wagner 1883; Schaefer 1885–1887: 3.345; Vince 1935: 514–515; Treves 1936: 252–258; Sealey 1960; Sealey 1967; Sealey 1993: 237–239. Dilts in his recent Oxford edition implicitly rejects authenticity by placing brackets around "Demosthenes" in the title to the speech. Those who have recently accepted the authenticity of the speech have followed Hansen's analysis, but, as the notes to the translation demonstrate, Hansen's arguments are not convincing and do not take into account the stylistic grounds for rejection. Several of those who reject Demosthenic authorship still believe that the speech was written in the fourth century BCE, but the errors about Athenian law and legal procedure and some of the vocabulary rule out this possibility.

[11]For the history of the Demosthenic corpus, see Canevaro 2013a: 319–342, with references to previous scholarship.

[12]See Canevaro forthcoming b.

[13]See the *hypothesis* to *Against Aristogeiton* I.

pressed doubts.[14] The vocabulary of the speeches differs in several ways from that of the genuine speeches of Demosthenes[15] and contains stylistic features unlike those found in Athenian forensic oratory. For instance, the first speech *Against Aristogeiton* contains several personifications (11n, 52n) and similes and metaphors (see 7n, 46n, 61n): although one finds similes in Demosthenes' speeches to the Assembly, they are generally absent from forensic oratory.[16] What is decisive against the authenticity of the first speech *Against Aristogeiton* is the presence of numerous errors about Athenian law and legal procedure, which demonstrate that they were written by authors after the Classical period.[17]

Whoever composed the two speeches drew on Dinarchus' speech *Against Aristogeiton* and possibly other sources but modified certain details about the information given there.[18] From the speech of Dinarchus (2.18) we learn that Aristogeiton was appointed as supervisor of the port, but he was rejected at his *dokimasia*; the speech in the Demosthenic corpus alludes to this (*Against Aristogeiton* II 21). The speech of Dinarchus (2.8, 11, 18) states that Cydimachus, the father of Aristogeiton, was condemned to death

---

[14]On the other hand, Plut. *Demosthenes* 15.1, Pliny *Letters* 9.26 and Longinus *On the Sublime* appear to believe that the first speech against Aristogeiton is a genuine speech of Demosthenes.

[15]See 11n, 22n, 24n, 28n, 31n, 41n, 42n, 43n, 46n, 49n, 50n, 51, 54n, 61n, 68n, 70n, 75n, 76n, 79n, 80n, 84n, 93n, 95n, 96n, and 101n. For philosophical terms, see 15n and 98n.

[16]For similes in Demosthenes' speeches to the Assembly, see Dem. 2.21, 29; 3.11; 4.26, 40. For a metaphor in a speech of Pericles to the Assembly, see Arist. *Rhetoric* 3.10.7 (Aegina as the "eyesore of the Piraeus"). Note that the metaphors and similes mentioned in this section of the *Rhetoric* appear to come either from deliberative or from epideictic speeches.

[17]See 13n, 23n, 27n, 28n, 58n, 60n, 65n, 79n, and 90n. Hansen 1976: 144–152 notes that the author of the first speech does have some correct information, but this does not indicate that the speech is genuine. The persons who composed the forged documents inserted into the Demosthenic corpus sometimes get details right, but the errors they make show that these documents cannot be genuine. See Canevaro 2013a: 27–36.

[18]On the speech of Dinarchus *Against Aristogeiton*, see Worthington 1992: 287–312.

and fled to Eretria where he died in poverty and that Aristogeiton did not send him food or pay for his funeral after his death; the speech in the Demosthenic corpus repeats the information about the failure to provide food or burial rites but states that Cydimachus died in prison (*Against Aristogeiton* I 54). The speech of Dinarchus (14) states that Aristogeiton was condemned and placed in prison and implies that he escaped. The speech in the Demosthenic corpus takes this information and adds colorful details (*Against Aristogeiton* I 56).[19] According to Dinarchus (2.18), Aristogeiton was in prison during the battle of Chaeronea. The second speech *Against Aristogeiton* (11) states that he brought a public action for proposing an illegal decree against Hyperides when the latter proposed that the slaves be liberated to defend Attica, but a recently deciphered palimpsest/parchment has shown that this information is not reliable.[20] The hypothesis to the first speech *Against Aristogeiton* states that Aristogeiton was accused of proposing an illegal decree by Phanostratus and was condemned to pay a fine of five talents. Aristogeiton then brought a public action against Hegemon but did not gain one-fifth of the votes and therefore owed a second debt of one thousand drachmas. When he did not pay these debts, they were doubled. When Aristogeiton continued to speak in the Assembly while a public debtor, Lycurgus brought a public action against him for violating the law probably in 324, if the information provided by the hypothesis is correct. There is no information about the outcome of this case. Aristogeiton was accused of receiving money from Harpalus in 324 (Dinarchus 2 passim) but may have been acquitted at his trial (Plato *Letters* 3.37, 42).

AGAINST ARISTOGEITON I

[1] I have been sitting here for a long time, men of the court, and listening like you to Lycurgus' accusations. I thought that

---

[19]For discussion of the differences between the details of the two speeches, see Sealey 1993: 238.

[20]See Horváth 2014: 81, 87.

the rest of his speech was good, but when I saw him making an extraordinary effort, one thing amazed me: is he not aware that what is just in this trial here draws its strength not from what he said nor from what I will say, but from the attitude each of you has when it comes to hating or tolerating evil?[21] [2] My own view is that one must make one's accusation and most of one's arguments paying respect to custom and to your willingness to listen. The outcome of this case, however, has been decided long ago by the personal character of each of you.[22] Now, if the majority of you have it in you to favor and protect evil men, I think that we will have sung our song in vain.[23] But if you have it in you to hate them, then with god's will this man will be punished.

[3] Although much has been said and all of it eloquently, I will not hesitate to tell you how I myself view the situation. I think that the present case is not at all similar to other cases. Look at it in this way. The judges come to all the courts to learn from the accuser and the defendant about the issue on which they will have to cast their votes, and the opposing parties come here, each to show that the justice of the laws is on his side.[24] [4] What is the situation with this case? You who have come here to judge know better than we who are making that charge that this man is a public debtor, that he is registered on the Acropolis, and that he does not have the right to speak.[25] As a result, each one of you

---

[21] Supporting speakers in other Attic orations never criticize other speakers on their side. See, for instance, Dem. 20.1, 51, 97, 100, 159; [Dem.] 59.16.

[22] Litigants in forensic speeches never discuss the moral character of the judges. Their admonitions to the judges usually remind them of their oath.

[23] The verb *rhapsōdō* ("sing a song") occurs only here in forensic oratory. The verb is found in an Assembly speech of Demosthenes (14.12), but there it is used to criticize ambassadors and is derogatory. It is hard to understand why a speaker would characterize his own speech with such a derogatory word.

[24] The speaker equates justice and the laws in the same way that litigants normally do. See E. M. Harris 2013a: 112–113.

[25] For public debtors being registered on the Acropolis, see Dem. 58.19; Lalonde, Langdon, and Walbank 1991: P26, lines 494–495, 505, 508–509; Harpocration (s.v. ψευδεγγραφή). Public debtors did not have the right to

takes on the position of accuser and knows the facts so there is no need for you to learn about the issues. [5] There is nothing at all that might save the man on trial, not just arguments in favor of his case, not his life as a human being, not any good deed whatsoever. Things that might cause an innocent man to be afraid, this man thinks will save him: he places his hope for safety in his boundless evil. [6] Given this situation, I think that one would not be wrong to say that in one respect Aristogeiton is on trial, yet in another you are the ones being examined; it is your reputation that is in danger. If people see that you get angry at offenses that are so obvious and serious and punish them, they will think that you have come here as judges and guardians of the law, which is what you are.[26] [7] But if some other consideration prevails over the laws, something that no one would ever admit, but will become obvious from your votes, I am afraid that some will think that you are training anyone living in the city who is bent on evil.[27] On his own, every evil man is weak, but if you lend him your support, this man becomes strong. The man who receives support from you gains a path to action and power, but you who give it to him receive a bad reputation.

[8] Before speaking about this man's personal life, I would like you for a few moments to examine seriously how much shame and dishonor all animals like him bring publicly upon the city. In this group he is the alpha, the omega, and everything in between. [9] I will not mention the rest, but these men enter meetings of the Assembly where you allow speakers to reveal their opinions, not their evil character, and come prepared with their arrogance, their shouting, their false charges, their blackmail, their lack of shame, and everything else like this. No one would find anything more detrimental to proper deliberation or, in my opinion, any-

address the Assembly. On public debtors, see Hunter 2000. For a similar appeal to the knowledge of the judges, see Aes. 1.77–78, 89–91.

[26]For the view that the judges are the guardians of the laws, cf. Dem. 24.36; Din. 3.16. For the idea that it is the judges and not just the defendant who are being judged, see Dem. 20.83.

[27]The word *paidotribein* ("to train young men") was normally used for the duties of the *paidotribēs*, and never as a metaphor in forensic oratory.

thing more shameful. By these shameful methods they triumph over all that is good in the city: the laws, the *proedroi*, the agenda, and discipline.[28] [10] If this is what you want and if they do this with your approval, Aristogeiton will go on his way, and one should leave him alone. But if you think now that you still must correct this problem and improve a situation so far neglected and allowed by their actions shamefully to deteriorate, you must today cast off habits like this and make the right decision. [11] You must give the highest consideration to Law and Order (*Eunomia*), which loves what is just and saves all cities and all countries, and to implacable[29] and august Justice,[30] which Orpheus, who taught us the most holy rites of initiation, says sits next to the throne of Zeus, watching over all the deeds of men.[31] You must cast your votes imagining that she looks at each of you and taking care and vigilance not to dishonor her. Each of you chosen by lot at any time to judge bears her name[32] and has received everything in the city that is good, just, and beneficial on that day as a deposit held on oath from the laws, the constitution, and the country.

---

[28] The *proedroi* were selected by lot by the *epistatēs* of the *prytaneis* and presided over meetings of the Assembly in the fourth century. See *Ath. Pol.* 44.2–3, with Rhodes 1981: 533–534. The *prytaneis* drew up an agenda for meetings of the Assembly (*Ath. Pol.* 43.3–4, 44.2–3).

[29] The word *aparaitētos* ("implacable") occurs only here in Athenian forensic oratory.

[30] *Dike* (Justice) is never personified in Athenian forensic oratory. For its personification in tragedy, see Sophocles *Oedipus at Colonus* 1381–1382.

[31] Orpheus was a legendary figure. Litigants sometimes refer to gods and heroes such as Zeus (Aes. 1.81, 87; 3.255; Is. 4.20, 24), Athena (Aes. 2.147; Dem. 24.22, 180, 199), Apollo (Aes. 1.81, 3.110; Dem. 50.13; Is. 6.61), Dionysus (Is. 1.31), and Heracles (Aes. 3.21; Is. 9.30; Lyc. *Against Leocrates* 77), but they are always those who are associated with public cults in Attica. Litigants never refer to legendary figures such as Orpheus who were associated with private rituals of initiation.

[32] The word "judge" (*dikastēs*) is formed from the word for "justice" (*dikē*). The word *epōnymos* never occurs in this sense ("named after") in Athenian forensic oratory; the adjective occurs only in reference to the Eponymous Heroes. See Dem. 20.94; 21.103; 24.8, 18, 25; 58.14, 15.

[12] Thus, if you do not adopt this attitude, but come and sit here with your usual naiveté, I am afraid that the situation will be reversed and that we, who seem to be accusing Aristogeiton, will be seen to be accusing you. The more you fail to heed our efforts to expose his evil character, the greater your shame will be. Enough about this topic.

[13] Men of Athens, I will tell you the truth with complete candor. When I saw you designating and selecting me at meetings of the Assembly to accuse this man, I was troubled and, by Zeus and all the gods, did not wish to do it[33] because I was not unaware that the man who does something like this in your city does not come away unscathed. If the harm to him is not so great that he notices it immediately, but he continues such actions and does not stop, he will know it soon enough. Just the same, I thought it necessary to obey your wishes. [14] I thought that Lycurgus would speak about the issues of justice concerning the denunciation (*endeixis*) and the laws, which he did, and I saw him summoning the witnesses to this man's evil conduct.[34] But as for the issues that men deliberating about the city and its laws ought both to consider and to examine, these are what I have chosen to discuss, and now I am moving on to these topics. Allow me, men of Athens, allow and permit me, by Zeus, to speak to you about these matters in a way that suits my nature and choice. For I would not be able to do it any other way.

[15] No matter whether they live in a large or small city, the entire life of human beings, men of Athens, is controlled by nature

---

[33]In the Athenian legal system, any citizen (and in some cases noncitizens) could bring a public charge, but in some cases the Assembly elected public prosecutors as in the case against Harpalus (Din. 2.6). On the other hand, there is no evidence indicating that the Assembly ever elected prosecutors in a case of *endeixis*. See Sealey 1993: 238. Hansen 1976: 146 speculates that because prosecutors were elected for other public cases, they might have been for *endeixis* but provides no evidence. The unparalleled nature of this procedure indicates that the speech is a forgery composed after the Classical period.

[34]*Synēgoroi* never criticize a previous speaker on their side.

and the laws.[35] Of these two, nature is disorderly and specific to each man who possesses it, but the laws are common, orderly, and the same for all. Thus, if one's nature is wicked, it often desires what is evil. You will therefore find men like these doing wrong. [16] But the laws desire and seek what is just, good, and beneficial. When that is found, it is established as a common order, equal and similar for all, and this is a law. All men should obey it for many reasons, but above all because every law is an invention and gift of the gods, a decision of wise men, a corrective for faults committed willingly or unwillingly, and a common agreement of the city in obedience to which all men should live in the city.

[17] But it is easy to show that Aristogeiton stands convicted by all the just charges in the denunciation and that there is no tolerable argument for him to make. All laws are established for two reasons: either to prevent anyone from committing injustice or to improve other men by punishing lawbreakers.[36] It will be clear that this man is subject to both considerations. For breaking the laws originally, he was given fines; for not respecting the penalty,[37] he is now being brought before you for punishment so that there remains no reason for anyone to acquit him. [18] One cannot say that the city suffers no harm from this. In my opinion, all the fines imposed by the city will be canceled if you accept his sophistries. If any people should be released from their fines, it is those who are most kind and good, who owe fines for the least serious offenses, not the worst man who has done the most wrong, whose fines are the most justified, and whose crimes are the most serious. [19] What could be more shocking than his blackmail and lawbreaking, both of which have caused him to

---

[35] No litigants speaking in court ever state that nature rules the lives of men or draws such a contrast between law and nature; this is a philosophical idea. On *nomos* vs. *physis* in Greek thought, see Heinimann 1965. Note that at Dem. 18.275 nature is linked to the unwritten laws and adheres to the same principles as the written laws of the city. See E. M. Harris 2006: 56.

[36] For the role of law in improving morals, see, for example, Dem. 21.227, 22.68; [Dem.] 59.77; Lys. 30.24, with E. M. Harris 2013a: 173–174.

[37] The penalty alluded to here is the penalty of losing one's right to address the Assembly.

be fined? Even if you allow all others to do this, you should certainly not yield to one who acts violently (that is surely outrageous). I will leave aside all arguments like this. But the entire order of the city and its laws, men of Athens, is thrown into turmoil and destroyed by this man. This is what I will clearly show you. [20] I will say nothing new, excessive, or unusual, but facts that all of you know as well as I do. If any of you go up to the Assembly, the courts are filled by lot, why officials willingly yield their place to new ones, and everything concerning the administration and security of the city is conducted, he will find that the laws are responsible for these activities and the fact that all men obey them. When they are destroyed and each man has the power to do what he wants, not only does the constitution vanish, but also our life would be no different from that of beasts. [21] What do you think this man who acts like this when the laws are strong would do if the laws were destroyed? Since it is agreed that next to the gods it is the laws that keep the city safe, all of you must act just as if you were sitting as people collecting contributions for a friendly loan for your country:[38] you should honor and praise the man obeying them as one who makes a full contribution to his country but punish him who disobeys. [22] Everything each one of us does when the laws command is a contribution to the city and the community. Whoever does not make a contribution, men of Athens, robs you and destroys many fine, righteous, and great benefits.[39] [23] To provide an example, I will tell you one or two of the best known. The Council of Five Hundred maintains its power over secrets by this weak barrier here, and private citizens do not enter.[40] The Council of the Areopagus, when it sits in the Stoa Basileios and is roped off, is by itself in complete peace,

---

[38]On the *eranos* loan and the meaning of the term *plerōtēs* ("one who collects an *eranos* loan") see E. M. Harris 2006: 335–336. For the image of the *eranos*, see Dem. 21.101, with Harris 2008: 122, note 158.

[39]The phrase *to kath' hauton* is puzzling. The Loeb translates the phrase "to the best of his ability." I have omitted it in my translation.

[40]For the *kingklis* ("barrier") at the entrance to the Bouleuterion, see Aristoph. *Knights* 641–642, with Rhodes 1972: 33. Mathieu and Dilts place brackets around the word *asthenous* ("weak").

and all leave and depart.[41] All the offices in which you serve when selected by lot, whenever the assistant says, "Depart!" have legal power over the duties to which they have been assigned, and even the most insolent refrain from violence. There are thousands of others. [24] Everything august and good that adorns the city and keeps it safe, self-discipline, the respect shown to your parents and elders by the young, good order, prevails with the help of the laws over what is disgraceful: lack of shame, arrogance, impudence. Vice is reckless, bold, and greedy; on the contrary, noble character is peaceful, restrained, slow, and adept at taking less. Therefore, those of you who at any time serve as judges must observe the laws and keep them strong. With their help the good prevail over the wicked. [25] If not, everything is destroyed, split open, thrown into confusion, and the city falls into the hands of the most wicked and shameless men. By the gods, just imagine if each man in the city were as bold and shameless as Aristogeiton and had the same attitude as he does, thinking that he has the right to say and do whatever he wishes in the democracy as long as he does not care what people think of him and that no one

---

[41]All contemporary sources state that the Council of the Areopagus met at the Areopagus and nowhere else. See Lys. 10.11; Euripides *Electra* 1258–1259; Athenaeus 13.566f; *IG* ii³ 320, lines 16–20. Cf. Pausanias 1.28.5. The Stoa Basileios was the office of the *basileus* (*Ath. Pol.* 7.1), one of the nine archons, whose jurisdiction included homicide trials (*Ath. Pol.* 57.2–4). There is no evidence that any other officials met in this building. The Areopagus, which gained each year nine new members, who were ex-archons (Plut. *Solon* 19.1, *Pericles* 9.3; *Ath. Pol.* 60.3; Pollux 8.118), and must have contained around one hundred and fifty members in total (Hansen 1991: 289), could not have fit inside the Royal Stoa, which was 17.72m by 7.1m on the exterior and therefore much too small to accommodate a group of this size (this point is missed by Wallace 1989: 218). See T. L. Shear 1971: 243–255 and T. L. Shear 1975: 365–370. Weil 1887: 24–25 saw no reason to doubt the information about this point on the basis of information found in the document at And. 1.82–85, but wrote before the Stoa Basileios was excavated and did not realize that the document in Andocides is a forgery. See Canevaro and Harris 2012: 110–116 and Canevaro and Harris 2016. Hansen 1976: 144–152 fails to deal with this issue. This mistake is another clear indication that the speech was composed after the Classical period.

would put him to death for any crime. [26] Imagine that someone with such aims not selected by lot tried to be equal and share the same rights with someone selected by lot or someone not elected with someone who was elected; or imagine that in general neither young nor older should do their duty but each man expelled discipline from his life and regarded his own wish as the law, authority, everything. If we should do this, would it be possible to run the city? How, then? Could the laws rule? How much violence, outrage, and lawbreaking do you think there would be every day in the entire city, how much foul language instead of praise and order? [27] Why is it necessary to say that everything is ordered by the laws and by our obedience to them? Out of all the Athenians participating in the selection (I know that all wished to be chosen by lot for this court), you alone are our judges. For what reason? Because you men were selected and then assigned by lot.[42] This is what the laws state. Will you who have entered here legally acquit a man whom you caught speaking and acting violently and illegally? Will none of you show that you feel rage[43] or anger at the violence this disgusting, shameful man does to the laws? [28] You, most foul of all men alive, your power to speak is not restrained by any barrier or doors that some man could secretly open, but by large and serious fines placed next to the goddess, and you force your way in and enter places from which the laws exclude you. Excluded by everything that is just in the city, by the verdicts of three courts,[44] by the register of the *thesmothe-*

---

[42]There were two selections by lot of judges for court cases. In the first selection, the judges were chosen for service on a given day. In the second, they were assigned to a specific court (*Ath. Pol.* 64–65).

[43]The Greek word *cholē* ("rage") appears only here and nowhere else in Athenian forensic oratory.

[44]The text of the manuscripts reads *gnōsesi dikastēriōn triōn* ("the verdicts of three courts"). Weil emends the text so that the speaker mentions "the verdict of three courts," which Hansen 1976: 147 interprets as "one sentence passed by three sections of 500 jurors (*sic*) each," but cites no parallel for the word *dikastēriōn* meaning a section of a court. If one does not emend the text, the expression is unparalleled because defendants were tried by one court, not three.

*tai*, and the other of the *praktores*,[45] by the charge of fraudulent registration,[46] which you yourself are bringing, almost by an iron chain,[47] you try to slip past these obstacles and to remove them, and by inventing excuses and concocting false charges, you think that you can overturn the common rules of justice. [29] Look, I will give you a great and clear example to show that you must not neglect any of this, not a single point. If someone should soon set apart a group and say that politicians should come from the youngest or wealthiest or liturgists or people from one of these groups, I know for certain that you would put him to death for overthrowing the democracy, and you would be right to do so. [30] Whichever of these you wish is less shocking than if someone from this man's group were to propose that men who use violence have the right to speak or those from prison or those whose fathers the people has put to death or those chosen by lot

---

[45] The *thesmothetai* received the plaint (*engklēma*) brought by the accuser and kept it on file after the case was decided. All public debts were registered with the *praktores*, not with the *thesmothetai* and the *praktores* as the speaker states. Hansen 1976: 147 claims that there was a "preliminary notice in the files of the *thesmothetai* immediately after the conviction," but there is no evidence for such a document. This mistake is evidence against the speech's authenticity.

[46] One brought a charge of fraudulent registration for public debt (*graphē bouleuseōs*) against an official who did not remove the name of a debtor from the public records after he paid (*IG* ii² 1631, lines 394–395), but this charge is not relevant to the case the speaker describes. When one charged an official with wrongly registering a public debtor, the charge was fraudulent registration (*graphē pseudengraphēs*) (Harpocration s.v.; Suidas s.v.). Hansen 1976: 146–147 claims that Lycurgus protested against Aristogeiton's incorrect use of the *graphē bouleuseōs* in his speech, which is the reason why the speaker does not discuss the issue in this speech. But there is no compelling reason to believe that Lycurgus discussed the matter in his speech, and nothing barred a supporting speaker from repeating or mentioning points made by the main speaker (see Dem. 20.51). Hansen's argument seeks to explain *ignotum per ignotius*. The speaker's error is strong evidence against the authenticity of the speech.

[47] The Greek word *halysis* ("chain") is not found elsewhere in Athenian forensic oratory.

but rejected for office as unqualified or those owing money to the Treasury or those disenfranchised for life or those who both appear and are the worst criminals.[48] This man and those who resemble him meet all these criteria. In my opinion, men of Athens, he would rightly be put to death for what he is doing now, yet much more or no less for what he clearly will do if you give him the right and opportunity—may this not happen! [31] What is amazing is that any of you is unaware that for anything good, noble, or worthy of the city this man is useless—I pray to Zeus and the gods that there never be such a dearth of men in the city that it receives anything good from Aristogeiton! As for those situations in which such a beast might prove useful, one must pray to the gods that they never occur. If it were to happen, it is better for the city that those wishing to do wrong have no one to carry out what they will do, than that this man be acquitted and be ready to serve them. [32] What incurable or dreadful act would this foul man, filled with ancestral hatred for the people,[49] hesitate to commit?[50] What other person more than this man would turn the city upside down (may this not happen!) if he had the power? Don't you see that it is not reason or shame that guides his character and his policies, but madness, that in fact all his policies are madness? This is the worst evil for the person afflicted by it, but also terrible and difficult for everyone, and intolerable for the city. Everyone who is out of his mind abandons himself and the safety

---

[48]Lipsius 1883 rightly observed that those who had been in prison, those who had been rejected at the *dokimasia* for office, and the children of those who were executed did not lose their civic rights. Hansen 1976: 149 claims that the passage is rhetorical and that the speaker exaggerates, but these inaccuracies cannot be dismissed as mere exaggerations. In fact, Hansen can cite no similar examples of litigants making comparable errors about Athenian law. These mistakes are strong evidence against the speech's authenticity.

[49]For the expression "ancestral hatred," cf. Dem. 21.49, where it is used for the traditional hostility between Greeks and barbarians, and Dem. 19.222, where Demosthenes uses the term about the other members of the embassy to Philip.

[50]The word *anamestos* ("filled") occurs nowhere else in Athenian forensic oratory.

of clear reason; if he survives, he survives against all expectation and logic. [33] What man in his right mind would place himself or the interests of the city in the company of this madness? Who would not avoid it as much as possible and keep his distance from one possessing it so that he would not fall into it against his will? Men deliberating about the country should not look for someone with whom to share madness, but intelligence, good sense, and much foresight. The latter lead men to happiness, but the former lead men to where this man should go. [34] Consider the matter not by looking at my speech, but at all the customs of men. In all cities there are altars and temples of all the gods, and among them one of Athena Pronoia because she is a good and mighty goddess. Next to Apollo at Delphi there is the most beautiful and greatest temple right as one goes into the shrine.[51] Being a god and a prophet, Apollo knows what is best. There is none for madness and shamelessness. [35] All men have altars for Justice, Law and Order,[52] and Shame, and the most beautiful and holy are in the very soul and nature of each man, set up for all men to honor in common. But there are none for Lack of Shame, Blackmail, Perjury, or Ingratitude, which are all the qualities of this man.

[36] I know that this man will not take the straight and just path in his defense, but will circle around outside the charges with insults and slanders, promising to judge them, to bring them to court, and to turn them over to you. If you listen to him in the correct way, all of this is unacceptable for him. How has he not been convicted on all these charges many times? [37] I will pass over other cases. But, Aristogeiton, you brought seven pub-

---

[51] For the shrine of Athena Pronaea ("in front of the temple" of Apollo) or Pronoia ("forethought") at Delphi, see Herod. 1.92; Aes. 3.108; Pausanias 9.10.2 and 10.8.6, who, however, places the shrine at a place that is not at the entrance to the shrine of Apollo but separated by several hundred meters. For the shrine in which the temple of Athena Pronaea is located, see Bommelaer 1997. This is another error that shows the speech was composed by a forger who was not familiar with sites on Mainland Greece.

[52] There is no evidence for shrines of *eunomia* in Attica before the Roman period. See *IG* ii² 1035, line 53; 3738, line 3; 4193A and B; and 4874.

lic charges against me and hired yourself out to Philip's agents, and you accused me twice at my audit. Being mortal, I bow down before Adrasteia[53] and give much thanks to the gods and to you, men of Athens, for saving me. You have obviously never yet said anything true, but have been proved a habitual blackmailer. If these men overturn the laws and acquit you today, will you prove me wrong? In what way? Consider it in the following way. [38] For two years, this man has usurped the right to speak when he did not have the right, but speaks just the same. Then during this time he saw the unfortunate Phocides and the smith from the Piraeus, and the tanner,[54] and all the others he accused of wronging the city before you, but he did not see me, the politician he was fighting, nor Lycurgus and the others about whom he soon will have much to say. Indeed, he deserves to die for both of these reasons, on the one hand, because he was able to show we were guilty but let us go and went after others, on the other, because, having no charge against us, he says these things to distract and deceive you.[55]

[39] If, on the other hand, there is the sort of person in our city who seeks someone capable of accusing someone without caring whether the charge is just or unjust, he would find no one less useful to him than this man. Why? Because the man who accuses others and judges everyone should be beyond reproach so that his vices do not cause them to be acquitted. But there is no man in the city stuffed with more and greater vices than this man.

---

[53]For the expression "I bow down before Adrasteia," see Plato *Republic* 451a. Adrasteia was an epithet for Nemesis, but the name of this god never occurs in Athenian forensic oratory.

[54]Phocides is listed as no. 967390 in *Persons of Ancient Athens* (as well as in the *Lexicon of Greek Personal Names*) but is not identified with any of the other persons in fourth-century BCE Athens who had the same name. The other two people are identified by their occupation only without their names being given. I know of no other example of this in Athenian forensic oratory.

[55]For the accusation in forensic oratory that the opponent is attempting to deceive the judges, see Kremmydas 2013.

[40] What is he, then? "Some people say, by Zeus, a watchdog of the people." What sort of watchdog?[56] One incapable of biting those whom he accuses of being wolves, but capable of gobbling down the sheep he claims to protect. To what politician has this man done as much harm as he has to the private citizens against whom he has proposed decrees for which he has been convicted? What politician has he brought to court in the time when he has started to speak again? Not even one, but many private individuals. Indeed, they say that dogs that touch sheep should be slaughtered so he could not be slaughtered too soon.[57] [41] In no regard, men of Athens, is this man useful for what he claims, but he has set his eyes on a filthy and shameful profession. He tosses insults in meetings of the Assembly and arrogantly picks fights with everyone, then after bamboozling all of you together over there, he leaves the podium and takes revenge on each of you one by one, blackmailing, accusing, extorting money, not, by Zeus, the speakers, no (they know how to give him a drenching[58]), but private individuals and those without experience. Those who have been struck know it.

[42] But, by Zeus, you will agree that this is so, but consider him a useful man for the city so that you turn a blind eye to all these crimes and save him. But what you have gained from experience, men of Athens, never judge this from what you are told. This man has not come before you in five years, the period he was sentenced not to speak.[59] Who, then, missed him during this

---

[56]For the image of the watchdog of the people, see Aristoph. *Knights* 1023; *Wasps* 835–994; Theophrastus *Characters* 29.4. Note that the image is not found elsewhere in forensic oratory.

[57]On the image of politician as watchdog, see E. M. Harris 2006: 10, note 17, and Brock 2013: 156.

[58]The verb *diabaptizesthai* (be drenched) is not found elsewhere in Athenian forensic oratory.

[59]The loss of the right to speak in the Assembly lasted only as long as someone remained a public debtor. If one lost one's rights (*atimia*) as a punishment after being convicted on a public charge, the loss was always permanent, never for a limited period of time. The Athenian courts did not sentence a defendant to *atimia* for a fixed period. Hansen 1976: 148 claims

time? What part of the city's business did anyone see neglected because of this man's absence? What has improved since he has now been speaking? Quite the contrary, I think: in the time he did not address you, the city gained a respite from the troubles this man caused everyone, and from the time he started speaking again, this man has laid siege to the city, giving divisive and subversive[60] speeches at every meeting of the Assembly.

[43] I want to touch upon a very risky[61] topic and speak to those who like him for this reason. Think about what kind of people you should judge them to be; I would not say anything except that those who associate with him lack a sense of virtue. I consider none of you here now in court like this. It is just, men of Athens, good, and beneficial for me to speak in this way and hold this opinion about you. [44] Of the other citizens, so as to cast aspersions on as few as possible, I consider only his pupil, or, if you wish, his teacher, Philocrates of Eleusis, to be like this. Not that I think that there are not more (may no one else take pleasure in Aristogeiton!), but that which I regard as an insult to you and hesitate to mention, I do not have the right to charge the rest of the citizens with. But my argument will have the same effect, even if it is directed at only one person. [45] I will refrain from closely examining what sort of character a person must have to enjoy Aristogeiton's company so that I am not forced to utter slanders and go on about them. This is what I will say. If Aristogeiton is simply wicked, harsh, a blackmailer and the sort of person he promises to be, I grant and yield to you, Philocrates of Eleusis,[62] who re-

---

that other statements in the speech contradict this view, but he provides no evidence to prove his assertion. Rubinstein 2000: 31, followed uncritically by MacDowell 2009: 311, attempts to twist the meaning of the Greek to evade the problem, but her analysis strains the meaning of the passage. This is another indication that the speech is a forgery.

[60]The words *stasiōdēs* ("divisive") and *tarachōdēs* ("subversive") occur nowhere else in Athenian forensic oratory.

[61]The adjective *parakinduneutikos* ("very risky") occurs nowhere else in Athenian forensic oratory.

[62]For Philocrates of Eleusis, who accused Demosthenes after the defeat at Chaeronea, see Dem. 18.249.

semble him, the right to save someone like yourself. For if everyone else thinks as he should and protects the laws, I do not think this would happen. [46] If he is a merchant of evil, one who sells it at retail and trades in it,[63] lacking only scales and weights, when selling everything he ever did, why do you whet him like a blade,[64] you foolish man? A cook gains no advantage from a knife that does not cut, and the man wishing to cause trouble and hardship for everyone gains nothing from a blackmailer selling this. [47] In fact, even though you know that he is like this, I will still tell you. You remember how he sold the indictment against Hegemon.[65] You know that he abandoned the prosecution of Demades.[66] He shouted and screamed about the oil-seller Agathon (this happened yesterday) and went "Woe! Woe!"[67] turning everything upside down at meetings of the Assembly, saying that one should torture him,[68] but after taking whatever sum, he was there when he was acquitted and was silent. After stirring up[69] the indictment against Democles, where did he take that? Thousands of more things, which it would be quite a task for me to recall all of them, but you, I am certain you have copies of them because you share in the profits. [48] What person, either wicked or good, is there to save him? Or for what reason? He is a traitor to men like him and an enemy to the good by nature and by birth, unless someone thinks that like a farmer the city should keep the seed and root of a wicked blackmailer.[70] This would not be good, men

---

[63] The word *metaboleus* ("trader") occurs nowhere else in Athenian forensic oratory. For commercial imagery in Athenian political discourse, see Brock 2013: 154, 173 note 73.

[64] The verb *akonō* ("whet like a blade") occurs nowhere else in Athenian forensic oratory.

[65] On Hegemon, see Dem. 18.285.

[66] On the Athenian politician Demades, see Brun 2000.

[67] The wording of this passage appears to imitate Dem. 19.209.

[68] It was illegal to have Athenian citizens tortured. See And. 1.43.

[69] The verb *anaseiō* ("stir up") occurs nowhere else in Athenian forensic oratory.

[70] The word *rhiza* ("root") occurs nowhere else in Athenian forensic oratory. I have translated the Greek term *sycophantes* as "blackmailer." The word refers to an accuser who brought false charges often with the aim of

of Athens, I believe, by the gods, and not the pious way to act. I do not think that our ancestors built these courts for you to cultivate such men[71] in them but the very opposite so that you repress and punish them and so that no one envies and lusts after evil. [49] There is a danger that evil is a difficult thing to repress.[72] Because Aristogeiton is being judged for crimes he has confessed to and was not put to death long ago, what must one do or say? This man is so evil that, although he has been denounced, he has not stopped shouting, blackmailing, and threatening, telling the generals, to whom you entrust the most important duties, that they should not be elected overseers of dung-pits,[73] after they did not give him money when he asked for it. [50] He was not insulting them, no, for they could have given him a little money and not listened to this, but splattering mud on your elections and making a display of his wickedness, tearing apart[74] the officials selected by lot, accusing, extorting money—what evil does he not cause? Finally, he sought to throw everyone into chaos and civil war, producing false documents, suited by his entire nature to harm everyone, making it quite clear by his life what kind of person he is. [51] Think about it. There are about twenty thousand Athenians in all.[75] Each of them does some private or pub-

---

extorting money from defendants. R. G. Osborne 1990 claims that the sycophant might play a positive role in Athenian democracy, but this view is rightly rejected by Harvey 1990, who shows that *sykophantia* was viewed as a crime and that sycophants were believed to have a detrimental effect on the democracy. Cf. MacDowell 2009: 304, note 40 ("Harvey convincingly refutes Osborne") and E. M. Harris 2013a: 62–63, 306–308, 344.

[71]The term *moscheuo* ("cultivate") is a botanical term used metaphorically and occurs nowhere else in Athenian forensic oratory. See Aeschylus *Eumenides* 910–912 for a similar metaphor.

[72]The adjective *dyskatapaustos* (difficult to repress) occurs nowhere else in Athenian forensic oratory.

[73]The word *koprōn* ("dung-pit") occurs nowhere else in Athenian forensic oratory.

[74]The verb *sparattō* ("tear away") occurs nowhere else in Athenian forensic oratory.

[75]For this number of Athenian citizens see Aristoph. *Wasps* 709; Plato *Critias* 112d.

lic business, by Heracles, as he walks around the Agora. But this man does not do any such business, nor could he point to any moderate or respectable activity he has spent his life pursuing. He does not spend his time thinking about what is good for the state. He practices no skill, neither farming or any other occupation; he shares no kindness, no company with anyone. [52] But he moves through the Agora like a viper or a scorpion with his sting erect,[76] leaping[77] here and there, looking for someone on whom to inflict disaster or slander or some disaster or to extort money by terrifying him. He does not frequent any of the barbershops or perfume shops or any other workshops in the city, not even one.[78] Pitiless,[79] without a fixed residence, antisocial, he knows nothing of gratitude, friendship, or any of the other qualities a decent man knows. Joined by those whom the painters depict in the company of the impious in Hades, he walks around with Curse, Slander, Envy, Discord, and Quarrel.[80] [53] A man who is likely not to receive any indulgence[81] even from the gods in Hades,[82] but to be seen among the impious for his evil life, whom you have caught committing crimes, will you not only not punish him but also acquit him and judge him worthy of greater rewards than given to your benefactors? Whom have you ever allowed, when he owes money to the Treasury, to enjoy the same rights as others without

---

[76]No Athenian litigant ever compares his opponent to a viper or a scorpion. This comparison appears in comedy (Eupolis fr. 245 K-A), but Hyperides (Harpocration s.v. *pareiai opheis*), however, compared sycophants to snakes.

[77]The verb *atto* ("leap") occurs nowhere else in Athenian forensic oratory.

[78]This passage may draw on Lys. 24.20. Cf. Isoc. 7.15; Dem. 34.13.

[79]The word *aspeistos* ("pitiless") occurs nowhere else in Athenian forensic oratory.

[80]These vices are never personified in Athenian forensic oratory.

[81]The word *hileōs* ("indulgent") occurs nowhere else in Athenian forensic oratory.

[82]Athenian forensic oratory never mentions punishment in the afterlife. In *Against Leptines* Demosthenes (20.87) expresses uncertainty about life after death. See Currie 2005: 38.

paying the fine? No one. Do not grant this now, but punish him and make him an example for others. [54] It is also worth hearing the rest, men of Athens. What you heard just now from Lycurgus was shocking, and there could be nothing worse; you will find the rest competes[83] with it and is of the same nature. Besides departing from Eretria after leaving his father in prison,[84] just as you have heard from Phaedrus, this impious and foul man did not bury him when he died or pay back the cost of burial to those who did, but brought a suit against them. [55] Besides not keeping his hands off his mother, just as you heard from witnesses, his sister, not born from the same father, but by that woman from who knows where (I leave that aside), his sister he sold for export as stated in the charge[85] for the case that this good brother here brought against him, the man who will join in his defense.[86] [56] Besides things like this, O Earth and gods![87] You will hear another shocking story. When he tunneled through the prison wall and ran away, he went to a woman named Zobia, whom he used to visit at one time, so it seems. She hid and saved him during the first days when the Eleven were searching for him and making announcements.[88] Later she gave him eight drachmas for travel money, a small tu-

---

[83]The adjective *enamillos* ("competing with") occurs here and nowhere else in Athenian forensic oratory.

[84]Din. 2.8, 11, 18 states that Cydimachus, the father of Aristogeiton, was condemned to death and fled to Eretria, where he died in poverty. His son did not send him food while he was alive and did not pay for his funeral after his death. Hansen 1976: 151 attempts to reconcile the two versions of the story, but it is hard to understand why the speaker would not mention that the Athenians condemned his father to death. According to the Suda, Cydimachus died in prison.

[85]For the written charge (*enklēma*) that an accuser submitted to an official to initiate legal proceedings, see E. M. Harris 2013a: 114–127.

[86]For a similar charge, see Dem. 24.203.

[87]The author of the speech imitates a standard exclamation in Demosthenes. See Dem. 18.139, 158, 294; 19.287, 311; 20.96; 22.78; 23.61; 24.186; 34.29; 39.21; 40.5; 45.73; 55.28.

[88]The Eleven were the officials in charge of the prison. See *Ath. Pol.* 52.1.

nic, and a cloak and sent him to Megara.⁸⁹ [57] After this woman did him such favors, when he was all puffed up⁹⁰ and famous in your city, she had some complaint and reminded him about this, then asked him to do her a favor. At first he thrashed her,⁹¹ then with threats he drove her out of his house. When she did not stop but acted like a woman, approached their acquaintances and complained, he grabbed her with his own hands and took her to the office for the metics' tax.⁹² If she had not happened to have paid, she would have been sold because of the man whom she was responsible for saving. [58] To show that I tell the truth, call for me that man who did not receive payment for burying his father and the arbitrator in the case that this man initiated about the sale of his sister against him,⁹³ and bring the charge. Call for me

---

⁸⁹For Megara as a city to which exiles from Athens went, see Xen. *Hellenica* 2.4.1; Lys. 12.17; Din. 1.58–59.

⁹⁰The verb *pneō* ("puff up") used in this metaphorical sense occurs here and nowhere else in Athenian forensic oratory and appears to be poetic.

⁹¹The verb *rapizō* ("thrash") occurs nowhere else in Athenian forensic oratory.

⁹²There is no other evidence for the existence of a building called the *pōlētērion tou metoikiou* in Classical Athens, although Harpocration (s.v. *pōlētai kai pōlētērion*) states that there was a building called the *pōlētērion* where the *pōlētai* met and cites a speech of Isaeus as evidence for the building. Photius and the Suda state that it was also mentioned in a speech of Hyperides. For discussion of the *pōlētērion* and its location, see Langdon in Lalonde, Langdon, and Walbank 1991: 65–67; for the activities of the *pōlētai*, see *Ath. Pol.* 47.2–3 with Langdon in Lalonde, Langdon, and Walbank 1991: 67–69. For the *metoikion* as the tax paid by metics at Athens, see Dem. 29.3, 57.55; Pollux 3.55 with Whitehead 1977: 76–77. Pollux 8.99 mentions that metics who defaulted were brought to the *pōlētai*. Hansen 1976: 149 admits that the phrase presents difficulties but follows Sauppe in bracketing the word *metoikiou*. Given the other inaccuracies in the speech, this should be viewed as more evidence against the speech's authenticity. This is the only evidence for metics being sold for as punishment for not paying the *metoikion* aside from Harpocration, who is probably relying on this passage.

⁹³The crime of selling someone into slavery was a public charge and prosecuted by *apagōgē* to the Eleven. See *Ath. Pol.* 52.1, with E. M. Harris 2006: 386–388. Such a charge would never have gone before an arbitrator, who

first of all the representative of Zobia[94] who sheltered him and the *pōlētai* to whom he brought her. Just now you were angry because he accused those who did not contribute to the friendly loan collected to save him.[95] A filthy, filthy beast, men of Athens, and unapproachable. Read the testimonies.

[WITNESS STATEMENTS]

[59] What charge would be sufficient for a man who has committed so many crimes like these? What penalty does he deserve? Death in my opinion appears too small.

[60] After discussing one more of the iniquities in his private life, I will pass over the rest. Before leaving prison, a man from Tanagra was put there about a surety[96] and had a document about it. Aristogeiton approached and talked to him for a while, then snatched the document away. The man accused him and made a scene, saying that no one else snatched it away. This man's

---

heard only private actions. On public arbitrators, see *Ath. Pol.* 53.1, 4–5; 55.5; 58.2. Dareste 1875: 2.344–346, followed uncritically by Hansen 1976: 149, claimed that the brother brought a private charge to obtain his part of the proceeds of the sale, but this makes no sense. The speaker is trying to show that the brother objected to Aristogeiton's crime of selling the sister. Had he been asking for some of the money, the speaker should have denounced his lack of support for a relative and his greed. It is also incredible that someone would have brought a case to court claiming money for an illegal sale.

[94]Metics were required to have an Athenian citizen as representative (*prostatēs*) who would represent them in court. See Whitehead 1977: 89–92.

[95]On the friendly loan (*eranos*), see 21n.

[96]This statement appears to be inconsistent with Athenian law and legal procedure. A surety was someone who promised to pay a loan or other obligation in case the original debtor defaulted. One could act as a surety either for a private or a public obligation, but only Athenian citizens could serve as sureties for public obligations and might be put in prison if they did not pay the money owed (Dem. 24.40, 87). On the other hand, a foreigner might serve as a surety for a private debt, but in that case he would not be put in prison for failing to pay. The basic work on personal security remains Partsch 1909 though it is now out of date. Note also that the term *katenguē* ("surety") occurs nowhere else in Athenian forensic oratory.

behavior was so disgusting that he tried to beat him. [61] Since he was fresh and recently caught,⁹⁷ this man got the better of this Aristogeiton, who was pickled in salt for having been there a long time.⁹⁸ When it reached this point, he eats off the man's nose. As a result, overcome by what happened to him, he stopped searching for the document. Later they found the document in a box for which this man had the key. After this, the men in the prison voted that no one should share fire, lamp, drink, or food with him, neither take it from him nor give it to him.⁹⁹ [62] To show that I am telling the truth, call for me the man himself whose nose this foul man ate and devoured.

[TESTIMONY]

What fine deeds this politician has crafted for you! It is worth hearing from the mouth of the man who did such things some story or speech! Read also this fine resolution (*dogma*) here about him.¹⁰⁰

[RESOLUTION]

[63] Are you not ashamed, men of Athens, that men put in prison for evil and the worst crimes, thought that this man was so much worse than themselves that they would not associate with him, yet you will let him associate with you after the laws have expelled him from politics? Do you commend anything he has done or any part of his life? Is there anything that does not make

---

⁹⁷For the term *prosphatos* used in a similar way, see Dem. 21.112.

⁹⁸The verb *taricheuō* ("pickle in salt") never occurs elsewhere in Athenian forensic oratory.

⁹⁹This phrase "no one should share fire, lamp, drink, or food with him" is taken from Din. 2.9.

¹⁰⁰This resolution would appear to be the one voted by Aristogeiton's fellow prisoners, but it is hard to believe that they would have written down their decision and placed it in a document. This certainly has no parallel in Athenian forensic oratory.

you angry? Isn't he impious? Isn't he savage? Not polluted? Not a blackmailer? [64] Although he does things like this and is this sort of man, he always shouts at every meeting of the Assembly, "I am all you have. All these men are conspiring. You have been betrayed. All that is left is my loyalty." I want to examine this mighty and great loyalty, where it comes from, and what gave rise to it so that if it exists as he says, you should make use of it and trust it, but if not, you should guard against it. [65] Is it because you condemned his father to death and sold his mother when she owed a fine for an action for disobedience that you consider him loyal to you?[101] But that is absurd, by Zeus and the gods. If he is loyal to them and obeys the law of nature, which has been established as one and the same for men and animals,[102] to love one's parents, [66] he obviously resents the people who destroyed them, and their laws, and their constitution. If he does not care for them, I would like to know what man, after seeing him betray the loyalty owed to

---

[101] Freed slaves were required to perform certain duties to their former masters, and their former masters could bring an action for disobedience (*dikē apostasiou*) against them (*Ath. Pol.* 58.3; Harpocration s.v. *apostasiou*). For the duties of freedmen, see Canevaro and Lewis 2014. The speaker therefore implies that Aristogeiton's mother was a former slave and insinuates that Aristogeiton was not an Athenian citizen since one needed to have two parents who were citizens to obtain citizenship (*Ath. Pol.* 42.1). Such slanders were not unusual in Athenian courts. Cf. Dem. 21.149. The penalty, however, for the former slave who lost in a case brought by this action was not sale by the state but return to the ownership of the former master. See Harrison 1968: 65, 182. This is another error about Athenian law and legal procedure that demonstrates the speech is a rhetorical exercise composed in the Hellenistic period. See Sealey 1993: 238. Hansen 1976: 144–152 does not address this evidence, which further undermines his defense of the speech's authenticity. MacDowell 1976: 82, following Lipsius, suggested emending *apostasiou* to *aprostasiou*.

[102] The phrase "law of nature" does not occur in Athenian forensic oratory. For the "unwritten law" that one must respect one's parents and the relationship between the unwritten laws and the written laws of the state, see E. M. Harris 2006: 53–57.

his parents, would trust the loyalty he promises now to have toward the people? I do not trust it and consider the man who neglects his parents hated by the gods, not just by men. [67] But, by Zeus, you voted against him in denunciations and twice placed him and his brother in prison—is he loyal to you for this? But that is also absurd. Is it because you disqualified him from the office for which he was selected by lot?[103] Is it because you condemned him for an illegal decree? [68] Is it because you set an additional penalty at five talents? Is it because you point your finger at him[104] in order to show that he is the most evil man of all? Is it because it is impossible for him to remove the disgraces as long as the existing laws and the constitution remain? So why is he loyal to you? Because, he says, he is shameless. Why does a shameless man have that name except that through lack of shame he dares to say what does not exist and could not, which in fact is what he does?

[69] Now I believe that it is better to tell you about what Lycurgus appears to have left for me to discuss, the denunciation. I think that you should examine the individual and the legal issues of the trial as if you were examining a private debt. If someone were to accuse a person of owing him money, and the other were to deny it, and if there clearly was a contract made for the loan and the stone-markers placed for it still standing,[105] you would consider the man denying the loan clearly shameless, but if they

---

[103]Din. 2.10 states that Aristogeiton was disqualified from the office of overseer of the port. All those who were selected for office had to undergo an examination of their qualifications. See Feyel 2009: 148–160. Anyone could bring a charge that the candidate was not qualified, and the court would decide about the issue. For the rejection of a candidate, see Lys. 26.14.

[104]The verb *daktulodeikto* ("point with one's finger") occurs nowhere else in Athenian forensic oratory.

[105]When a debtor received a loan, the creditor might ask for the debtor to pledge some land as real security to ensure repayment. Markers would then be placed on this land to indicate that it was legally encumbered. On real security, see E. M. Harris 2006: 163–239 and E. M. Harris 2013c. Finley 1985 is a useful collection of the texts of the security *horoi* published before 1985, but his analysis of the institution should be used with caution.

were destroyed, you would consider the plaintiff shameless. That
is the natural conclusion. [70] The laws according to which all
debtors are recorded are equivalent to the contract according to
which Aristogeiton owes money to the city, and the stone-marker
is the board placed next to the goddess.[106] If these have been destroyed and the fine has been erased, then I am talking nonsense,
or rather I am lying. If this is still there, will be, and remains until he pays it off, this man says nothing truthful, and his attempt
to destroy common justice is wrong and shocking.[107] [71] The
trial and the issue are not about whether he does not owe the full
amount that he owed, but whether he owes anything. Those who
are registered as owing only a drachma would be treated abom-
inably if their debt will hold firm against them for some minor
or nonexistent offense, when someone who has committed a major crime will recover his rights for one or two payments. Now
there are three debts that have been recorded and for which he
has been denounced. Two of them are recorded in the inventory,
and one was not, but he accuses Ariston of Alopeke of false registration. [72] "Yes," he says, "he registered me unjustly." You
must, so it seems, receive satisfaction. But at first you must put
up with the situation and abide by the terms of your punishment.
For what will you receive compensation? If you can do everything
other people do, how have you been wronged? [73] Come, by the
gods, consider this point too. If he convicts Ariston for false registration, what will happen? His name will be erased, by Zeus,
and that man's name will be registered in its place. That is what
the laws say. Good. From this day on, then, will this man whose
name is erased owe a fine, and that man whose name is registered
recover his rights? This follows from what he now claims, for if
when he is registered he does not owe, then when his name is
erased, he clearly will owe. But this cannot, cannot be. But when
his name is erased, then he will not owe. Therefore, surely he now

---

[106]Records of public debtors were placed on the Acropolis. See Dem.
58.19–20, 50–52. After the fine was paid, the name was erased.

[107]The word *teōsper* occurs only here in Athenian forensic oratory and
nowhere else.

owes money. [74] What then? If he does not convict Ariston, who will pay the city for the things this man does that he has no right to do? Those men for whom this man as he goes around the court proposes death or imprisonment as a penalty, how will they get their lives back or avoid terrible suffering? This man to whom the laws grant neither equal nor standard rights, this man is responsible for causing irreparable harm to others. This is not right, nor worthy of a citizen, nor in our interests. [75] When I see them, I am amazed why you think the situation is upside down. Is it that the earth is on top and the stars below?[108] That cannot be— and may it not happen! But when your will gives rights to men to whom the laws deny rights, when evil is honored, and the good thrown out, when justice and your interests are overcome by envy, one must think that everything has been turned upside down.

[76] I have already seen some men on trial who have been convicted by their own actions and are unable to show that they are not guilty. Some base their defense on their moderate and restrained lives, others on the deeds and liturgies of their ancestors, and still others on other such things, which they use to lead the judges to pity and clemency. But this man can tread[109] in none of these places; everywhere for him are precipices, ravines, and chasms.[110] [77] What will he actually say? For all the things his father did, by Zeus. But you condemned him to death in this court because he was clearly evil and deserved to die. No, by Zeus, if he finds this story about his father painful, will he base his defense on his own life for being virtuous and moderate? What sort of life? The one he has lived? That is not the kind of life that you all have seen. [78] "But, my good friend, he will turn to his liturgies." When or where did he ever perform any? His father's? There

---

[108] The word *astra* ("stars") occurs nowhere else in Athenian forensic oratory.

[109] The word *basimon* ("place where one can tread") occurs nowhere else in Athenian forensic oratory.

[110] The words *apokrēmna* ("precipices") and *pharangas* ("ravines") occur nowhere else in Athenian forensic oratory. The word *barathron* ("chasm") refers only to the place of execution (Dem. 8.45; 10.16) and is never used as a metaphor for perils.

are none. His own? You will find accusations, arrests, and denunciations, but no liturgies. But by Zeus, apart from this, many of his relatives and respectable men will stand next to him and beg for his acquittal. But there are none and never were. How could there be for a man who is not even free born? [79] Except, by Zeus, there is this brother of his who is here and brought that fine case against him. Why should one say anything else about him? This is his brother by the same mother and same father and, to make it even worse, his twin.[111] This man—I do not talk about the rest, but as for the drugs and incantations[112] for which you put the foul potion-maker Theoris from Lemnos and her entire family to death,[113] [80] he took them from her slave girl who informed against her and with whom this charlatan has had children. He uses charms,[114] cheats, and says that he cures epileptics when he himself has seizures of depravity.[115] This man will beg for Aristogeiton's acquittal, this scapegoat,[116] this plague,[117] whom one would rather avoid as a bad omen[118] when seeing him rather than wish to speak with, who sentenced himself to death when he brought a case like this.

[81] What then is left, men of Athens? That which is com-

---

[111] The word *didymos* ("twin") occurs nowhere else in Athenian forensic oratory.

[112] The word *epōdai* ("incantations") occurs nowhere else in Athenian forensic oratory.

[113] There is no other case in Athenian law in which a person and his or her family are collectively executed. For some offenses, the defendant and his descendants lost their rights, but that is a different matter.

[114] The word *manganeuō* ("use charms") occurs nowhere else in Athenian forensic oratory.

[115] The term *epilēptos* ("epileptic"), used in both a literal and metaphorical sense, occurs here and nowhere else in Athenian forensic oratory.

[116] The term *pharmakos* ("scapegoat") occurs nowhere else in Athenian forensic oratory. On the scapegoat in Greek religion see Bremmer 1983.

[117] The word *loimos* ("plague") occurs nowhere else in Athenian forensic oratory.

[118] The verb *oiōnizomai* ("regard as an omen") occurs nowhere else in Athenian forensic oratory.

monly provided to all men on trial by the character of the rest of you. No man on trial brings this for himself, but each of you comes bringing it from home: pity, sympathy, and generosity. But it is neither right nor righteous to give this foul man a share of it. Why? Because the law that each man applies to everyone from his own nature, he deserves to have everyone apply to himself. [82] What law or attitude do you think Aristogeiton applies to everyone? Is it to see everyone living in happiness and prosperity with a good reputation? But what will he do to earn his living? The misfortunes of others are this man's bread and butter. He certainly wants everyone to be on trial and dragged into court on malicious charges. This is what he cultivates, the way he works. What would one call this thrice cursed,[119] common enemy with spite for everyone, a man for whom the earth bears no fruit nor would receive him for burial? Isn't this the way he is? I think so.

[83] What sympathy or kind of pity did the victims of his malicious charges receive from him, who asked for the death penalty for everyone in these courts and proposed it even before the first vote was cast? The men whom this charlatan treated so savagely and so harshly, those whom you selected by lot did what was right by saving, acquitting and not giving him one-fifth of the votes.[120] [84] His harshness, murderousness, and savagery were present and exposed. When he saw the children, old mothers standing beside the men on trial, he felt no pity. Sympathy for you then? For what? From whom? Pity for your children? Far from it. You have thrown away pity for them, Aristogeiton, or rather you have destroyed them completely. After heaping up and filling these harbors with shoals, do not cast your anchor there.[121] It would not be right.

[85] Now if you should hear the slanders that he goes around

---

[119]The word *triskatarâtos* ("thrice cursed") occurs nowhere else in Athenian forensic oratory.

[120]On the penalty for not receiving one-fifth of the votes, see *Against Timocrates* 3n.

[121]The word *probolâs* with the meaning "shoals" and the word *ankyra* are never found in forensic oratory, in which metaphors like this tend to be avoided.

the Agora telling about you, you would hate him all the more and rightly so. He says that many owe money to the Treasury, and that these men are just like him. That there are many unlucky men, even if there are only two, I agree. That is more than there should be. None of the rest should have been debtors. But they are not, by the gods, similar to this man, I think, far from it, but quite the opposite. [86] Think about it in this way. Do not think, men of Athens, that I am speaking to you as if you owed money to the Treasury. This is not so, and may it never be; I do not believe it. But if there is some friend or acquaintance among them, I wish to show you that it is right to hate him for his sake. First, because good men who happen to have come on hard times on account of sureties, acts of generosity, or private debts but have committed no public offenses, he drags into court and places in the same category as himself. This is neither right nor decent. [87] It is not the same thing, Aristogeiton, far from it, for you to propose that three citizens be put to death without a trial and for you to be convicted for proposing an illegal decree and sentenced to a fine when you should have been put to death, and for someone to act as surety for a friend and then not be able to pay a penalty one did not expect. It is not the same thing; no. Moreover, the common generosity that you have in your character toward others, this man destroys and corrupts as best he can. Men of Athens, you feel a natural generosity toward one another as I said, and just as families are guided by it when they manage their private households, so too do you when you manage the public affairs of the city.[122] [88] How then do families act? Where there is a father, adult sons, and perhaps their children, there are necessarily many different wishes. Youth does not speak or act the same way that old age does. Nevertheless, the young do everything that they do if they are moderate so as to try to remain as inconspicuous as possible, or, if not, so that everyone sees they wish to act this way. Their elders, by contrast, if they see them spending or

[122]For the parallel between conduct in private life and conduct in public affairs, cf. Sophocles *Antigone* 672–680; Aes. 1.30, 3.78; Xen. *Memorabilia* 3.4.12, 6.14.

drinking or playing around excessively, they view this in such a way as to avoid appearing to see it. As a result, everything proceeds according to their natural inclinations, and all goes well. [89] In the same way, men of Athens, you run your city as if it were your family[123] and with generosity; some regard the things done by victims of misfortune in such a way that, as the proverb goes,[124] they look without looking and hear without hearing, while others do what they do in such a way that they are clearly watchful and feel ashamed. As a result, the common cause of the city's prosperity remains and has been its concord. [90] These habits so nobly ingrained in your nature and character Aristogeiton shakes, destroys, and tosses away.[125] What the victims of misfortune do without making a sound,[126] this man performs with everything but bells tied to him.[127] Neither the *prytanis*, nor the herald, nor the president (*epistatēs*), nor the presiding tribe can control this man.[128] [91] When one of you becomes irritated by his outrageous behavior and says: "This man here is doing this when he owes this debt to the Treasury!" "What of it? Isn't so-and-so a debtor?" says everyone, subtly adding the name of his en-

---

[123] The adverb *syngenikōs* ("like a family") occurs nowhere else in Athenian forensic oratory.

[124] The word *paroimia* ("proverb") occurs nowhere else in Athenian forensic oratory.

[125] The verb *metarhiptō* ("toss away") occurs nowhere else in Athenian forensic oratory.

[126] The adverb *apsophētei* ("without a sound") occurs nowhere else in Athenian forensic oratory.

[127] The word *kōdōn* ("bell") occurs nowhere else in Athenian forensic oratory.

[128] This appears to refer to officials who kept order at meetings of the Assembly. Before around 380 BCE the *prytaneis* presided over these meetings of the Assembly, but after this a board of *proedroi* headed by an *epistatēs* presided over meetings. The use of the singular *prytanis* makes little sense next to the phrase *proedreuousa phylē* ("presiding tribe") because the *proedreuousa phylē* consisted of all the *prytaneis*. The author may have been influenced by the use of the term at Thuc. 6.14, which reflected practice in 415 BCE but was no longer in effect in the late fourth century BCE. The mistakes about procedure are another sign of forgery.

emy. And thus this man's villainy is responsible for the slanders made because of him against people quite unlike him.

[92] It remains for those wishing to get rid of this man and having caught him in a clear and obvious violation of the laws to sentence him to death or, if not, to impose so great a monetary penalty that he will not be able to pay it. There is no other way to get rid of him; you know it for certain. [93] In fact, men of Athens, one would see that the best and most moderate men by nature willingly do what they should, but those not as good without being called wicked are careful not to do wrong because they fear you and are hurt by shameful words and reproaches. But they say that those men who are the most wicked and called accursed[129] are disciplined by suffering. [94] This Aristogeiton here so much surpasses all men in wickedness that even when he suffers, he does not take the warning,[130] but has been caught again for the same crimes and acts of greed. Indeed, he deserves your anger much more now than before: then he thought that he should only propose illegal motions, but now he thinks that he should do everything, make accusations, speak, slander, tell lies, demand the death penalty, bring denunciations (*eisangelias*), and insult those with rights while he is in debt to the Treasury. Nothing is more shocking than he is.

[95] Giving him advice is lunacy: would the man who never yields or turns aside at the shouts the entire persons use to warn people who irritate them quickly pay attention to something said by one person? Incurable, men of Athens, is the problem with this man. Just as doctors, when they see a cancer or an ulcer or some incurable disease,[131] burn or cut it out, all of you in the same way should ban this monster, throw him out off the city, destroy him, and not wait for something to happen (may this not hap-

---

[129]The adjective *exagistos* ("accursed") occurs nowhere else in Athenian forensic oratory.

[130]For the proverbial idea of learning by suffering, see Aeschylus *Agamemnon* 177.

[131]Although Demosthenes uses some medical language (see Wooten 1979), one never finds such technical medical terms for diseases in Athenian forensic oratory.

pen to any individual or to the community), but take precautions. [96] Look at it this way. Perhaps none of you has been bitten by a viper or tarantula,[132] and may this never happen to you. But nevertheless you kill all creatures like this when you see them. In similar fashion, men of Athens, when you see a spiteful blackmailer, a man with a viper's nature, do not wait for him to bite each of you, but let anyone who happens to be there punish him.

[97] Lycurgus called on Athena and the Mother of the Gods to witness, and he was right. I summon your ancestors and their virtues, whose memory time has not erased, and rightly so. In their public life, they did not allow themselves to cooperate with the wickedest men and blackmailers; they did not practice envy toward each other even behind the walls of their houses,[133] but honored politicians and private citizens who were virtuous and good and hated and punished the evil and the bold. For these reasons they were athletes of noble deeds.[134]

[98] After saying one more thing, I wish to stop.[135] Soon you will leave the court, and those standing around, both foreigners and citizens, will see you. They will look at you one by one and recognize by your expression[136] those who voted to acquit. What will you then say, men of Athens, if you leave after casting aside the laws? With what expression or look will you return the gaze of each man? [99] How will you go to the Metroon if you wish for some reason? Surely each one of you individually will not approach the laws as if they were sovereign if you leave without all of you collectively making them strong? How will you go up to

---

[132]The terms *echis* ("viper") and *phalangion* ("tarantula") occur here and nowhere else in Athenian forensic oratory.

[133]On the Athenians as lacking in envy, see Thuc. 2.37.

[134]Here we find another metaphor. Demosthenes (18.319) uses the word "athlete" but never uses it in a metaphor like this one in a forensic speech.

[135]The author here imitates the language Demosthenes uses to introduce the *epilogos*. Cf. Dem. 20.154, 21.184.

[136]The verb *physiognōmoneō* ("recognize by one's expression") never occurs in Athenian forensic oratory. The practice of "reading the soul" through a study of one's physiognomy was a philosophical idea, would have been out of place in a speech delivered in court. See Swain 2007.

the Acropolis on the first day of the month[137] and each of you pray to the gods for blessing for the city and for himself when he and his noble father are there and after you have made a decision contrary to your oaths and the records there? [100] What will you say, men of Athens, what will you say if someone recognizes that you acquitted him? What will you say? That you like him? Who will dare to say that? Who will wish to inherit a share of his wickedness with its curse and ill repute? That he himself did not vote to acquit? Certainly you will curse the men who acquitted him, and each one of you proving in this way that he was not among them. [101] Why should one do this when everyone can speak respectfully and pray for every kind of blessing for everyone, you for yourselves, and all other Athenians for you, and I will add even foreigners, children, and wives. His malice has struck, yes, struck everyone;[138] everyone wishes to get rid of his wickedness and to see him punished.

## AGAINST ARISTOGEITON II

[1] Because this man here Aristogeiton owes money to the Treasury and does not have the rights of a citizen and because the laws explicitly forbid such people to speak, he has been clearly denounced, men of Athens. You must restrain and prohibit all men who break the law, above all those who are in office and are active in politics. [2] These men are responsible for damaging the public interest if they are bad but bring the greatest benefits to the city if they are honest and wish to abide by the laws. If you give those who manage public business the opportunity just once to break the law and to despise what has been determined to be just, all those who share in our city must feel its effects. [3] It is just like errors that occur on ships when they are sailing: when one

---

[137] The first day of each month in Athens (and other Greek communities: see Herod. 6.57) was a festival day. Offerings called *epimēnia* consisting of a honey cake were made on the Acropolis to a snake that lived there (Herod. 8.41). See Mikalson 1975: 14–15.

[138] The word *kakopragmosynē* ("malice") occurs nowhere else in Athenian forensic oratory.

of the sailors makes a mistake, he causes little damage, but when the helmsman blunders, he causes a disaster affecting all the passengers.[139] In the same way, the wrongs done by private citizens do not cause damage to the people but only for themselves, while the wrongs done by officials and those in politics affect everyone. [4] For this reason, Solon made retribution slow for private citizens, but swift for officials and leaders of the people[140] because he thought that it was possible to gain one's rights even after a long time, but it was not possible to wait in the case of the latter. For there is no opportunity to punish in the future once the constitution has been overthrown.

No person is so shameless or so lacking in respect for you that he will attempt to deny these principles of justice with one exception: this man here Aristogeiton and his evil character. On the contrary, we will discover that when you convict officials and politicians just once, they then follow these rules.[141] [5] When certain officials are removed from office, they immediately stop holding office and remove their crowns.[142] All the *thesmothetai* who cannot go up to the Areopagus avoid being removed by force and abide by your decisions. And rightly so: just as they believe that private citizens should obey them when they are in office, in the same way when they become private citizens again, they would rightly obey the laws that rule our city. [6] All men active in political life, if you wish to examine their conduct starting in ancient times, clearly abide by your principles of justice. They say that Aristides when sent into exile lived on Aegina until the people brought him back, and Miltiades and Pericles when they owed fines, one thirty talents, the other fifty talents, paid the money

---

[139]On the image of the ship as state, see Dem. 19.250; Aes. 3.158 with Brock 2013: 53–68.

[140]This is the only passage in which the term *dēmagōgos* ("leader of the people") appears in the Demosthenic corpus.

[141]For the theme of the influence of judicial verdicts on the conduct of citizens, see E. M. Harris 2013a: 173–174.

[142]Those who held office wore crowns to distinguish them from private citizens. See Dem. 21.31–33.

and in this way continued to speak in public.[143] [7] The most shocking thing that could happen would be that those who have brought you the most and greatest benefits should not gain this reward, the right to break the law, so that this man who has done nothing good and who violates your established laws has clearly gained the right from you to break the law, which is contrary to the public interest and to justice. But why should I speak about the distant past? Compare the men of your own time to see if any of them has acted this shamefully. You could find no one if you wish to examine them closely.

[8] Apart from this, when someone brings a public charge against a decree or a law before the *thesmothetai*, the law or the decree is repealed, and the one who enacted or proposed the decree or law feels no shame in submitting to this decision, but abides by whatever you vote even if he is the leading citizen in terms of his ability either to speak or to act. And yet how is it not strange for those measures that all of you voted when you met to be repealed by the laws and yet for you to think it necessary to make Aristogeiton's wish to violate the law superior to the laws themselves? [9] By contrast, when someone brings a case to court and does not gain one-fifth of the votes, for which the laws order as a punishment that in the future he lose the right to bring public charges, to make arrests, or to bring him to an official (*ephēgeisthai*), in the same way no one of those subject to these penalties thinks that he should carry out these procedures.[144] But for Aristogeiton, alone out of everyone it seems, no court and no law is superior to his own wishes. [10] Neither you nor your ancestors ever changed

---

[143]Aristides was ostracized around 483 but allowed to return as the result of a measure passed during the Persian invasion (*Ath. Pol.* 22.7–8). According to Herodotus (6.136), Miltiades was accused by Xanthippus and fined fifty talents. According to Thucydides (2.65.3), Pericles was removed from office and sentenced to a fine in 430, but was reelected soon afterwards.

[144]The penalty for bringing a public charge and failing to gain one-fifth of the votes cast at the trial was a fine of one thousand drachmas and loss of the right to bring any public charges again. See E. M. Harris 2006: 405–422.

your mind about preserving all these rules. For what protects the democracy is victory over our enemies either through giving advice or by fighting and submission to the laws either by choice or by compulsion. That this is the way things should be done, even this man has agreed. [11] After the disasters at Chaeronea struck the Greeks, and the city was reduced to the gravest danger to protect our land, when Hyperides proposed that those who had lost their rights would regain them so that everyone would be united and fight enthusiastically to protect freedom if any danger, however great, faced the city, Aristogeiton brought a charge of passing an illegal decree against the proposal and challenged it in court.[145] [12] And yet how is it not shocking that this Aristogeiton here did not agree that any citizen recover his rights to defend the country, yet now demands to receive from you this very reward for his own lawbreaking? Yet that decree was much more lawful and more just than the one you are asking these men here to vote. [13] The one was equal and common for all citizens; the other was unequal and brought an advantage for you alone. The aim of the former was that there be no peace whose terms would place one person in control of the constitution; the aim of the other was that you alone be given the power to violate with impunity the decisions and laws of these men here, which had been handed down by the ancestors, and to do whatever you wish. [14] I would like to ask you whether the accusation he brought was legal and just or the very opposite, unjust and illegal. If it was against our interests and harmful for the people, he would for this very reason deserve to die. If his charge was advantageous and beneficial for the many, why are you

---

[145]After the defeat at Chaeronea, Hyperides proposed that the Athenians free their slaves and draft them into the army. See also Hyperides fragments 27–39 Kenyon; Lycurgus *Against Leocrates* 41. The new papyrus text of Hyperides' *Against Diondas* indicates that Diondas, not Aristogeiton, brought the case against Hyperides. See Horváth 2014: 81, 87. I would like to thank J. Kucharski for drawing my attention to this passage. This is another indication that this speech was a later forgery. [Plut.] *Lives of the Ten Orators* 848f–849a states that Aristogeiton brought a *graphē paranomōn* against this decree, but is probably relying on this passage. This would indicate that *Against Aristogeiton* II was written before the second century CE.

now asking these men to vote the opposite of what you yourself proposed? But that was neither just, nor legal, nor in the interests of all. [15] I see that you, men of Athens, hold this view also about your own interests. For you have voted in the past to condemn in many denunciations against private individuals. And yet how is it not shocking that you have the power to examine the laws carefully, but those who meddle and irritate everyone in common and claim to be superior to everyone have it so easy?

[16] There is surely no one of you who accepts that the situation should be as I say it should but because he is respectable and useful to you and thinks that it must be overlooked that he is breaking the law. In my opinion, Lycurgus has amply demonstrated in the previous speech that he is wicked and his character is shockingly unjust. Anyone can see from his policies that he is not helpful. [17] Which of the people whom he has charged has he brought into court and convicted? What sort of resources has he provided for you? What decree has he proposed that you found convincing yet later did not choose to regret? It's like this: he is so inept and his character so barbaric that when he sees you angry more than you should be, he adapts his advice to suit your anger and opposes what the situation calls for. [18] A politician working on your behalf should not follow the sudden shifts in mood that come upon you and stir your anger but look to reasoning, the facts, and the opportunities that exist. The former tends to change quickly, but the latter to endure and remain for a long time. But this man pays no attention to any of these precepts and tests the secrets of the constitution[146] so that he is forced to enact and then repeal the same measures.

[19] Perhaps because he always prefers to slander and shout down and find fault with everyone's speeches, it now is a good idea to keep him around. But by the goddess Athena, what happens on the speaker's platform, judges, is a disgrace for the city, and the madness of these men has made politics disgraceful for the honest citizens among you. If anyone of you likes what has

---

[146]This phrase "secrets of the constitution" is never found in Athenian oratory.

happened, you will not be at a loss for people to act this way because even now the speaker's platform is full of them. It is not difficult to criticize those who give you advice, but it is difficult to give advice and to persuade you to vote for something that needs to be done. [20] Moreover, if he had not deceived you earlier by using the same arguments when he was on trial for the previous denunciation, then it would not be right to allow him some concession contrary to the laws now in effect (one should not grant some the right to violate the laws while demanding that others obey them). But perhaps it would be more reasonable to trust him, to do him this favor, and to overlook one of these offenses. [21] But after you then let him go on the basis of what you agreed were hopes, then a little later you punished this same man for not doing and saying what is best for the people, what reasonable excuse is left for you if you are now being deceived?[147] Why should you believe his words about what you yourselves have experienced through his actions? Perhaps it is necessary to judge from what is said those things that you have not yet been able to examine carefully on your own. [22] I myself am astonished at men who entrust their private property to men who have been honest for many years, but turn over public interests of the city to those who have been proven to be worthless by common agreement.[148] No one would think of having a half-breed and worthless dog protecting his flock.[149] Yet some say that we should send as guards over politicians men who pretend to denounce wrongdoers but require the maximum amount of surveillance themselves.

[23] If you are sensible, you will keep this in mind and say goodbye to men who claim to be your friends. You will use every available means to make sure that you give no one the right to annul your laws, above all to none of those who pretend that they can speak and draft proposals for your benefit. How com-

---

[147] This passage states that Aristogeiton was acquitted at the first *endeixis* but convicted on the second, but this is contradicted by *Against Aristogeiton* I 67, which states that he was convicted at the previous *endeixis*.

[148] For a similar view, see Isoc. 8.52.

[149] For the image of the watchdog, see *Against Aristogeiton* I 40n.

pletely shocking is it for our ancestors to have had the courage to die to stop the laws from being destroyed, but for you not to punish those who break them? Or for them to erect in the Agora a bronze statue of Solon who wrote the laws,[150] but for you clearly to despise the laws on account of which he happened to gain exceptional honors? [24] How could this situation make any sense if you are angry with criminals when you pass laws, but you let them go unpunished after catching them when their guilt is obvious? And for one lawgiver acting on your behalf to be hated by worthless men but for you not even to show that you hate evil men when you meet together to protect yourselves but to be defeated by one man's bad character? And for you to stipulate death as the punishment if anyone cites a law that does not exist,[151] but to put those who place the laws that do exist in the category of those that do not, these you let go unpunished? [25] You would realize very precisely what a great advantage it is to obey the established laws and what a great evil it is to despise and not obey them, if you should consider the benefits that accrue from the laws separately from the consequences of lawlessness by keeping both before your eyes. You will find that from the latter come madness, lack of self-control, and greed: from the former good sense, self-control, and justice. [26] It is obvious: we can see that the best-run cities are those that had the best legislators. For the illnesses of the body are cured by the inventions of doctors, but the thoughts of legislators amputate the wildness of the soul.[152] We will never find anything holy or worthwhile that does not partake of the law, [27] because law and order, if we should be-

---

[150]There was a statue of Solon on Salamis (not in the Agora) in the fourth century. In 346 BCE Aeschines (1.25–26) assumed that it was erected there during Solon's day, but Demosthenes (19.251–254) states it was erected less than fifty years before, that is, after 396 BCE. Aelian (*Varia Historica* 8.16) mentions a statue of Solon in the Agora, but he may be drawing on this passage. There is no other evidence for a statue of Solon in the Agora.

[151]There is no other evidence for this statute in our sources.

[152]On medical imagery in political discourse, see Brock 2013: 69–82. Legislators are never compared to doctors in Athenian forensic oratory.

lieve what we observe, clearly control the entire universe, divine actions, and the so-called seasons.[153] Rouse yourselves to action, support the laws, and vote to condemn those who chose to commit impiety against the divine. If you do this, you will do your duty and cast the best vote.

---

[153]This view that law forms part of the natural order of the physical world is a philosophical idea, which is never found in Attic oratory.

# BIBLIOGRAPHY FOR THIS VOLUME

Allen, D., 2000: "Changing the Authoritative Voice: Lycurgus' *Against Leocrates*," *Classical Antiquity* 19.1: 5–33.

Ando, C., and J. Rüpke, eds., 2015: *Public and Private in Ancient Mediterranean Law and Religion*. Berlin.

Archibald, Z. H., 1998: *The Odrysian Kingdom of Thrace: Orpheus Unmasked*. Oxford.

Azoulay, V., 2014: *Les tyrannicides d'Athènes: vie et mort de deux statues*. Paris.

Azoulay, V., and P. Ismard, eds., 2011: *Clisthène et Lycurge d'Athènes: autour du politique dans la cité classique*. Paris.

Badian, E., 1983: "Philip II and Thrace," *Pulpudeva* 4: 51–71.

Badian, E., 1991: "The King's Peace," in Flower and Toher (1991): 25–48.

Badian, E., 2000: "The Road to Prominence," in Worthington (2000): 9–44.

Bakewell, G., and J. Sickinger, eds., 2003: *Gestures: Essays in Ancient History, Literature, and Philosophy presented to Alan L. Boegehold on the Occasion of his Retirement and His Seventy-fifth Birthday*. Oxford.

Balot, R. K., 2001: *Greed and Injustice in Classical Athens*. Princeton, NJ.

Best, J., 1969: *Thracian Peltasts and Their Influence on Greek Warfare*. Groningen.

Bettalli, M., 2013: *Mercenari: il mestiere delle armi nel mondo greco antico: età arcaica e classica*. Rome.

Bianco, E., 2002: "Carete: cane del popolo?" *Ancient Society* 32: 1–28.

Bianco, E., 2014: "Caridemo: storia di un *freelance*," *Erga-Logoi* 2: 7–29.

Bingham, T., 2010: *The Rule of Law*. London.

Blass, F., 1897–1898: *Die attische Beredsamkeit*. Leipzig.

Blok, J., 2010: "Deme Accounts and the Meaning of *hosios* Money in Fifth-Century Athens," *Mnemosyne* 63: 61–93.

Blok, J. H., and A. P. M. H. Lardinois, eds., 2006: *Solon of Athens: New Historical and Philological Approaches*. Brill.

Boeckh, A., 1840: *Urkunden über das Seewesen*. Berlin.

Bogaert, R., 1974: "Die Krise der Banken in Athen im 4. Jahrhundert v. u. Z.," in Welskopf 1974: 2.521–530.

Bommelaer, J. F., 1997: *Marmaria: le sanctuaire d'Athéna à Delphes*. Athens.

Borza, E. N., 1992: *In the Shadow of Olympus: The Emergence of Macedon*. Princeton, NJ.

Braun, R., 1873: "De duabus adversus Aristogeitonem orationibus, quas Demosthenis scripsisse fertur." Diss. Greifswald.

de Brauw, M., 2001–2002: "Listen to the Laws Themselves: Citation of Law and Portrayal of Character in Attic Oratory," *Classical Journal* 97: 161–176.

Bravo, B., 1982: "*Androlēpsíai*. La 'prise d'hommes' comme vengeance d'un meurtre commis dans une cité étrangère," in Modrzejewski and Liebs 1982: 131–156.

Bremmer, J., 1983: "Scapegoat Rituals in Ancient Greece," *Harvard Studies in Classical Philology* 87: 299–320.

Brenne, S., 2001: *Ostrakismos und Prominenz in Athen: Attische Bürger des 5. Jhs. v. Chr. auf den Ostraka*. Vienna.

Bresson, A., 2000: *La cité marchande*. Bordeaux.

Brock, R., 2013: *Greek Political Imagery from Homer to Aristotle*. New York.

Brun, P., 2000: *L'orateur Démade: essai d'histoire et d'historiographie*. Bordeaux.

Brunt, P. A., 1969: "Euboea in the Time of Philip II," *Classical Quarterly* 19: 245–265.

Buckler, J., 1980: *The Theban Hegemony, 371–362 BC*. Cambridge, MA.

Buckler, J., 1989: *Philip II and the Sacred War (Mnemosyne Supplement 108)*. Leiden.

Buckler, J., 2003: *Aegean Greece in the Fourth Century* BC. Leiden.

Bugh, G. 1988: *The Horsemen of Athens*. Princeton, NJ.

Bultrighini, U., 1999: *"Maledetta" Democrazia: studi su Crizia*. Alessandria.

Burke, E. M., 2002: "The Early Political Speeches of Demosthenes: Elite Bias in the Response to Economic Crisis," *Classical Antiquity* 21: 163–193.

Canevaro, M., 2009: "L'accusa contro Leptine: crisi economica e consensus post-bellico," *Quaderni del Dipartimento di Filologia, Linguistica, e Tradizione Classica A. Rostagni* n.s. 8: 117–141.

Canevaro, M., 2012: Review-article of Wohl 2010. *Rivista di diritto ellencio* 2: 439–444.

Canevaro, M., 2013a: *The Documents in the Attic Orators: Laws and Decrees in the Public Speeches of the Demosthenic Corpus.* Oxford.

Canevaro, M., 2013b: "*Nomothesia* in Classical Athens: What Sources Should We Believe?" *Classical Quarterly* 63: 139–160.

Canevaro, M., 2013c: "Thieves, Parent Abusers, Draft Dodgers . . . and Homicides? The Authenticity of Dem. 24.105," *Historia* 62: 25–47.

Canevaro, M., 2016a: *Demostene. Contro Leptine. Introduzione, Traduzione e Commento.* Berlin.

Canevaro, M., 2016b: "The Procedure of Demosthenes' *Against Leptines*: How to Repeal (and Replace) an Existing Law," *Journal of Hellenic Studies* 136, 39–58.

Canevaro, M., forthcoming a: "The Documents in the Attic Orators: Early Antiquarians and Unintentional Forgers," in Papy and Gielen forthcoming.

Canevaro, M., forthcoming b: "The Authenticity of the Document at Dem. 24.20–23, the Procedures of *Nomothesia* and the so-called ἐπιχειροτονία τῶν νόμων" *Klio*.

Canevaro, M., and E. M. Harris, 2012: "The Documents in Andocides' *On the Mysteries*," *Classical Quarterly* 62: 98–129.

Canevaro, M., and E. M. Harris, 2016: "The Authenticity of the Documents at Andocides' *On the Mysteries* 77–79 and 83–84" *Dike* 19 (forthcoming).

Canevaro, M., and D. Lewis, 2014: "*Khoris oikountes* and the Obligation of Freedmen in Late Classical and Early Hellenistic Athens," *Incidenza dell' antico: dialoghi di storia greca* 12: 91–121.

Cantarella, E., ed., 2007: *Symposion 2005: Vorträge zur griechischen und hellenistischen Rechtsgeschichte.* Vienna.

Capdetrey, L., and C. Hasenohr, eds., 2012: *Agoranomes et édiles: institutions et marchés antiques.* Paris.

Carawan, E., 1984: "*Akriton Apokteinein*: Execution without Trial in Fourth-Century Athens," *Greek, Roman and Byzantine Studies* 25: 111–121.

Carawan, E., 1998: *Rhetoric and the Law of Draco.* Oxford.

Carawan, E., ed., 2007: *Oxford Readings in the Attic Orators.* Oxford.

Carey, C., 1995: "Rape and Adultery in Athenian Law," *Classical Quarterly* 45: 407–417.

Cargill, J. L., 1981: *The Second Athenian League: Empire or Free Alliance?* Berkeley.

Carlier, P., 1990: *Démosthéne.* Paris.

Carmigiato, A., 1999: "A proposito dell'autenticità della XXV orazione del corpus demostenico (*Contro Aristogitone* I)," *Aevum Antiquum* 12: 91–112.

Cartledge, P., P. Millett, and S. C. Todd, eds., 1990: Nomos: *Essays in Athenian Law, Politics, and Society.* Cambridge.

Cartledge, P., E. E. Cohen, and L. Foxhall, eds., 2002: *Money, Labour and Land. Approaches to the Economies of Ancient Greece.* London.

Casabona, J., 1966: *Recherches sur le vocabulaire des sacrifices en grec des origines à la fin de l'époque classique.* Aix-en-Provence.

Cawkwell, G. L., 1962: "Notes on the Social War," *Classica et Mediaevalia* 23: 34–49.

Cawkwell, G. L., 1963: "Eubulus," *Journal of Hellenic Studies* 83: 47–67.

Cawkwell, G. L., 1981: "Notes on the Failure of the Second Athenian Confederacy," *Journal of Hellenic Studies* 101: 40–55.

Ceccarelli, P., 2013: "The Use (and Abuse) of Letters in the Speeches of the Attic Orators," in Yiftach-Firanko 2013: 83–104.

Charles, J. F., 1938: "Statutes of Limitations at Athens." Dissertation. University of Chicago.

Christ, M. R., 1998: *The Litigious Athenian.* Baltimore.

Cohen, D., 1983: *Theft in Athenian Law.* Munich.

Cohen, D., 1995: *Law, Violence and Community in Classical Athens.* Cambridge.

Cohen, D., ed., 2002: *Demokratie, Recht, und soziale Kontrolle im klassischen Athen (Schriften des Historischen Kollegs. Kolloquien 49).* Munich.

Cohen, E. E., 1992: *Athenian Economy and Society: A Banking Perspective.* Princeton, NJ.

Conwell, D. H., 2008: *Connecting a City to the Sea: the History of the Athenian Long Walls.* Leiden.

Cooper, C., 2000: "Philosophers, Politics and Academics: Demosthenes' oratorical reputation in antiquity," in Worthington 2000: 224–245.

Couvenhes, J.-C., 2012: "L'introduction des archers scythes, esclaves publics, à Athènes: la date et l'agent d'un transfert culturel," in Legras 2012: 99–118.

Cribiore, R., 2001: *Gymnastics of the Mind: Greek Education in Hellenistic and Roman Egypt.* Princeton, NJ.

Dareste, R., 1875: *Les plaidoyers civils de Démosthène/traduits en français, avec arguments et notes.* 2 vols. Paris.

Daverio Rocchi, G., 1988: *Frontiera e confini nella Grecia antica.* Rome.

Davies, J. K., 1971: *Athenian Propertied Families, 600–300 BC.* Oxford.

Davis, G., 2011: "*Axones* and *Kyrbeis*: A New Answer to an Old Problem," *Historia* 60.1: 1–35.

Deacy, S., and K. F. Pierce, eds., 1997: *Rape in Antiquity: Sexual Violence in the Greek and Roman Worlds.* London.

Dmitriev, S., 2011: *The Greek Slogan of Freedom and Early Roman Politics in Greece.* Oxford.

Dorjahn, A. P., 1935: "The Anticipation of Arguments in Athenian Courts," *Transactions of the American Philological Association* 66: 275–295.

Dover, K. J., ed., 1968a: *Aristophanes: Clouds.* Oxford.

Dover, K. J., 1968b: *Lysias and the Corpus Lysiacum.* Berkeley.

Dreher, M., 1995: *Hegemon und Symmachoi: Untersuchungen zum zweiten athenischen Seebund.* Berlin.

Drerup, E., 1898: "Über die bei den attischen Rednern eingelegten urkunden," *Jahrbücher für classische Philologie*, Suppl. 24: 221–336.

Drerup, E., 1923: *Demosthenes im Urteile des Altertums*. Würzburg.

Ducat, J., 1990: *Les hilotes* (*Bulletin de Correspondance Hellénique Supplément 20*). Paris.

Ducat, J., 1994: *Les Pénestes de Thessalie*. Paris.

Edwards, M., 1995: *Greek Orators IV: Andocides*. Warminster.

Engen, D. T., 2010: *Honor and Profit: Athenian Trade Policy and the Economy and Society of Greece, 415–307 B.C.E.* Ann Arbor, MI.

Faraguna, M., 2011: "Lycurgan Athens?" in Azoulay and Ismard 2011: 67–88.

Faraguna, M., ed., 2013: *Legal Documents in the Ancient World*. Trieste.

Feyel, C., 2009: *Δοκιμασία: La place et le rôle de l'examen préliminaire dans les institutions des cités grecques*. Nancy.

Finley, M. I., 1985: *Studies in Land and Credit in Ancient Athens, 500–200 B.C.* Revised with a new introduction by P. Millett. New Brunswick, NJ.

Flensted-Jensen, P., T. Nielsen, and L. Rubinstein, eds., 2000: *Polis and Politics: Studies in Ancient Greek History*. Copenhagen.

Flower, M. A., and M. Toher, eds., 1991: *Georgica: Greek Studies in Honour of George Cawkwell*. London.

Gabrielsen, V., 1981: *Remuneration of State Officials in Fourth Century B.C. Athens*. Odense.

Gabrielsen, V., 1994: *Financing the Athenian Fleet: Public Taxation and Social Relations*. Baltimore.

Gagarin, M., 1978: "Self-Defence in Athenian Homicide Law," *Greek, Roman and Byzantine Studies* 19: 111–120.

Gagarin, M., 1981: *Drakon and Early Athenian Homicide Law*. New Haven, CT.

Gagarin, M., 2008: *Writing Greek Law*. Cambridge.

Gagarin, M., 2012: "Law, Politics, and the Question of Relevance in the Case *On the Crown*," *Classical Antiquity* 31.2: 293–314.

Garnsey, P., 1988: *Famine and Food Supply in the Graeco-Roman World: Responses to Risk and Crisis*. Cambridge.

Gauthier, P., 1976: *Un commentaire historique sur les Poroi de Xénophon*. Paris.

Gentili, B., and F. Perusini, 2002: *Le orse di Brauron: un rituale di iniziazione femminile nel santuario di Artemide*. Pisa.

Gernet, L., and J. Humbert, 1959: *Démosthène: plaidoyers politiques*. Volume 2. Paris.

Giannadaki, I., 2014: "The Time Limit (*Prothesmia*) in the *Graphe Paranomon*," *Dike* 17: 15–34.

Gibson, C. A., 2002: *Interpreting a Classic: Demosthenes and His Ancient Commentators*. Berkeley.

Grafton, A., 1990: *Forgers and Critics: Creativity and Duplicity in Western Scholarship*. Princeton, NJ.

Hamel, D., 1998: *Athenian Generals: Military Authority in the Classical Period* (*Mnemosyne Supplement* 182). Brill.

Hammond, N. G. L., 1972–1988: *A History of Macedonia*. Oxford.

Hansen, M. H., 1974: *The Sovereignty of the People's Court in Athens in the Fourth Century B.C. and the Public Action against Unconstitutional Proposals*. Odense.

Hansen, M. H., 1975: Eisangelia*: The Sovereignty of the People's Court in Athens in the Fourth Century B.C. and the Impeachment of Generals and Politicians*. Odense.

Hansen, M. H., 1976: *Apagoge, Endeixis, and Ephegesis against Kakourgoi, Atimoi, and Pheugontes: A Study in the Athenian Administration of Justice in the Fourth Century B.C.* Odense.

Hansen, M. H., 1978: "*Nomos* and *psephisma* in Fourth-Century Athens," *Greek, Roman and Byzantine Studies* 19: 315–330.

Hansen, M. H., 1979: "*Misthos* for Magistrates in Fourth Century Athens," *Symbolae Osloenses* 54: 5–22.

Hansen, M. H., 1979–1980: "Athenian *Nomothesia* in the Fourth Century BC and Demosthenes' Speech *Against Leptines*," *Classica et Mediaevalia* 32: 87–104.

Hansen, M. H., 1980: "Perquisites for Magistrates in Fourth Century Athens," *Classica et Mediaevalia* 32: 105–25.

Hansen, M. H., 1982: "When Did the Athenian *Ecclesia* Meet?" *Greek, Roman and Byzantine Studies* 23:331–350.

Hansen, M. H., 1983: *The Athenian Ecclesia: A Collection of Articles 1976–1983* (*Opuscula Graecolatina* 26). Copenhagen.

Hansen, M. H., 1987: "*Graphe Paranomon* against *Psephismata* not yet Passed by the Ekklesia," *Classica et Mediaevalia* 38: 63–73.

Hansen, M. H., 1991: *The Athenian Democracy in the Age of Demosthenes*. Oxford.

Hansen, M. H., ed., 2009: *Démocratie athénienne, démocratie moderne: tradition et influences*. Geneva.

Hansen, M. H., 2014: "*Misthos* for Magistrates in Fourth Century Athens?" *Greek, Roman and Byzantine Studies* 54: 404–419.

Hansen, M. H., 2015: "Is Patrokleides' Decree (Andoc. 1.77–79) a Genuine Document?" *Greek, Roman and Byzantine Studies* 55: 884–901.

Hansen, M. H., 2016a: "The Authenticity of the Law about *Nomothesia* Inserted in Demosthenes *Against Timokrates* 20–23," *Greek, Roman and Byzantine Studies* 56: 438–474.

Hansen, M. H., 2016b: "Is Teisamenos' Decree (Andoc. 1.83–84) a Genuine Document?" *Greek, Roman and Byzantine Studies* 56: 34–48.

Hansen, M. H., and T. Heine Nielsen, eds., 2004: *An Inventory of Archaic and Classical* Poleis. Oxford.

Hansen, M. H., and F. Mitchel, 1984: "The Number of *Ecclesiai* in Fourth-Century Athens," *Symbolae Osloenses* 59: 13–19.

Harding, P., 1976: "Androtion's Political Career," *Historia* 25: 186–200.

Harding, P., 2006: *Didymos on Demosthenes: Introduction, Text, Translation and Commentary*. Oxford.

Harris, D., 1995: *The Treasures of the Parthenon and Erechtheion*. Oxford.

Harris, E. M., 1989: "Iphicrates at the Court of Cotys," *American Journal of Philology* 110: 264–271.

Harris, E. M., 1990: "The Constitution of the Five Thousand," *Harvard Studies in Classical Philology* 93: 243–280.

Harris, E. M., 1995: *Aeschines and Athenian Politics*. New York.

Harris, E. M., 1998: Review of Deacey and Pierce 1997. *Échos du monde classique/Classical Views* 40 (16): 483–496.

Harris, E. M., 1999: "Notes on the New Grain-Tax Law," *Zeitschrift für Papyrologie und Epigraphik* 128: 269–272.

Harris, E. M., 2000: "The Authenticity of Andocides' *De Pace*: A Subversive Essay," in Flensted-Jensen, Nielsen, and Rubinstein 2000: 479–506.

Harris, E. M., 2002: "Workshop, Marketplace and Household:

The Nature of Technical Specialization in Classical Athens and its Influence on Economy and Society," in Cartledge, Cohen, and Foxhall 2002: 67–99.

Harris, E. M., 2006: *Democracy and the Rule of Law in Classical Athens: Essays on Law, Society, and Politics*. Cambridge.

Harris, E. M., 2008: *Demosthenes Speeches 20-22*. Austin TX.

Harris, E. M., 2009/2010: Review-article of Lanni 2006. *Dike* 12/13: 323–331.

Harris, E. M., 2010: "Is Oedipus Guilty? Sophocles and Athenian Homicide Law," in Harris, Leão, and Rhodes 2010: 122–146.

Harris, E. M., 2013a: *The Rule of Law in Action in Democratic Athens*. Oxford.

Harris, E. M., 2013b: "The Plaint in Athenian Law and Legal Procedure," in Faraguna 2013: 143–162.

Harris, E. M., 2013/2014: "The Authenticity of the Document at Andocides 1.96–98," *Tekmeria* 12: 121–153.

Harris, E. M., 2015: "The Family, the Community and Murder: The Role of Pollution in Athenian Homicide Law," in Ando and Rüpke 2015: 11–35.

Harris, E. M., 2016a: "From Democracy to the Rule of Law?" in Tiersch 2016: 71–84.

Harris, E. M., 2016b: "The Nature of Self-Defense in Draco's Homicide Law: The Restoration of *IG* I³ 104, lines 33–35," *Hyperboreus* 22.2: 203–216.

Harris, E. M., forthcoming a: "The Athenian View of an Athenian Trial" in Carey and Giannadaki, eds., *The Use and Abuse of Law*.

Harris, E. M., forthcoming b: "Applying the Law about the Award of Crowns to Magistrates (Aeschin. 3.9–31; Dem. 18, 113–117): Epigraphic Evidence for the Legal Arguments at the Trial of Ctesiphon," in *Zeitschrift für Papyrologie und Epigraphik*.

Harris, E. M., and L. Rubinstein, eds., 2004: *The Law and the Courts in Ancient Greece*. London.

Harris, E. M., D. Leão, and P. J. Rhodes, eds., 2010: *Law and Drama in Ancient Greece*. London.

Harris, E. M., and G. Thür, eds., 2008: *Symposion 2007: Vorträge zur griechischen und hellenistischen Rechtsgeschichte*. Vienna.

246 DEMOSTHENES, SPEECHES 23–26

Harrison, A. R. W., 1968: *The Law of Athens: Family and Property*. Oxford.

Harrison, A. R. W., 1971: *The Law of Athens: Procedure*. Oxford.

Harvey, D., 1990: "The Sycophant and Sycophancy: Vexatious Redefinition?" in Cartledge, Millett, and Todd 1990: 103–121.

Heinimann, F., 1965: Nomos *und* Physis: *Herkunft und Bedeutung einer Antithese im griechischen Denken des 5. Jahrhunderts*. Basel.

Henry, A. S., 1977: *The Prescripts of Athenian Decrees*. Leiden.

Herman, G., ed., 2011: *Stability and Crisis in the Athenian Democracy* (*Historia Einzelschriften 220*). Stuttgart.

Heskel, J., 1996: "Philip II and Argaios: A Pretender's Story," in Wallace and Harris 1996: 37–56.

Heskel, J., 1997: *The North Aegean Wars, 371–360 B.C.* (*Historia Einzelschriften 102*). Stuttgart.

Hölkeskamp, K.-J., 2002: "Nomos, Thesmos und Verwandtes: Vergleichende Überlegungen zur Konzeptualisierung geschriebenen Rechts im klassischen Griechenland," in D. Cohen 2002: 115–146.

Hopper, R. J., 1971: *The Acropolis*. London.

Hornblower, S., 1982: *Mausolus*. Oxford.

Horváth, L., 2014: *Der Neue Hypereides: Textedition, Studien und Erläuterungen*. Berlin.

Hunt, P., 1998: *Slaves, Warfare, and Ideology in the Greek Historians*. Cambridge.

Hunt, P., 2010: *War, Peace, and Alliance in Demosthenes' Athens*. Cambridge.

Hunter, V. J., 1994: *Policing Athens: Social Control in the Attic Lawsuits, 420–320 B.C.* Princeton, NJ.

Hunter, V. J., 2000: "Policing Public Debtors in Classical Athens," *Phoenix* 54: 21–38.

Hurwit, J., 2004: *The Acropolis in the Age of Pericles*. Cambridge.

Ismard, P., 2012: "Le périmètre de la légalité dans l'Athènes classique: réponse à Robert Wallace," in Legras and Thür 2012: 127–134.

Ismard, P., 2015: *La démocratie contre les experts: les esclaves publics en Grèce ancienne*. Paris.

Jaeger, W., 1938: *Demosthenes: The Origin and Growth of His Policy*. Berkeley and London.

Jehne, M., 1992: "Die Anerkennung der athenischen Besitzan-spruche auf Amphipolis und die Cheronnes," *Historia* 41: 272–282.

Jim, T. S. F., 2014: *Sharing with the Gods:* Aparchai *and* Dekatai *in Ancient Greece.* Oxford.

Johnstone, S., 1999: *Disputes and Democracy: The Consequences of Litigation in Ancient Athens.* Austin, TX.

Jost, K., 1936: *Das Beispiel und Vorbild der Vorfahren bei den attischen Rednern und Geschichtschreibern bis Demosthenes.* Paderborn.

Joyce, C., 2014: "The Meaning of *mnesikakein* and the Amnesty of 403 BCE," *Antichthon* 48: 37–54.

Kästle, D.-J., 2012: "Νόμος μεγίστη βοηθεία : Zur Gesetzar-gumentation in der attischen Gerichtsrede." *Zeitschrift für Savigny-Stiftung: Romanistische Abteilung* 129: 161–205.

Kavvadias, G., and A. P. Matthaiou, 2014: "A New Attic In-scription of the Fifth Century B.C. from the East Slope of the Acropolis," in Matthaiou and Pitt 2014: 51–72.

Keaney, J. J., 1991: *Harpocration: Lexeis of the Ten Orators.* Amsterdam.

Köhler, U., 1867: "Attische Inschriften," *Hermes* 2: 16–36.

Konstan, D., 2000: "Pity and the Law in Greek Theory and Prac-tice," *Dike* 3: 125–145.

Kosmetatou, E., 2004: "'Persian' Objects in Classic and Hellenis-tic Inventory Lists," *Museum Helveticum* 61: 139–170.

Kraay, C., 1976: *Archaic and Classical Greek Coins.* London.

Kramer, C., 1930: "De priore Demosthenis adversus Aristogito-nem oratione." Diss. Greifswald.

Kremmydas, C., 2007: "*P. Berlin* 9781: The Early Reception of Demosthenes 20," *Bulletin of the Institute of Classical Studies* 50: 19–48.

Kremmydas, C., 2012: *A Commentary on Demosthenes' Against Leptines with Introduction, Text and Translation.* Oxford.

Kremmydas, C., 2013: "The Discourse of Deception and Char-acterization in Attic Oratory," *Greek, Roman and Byzantine Studies* 53.1: 51–89.

Krentz, P., 1982: *The Thirty at Athens.* Ithaca, NY.

Kroll, J. H., and N. M. Waggoner, 1984: "Dating the Earliest

Coins of Athens, Corinth and Aegina," *American Journal of Archaeology* 88: 325–340.

Kurihara, A., 2003: "Personal Enmity as a Motivation in Forensic Speeches," *Classical Quarterly* 53: 464–477.

Lalonde, G. V., M. K. Langdon, and M. B. Walbank, 1991: *Inscriptions: Horoi, Poletai Records, Lease of Public Land* (*Agora* XIX). Princeton, NJ.

Lambert, S. D., ed., 2011a: *Sociable Man. Essays on Ancient Greek Social Behaviour, in Honour of Nick Fisher*. Swansea.

Lambert, S. D., 2011b: "What Was the Point of Inscribed Honorific Decrees in Classical Athens?" in Lambert 2011a: 193–214.

Lane Fox, R., 1997: "Demosthenes, Dionysius and the Dating of Six Early Speeches," *Classica et Mediaevalia* 48: 167–203.

Langdon, M., 1994: "Public Auctions in Ancient Athens," in R. G. Osborne and Hornblower 1994: 253–265.

Lanni, A., 2006: *Law and Justice in Classical Athens*. Cambridge.

Lanni, A., 2009: "Judicial Review and the Athenian 'Constitution,'" in Hansen 2009: 235–263.

Lee, E. N., A. P. D. Mourelatos, and R. M. Rorty, eds., 1973: *Exegesis and Argument: Studies in Greek Philosophy Presented to Gregory Vlastos*. Assen.

Lefèvre, F., 1998: *L'Amphictionie pyléo-delphique: histoire et institutions* (*Bibliothèque des Écoles françaises d'Athènes et de Rome 298*). Paris.

Legon, R. P., 1981: *Megara. The Political History of a Greek City-State to 336 B.C.* Ithaca, NY.

Legras, B., ed., 2012: *Transferts culturels et droits dans le monde grec et hellénistique*. Paris.

Legras, B., and G. Thür, eds., 2012: *Symposion 2011: Vorträge zur griechischen und hellenistischen Rechtsgeschichte*. Vienna.

Lévy, E., ed., 2000: *La codification des lois dans l'antiquité*. Paris.

Lewis, D. M., 1954: "Notes on Attic Inscriptions I," *Annual of the British School at Athens* 50: 1–36.

Lewis, D. M., 1997: *Selected Papers in Greek and Near Eastern History*, edited by P. J. Rhodes. Cambridge.

Lewis, S., ed., 2006: *Ancient Tyranny*. Edinburgh.

Liddel, P., 2007: *Civic Obligation and Individual Liberty in Ancient Athens*. Oxford.

Linders, T., 1975: *The Treasurers of the Other Gods and Their Functions*. Meisenheim am Glan.

Lintott, A., 2004: "*Sula*—Reprisal by Seizure in Greek Inter-Community Relations," *Classical Quarterly* 54: 340–353.

Lipsius, J. H., 1883: "Über die Unechtheit der ersten Rede gegen Aristogeiton: *Leipziger Studien* 6: 319–333.

Lipsius, J. H., 1905–1915: *Das attische Recht und Rechtsverfahren.* 3 vols. Leipzig.

Lonis, R., ed., 1988a: *L'Étranger dans le monde grec. Actes du colloque organisé par l'Institut d'Études anciennes, Nancy mai 1987.* Nancy.

Lonis, R., 1988b: "Extradition et prise de corps des refugiés politiques," in Lonis 1988a: 69–88.

Loomis, W. T., 2003: "Athenian Slander: A Common Law Perspective," in Bakewell and Sickinger 2003: 287–300.

MacDowell, D. M., 1963: *Athenian Homicide Law in the Age of the Orators.* Manchester.

MacDowell, D. M., 1975: "Law Making at Athens in the Fourth Century BC," *Journal of Hellenic Studies* 95: 62–74.

MacDowell, D. M., 1976: *The Law in Classical Athens.* London.

MacDowell, D. M., 2007: "Hereditary *Sitesis* in Fourth-Century Athens," *Zeitschrift für Papyrologie und Epigraphik* 162: 111–113.

MacDowell, D. M., 2009: *Demosthenes the Orator.* Oxford.

Maffi, A., 2009/2010: "Recenzioni," *Dike* 12/13: 332–371.

Martin, G., 2009: *Divine Talk: Religious Argumentation in Demosthenes.* Oxford.

Mathieu, G., 1947: *Démosthène: Plaidoyers politiques IV: Sur la couronne, Contre Aristogiton I, II.* Paris.

Matthaiou, A. P., and R. K. Pitt, eds., 2014: ὢΑθηναίων ἐπίσκοπος . *Studies in Honour of Harold B. Mattingly.* Athens.

Meritt, B. D., and J. S. Traill, 1974: *The Athenian Councillors (Agora* XVI). Princeton, NJ.

Migeotte, L., 2005: "Les pouvoirs des agoranomes dans les cités grecques," in Wallace and Gagarin 2005: 287–301.

Migeotte, L., 2014: *Les finances des cités grecques: aux périodes classique et hellénistique.* Paris.

Mikalson, J. D., 1975: *The Sacred and Civil Calendar of the Athenian Year.* Princeton, NJ.

Mirhady, D. C., 2007: "The Dikasts' Oath and the Question of Fact," in Sommerstein and Fletcher 2007: 48–59, 228–233.

Modrzejewski, J., and D. Liebs, eds., 1982: *Symposium 1977: Vorträge zur griechischen und hellenistischen Rechtsgeschichte.* Cologne.

Moreno, A., 2007: *Feeding the Democracy: The Athenian Grain Supply in the Fifth and Fourth Century* BC. Oxford.

Moscati Castelnuovo, L., 1980: "La carriera politica dell' Attidografo Androzione," *Acme* 33: 252–278.

Mosley, D. J., 1973: *Envoys and Diplomacy in Ancient Greece (Historia Einzelschriften 22).* Wiesbaden.

Naiden, F. S., 2006: *Ancient Supplication.* Oxford.

Navarre, O., and P. Orsini, 1954: *Démosthène: Plaidoyers politiques* I: *Contre Androtion, Contre la Loi de Leptine, Contre Timocrate.* Paris.

Nouhaud, M., 1982: *L'utilisation de l'histoire par les orateurs attiques.* Paris.

Novotny, M., 2014: Review of Canevaro (2013a). *Eirene* 50: 341–345.

Ober, J., 1989: *Mass and Elite in Democratic Athens: Rhetoric, Ideology, and the Power of the People.* Princeton, NJ.

Ogden, D., 1996: *Greek Bastardy in the Classical and Hellenistic Periods.* Oxford.

Omitowoju, R. S., 1997: "Regulating Rape: Soap Operas and Self-Interest in the Athenian Courts," in Deacy and Pierce 1997: 1–24.

Omitowoju, R., 2002: *Rape and the Politics of Consent in Classical Athens.* Cambridge.

Osborne, M. J., 1973: "Orontes," *Historia* 22: 515–551.

Osborne, M. J., 1981: "Entertainment in the Prytaneion at Athens," *Zeitschrift für Papyrologie und Epigraphik* 41: 153–170.

Osborne, M. J., 1981–1983: *Naturalization in Athens.* 4 vols. Brussels.

Osborne, R. G., 1990: "Vexatious Litigation in Classical Athens: Sykophancy and the Sykophant," in Cartledge, Millett, and Todd 1990: 83–102.

Osborne, R. G., and S. Hornblower, eds., 1994: *Ritual, Finance,*

*Politics: Athenian Democratic Accounts Presented to David M. Lewis.* Oxford.

Ostwald, M., 1969: Nomos *and the Beginnings of Athenian Democracy.* Oxford.

Ostwald, M., 1973: "Was There a Concept of ἄγραφος νόμος in Classical Greece?" in Lee, Mourelatos, and Rorty 1973: 70–104.

Ostwald, M., 1986: *From Popular Sovereignty to the Sovereignty of Law: Law, Society and Politics in Fifth-Century Athens.* Berkeley.

Pack, R., 1965: *The Greek and Latin Literary Texts from Greco-Roman Egypt.* Ann Arbor, MI.

Papillon, T. L., 1998: *Rhetorical Studies in the Aristocratea of Demosthenes.* Frankfurt am Main.

Papy, J., and E. Gielen, eds., forthcoming: *Falsifications and Authority in Antiquity, the Middle Ages and the Renaissance.* Brussels.

Parke, H. W., 1928: "When Was Charidemus Made an Athenian Citizen?" *Classical Review* 42: 170.

Parke, H. W., 1933: *Greek Mercenary Soldiers: From the Earliest Times to the Battle of Ipsus.* Oxford.

Parker, R., 1983: *Miasma: Pollution and Purification in Early Greek Religion.* Oxford.

Parker, R., 2005: *Polytheism and Society at Athens.* Oxford.

Parkins, H., and C. Smith, eds., 1998: *Trade, Traders, and the Ancient City.* London.

Partsch, J., 1909: *Griechische Bürgschaftsrecht.* Leipzig.

Passow, W., 1890: "Verjährung in Blutsachen," *Hermes* 25: 466–468.

Pébarthe, C., 2015: Review of Ismard 2015. *Revue des études anciennes* 117.1: 241–247.

Pecorella Longo, C., 2004: "Il condono della pena in Atene in età classica," *Dike* 7: 85–111.

Pelloso, C., 2008: *Studi sul furto nell'antichità mediterranea.* Padua.

Pepe, L., 2012: *Phonos: l'omicidio da Draconte all'età degli oratori.* Milan.

Pernot, L., 2006: *L'ombre du tigre: recherches sur la réception de Démosthène.* Naples.

Phillips, D. D., 2008: *Avengers of Blood: Homicide in Athenian Law and Custom from Draco to Demosthenes* (*Historia Einzelschriften 202*). Stuttgart.

Phillips, D. D., 2013: *The Law of Ancient Athens*. Ann Arbor, MI.

Picard, O., 1979: *Chalcis et la confédération eubéenne: étude de numismatique et d'histoire (IVᵉ-Iᵉʳ siècle)*. Athens.

Piérart, M., 2000: "Qui étaient les nomothètes à l'époque de Démosthène?" in Lévy 2000: 229–256.

Pritchard, D., 2014: "The Public Pay of Magistrates in Fourth Century Athens," *Greek, Roman and Byzantine Studies* 54: 1–16.

Pritchett, W. K., 1971: *Ancient Greek Military Practices*. Berkeley.

Pritchett, W. K., 1974–1991: *The Greek State at War*. 5 vols. Berkeley and Los Angeles.

Psoma, S. E., 2001: *Olynthe et les Chalcidiens de Thrace: Études de numismatique et d'histoire*. Stuttgart.

Rhodes, P. J., 1972: *The Athenian Boule*. Oxford.

Rhodes, P. J., 1981: *A Commentary on the Aristotelian Athenaion Politeia*. Oxford.

Rhodes, P. J., 1985: "*Nomothesia* in Fourth Century Athens," *Classical Quarterly* 35: 55–60.

Rhodes, P. J., and R. G. Osborne, 2004: *Greek Historical Inscriptions, 404–323 B.C.* Oxford.

Roisman, J., 2006: *The Rhetoric of Conspiracy in Ancient Athens*. Berkeley.

Rosivach, V., 1994: *The System of Public Sacrifice in Fourth-Century Athens*. Atlanta, GA.

Rousset, D., 1994: "Les frontières des cités grecques. Premières réflexions à partir du recueil des documents épigraphiques," *Cahiers du Centre G. Glotz* 5: 97–126.

Rubel, A., 2009: "Die ökonomische und politische Bedeutung von Bosporos und Hellespont in der Antike," *Historia* 58: 336–355.

Rubinstein, L., 1993: *Adoption in IV. Century Athens*. Copenhagen.

Rubinstein, L., 2000: *Litigation and Cooperation: Supporting Speakers in the Courts of Classical Athens*. Stuttgart.

Rubinstein, L., 2005: "Main Litigants and Witnesses in the Athenian Courts," in Wallace and Gagarin 2005: 99–120.

Rubinstein, L., 2007: "Arguments from Precedent in Athenian Oratory," in Carawan 2007: 359–371.

Ruschenbusch, E., 1960: "ΘΟΝΟΣ: Zum Recht Drakons und seiner Bedeutung für das Werden des athenischen Staates," *Historia* 9: 129–154.

Ruschenbusch, E., 1979: "Die Einführung des Theorikon," *Zeischrift für Papyrologie und Epigraphik* 36: 303–308.

Ruschenbusch, E., ed., 2010: *Solon: Das Gesetzeswerk - Fragmente: Übersetzung und Kommentar* (*Historia Einzelschriften 215*). Stuttgart.

de Ste. Croix, G. E. M., 1963: "The Alleged Secret Pact between Athens and Philip II concerning Amphipolis and Pydna," *Classical Quarterly* 13: 110–119.

Sánchez, P., 2001: *L'Amphictionie des Pyles et de Delphes: recherches sur son rôle historique, des origines au II siècle de notre ère* (*Historia Einzelschriften 148*). Stuttgart.

Scafuro, A. S., 2004: "Dem. 21.10: The Role of the Prosecutor and Athenian Legal Procedure," *Dike* 7: 113–133.

Scafuro, A. S., 2005: "Parent Abusers, Military Shirkers, and Accused Killers: The Authenticity of the Second Law Inserted at Dem. 24.105," in Gagarin and Wallace 2005: 51–70.

Scafuro, A., 2006: "Identifying the Kernel of Solonian Laws," in Blok and Lardinois 2006: 165–187.

Schaefer, A., 1885–1887: *Demosthenes und seine Zeit*. Leipzig.

Schläfke, R., 1913: "De Demosthenis quae dicuntur adversus Aristogitonem orationibus." Diss. Greifswald.

Schmalz, G., 2006: "The Athenian Prytaneion Discovered?" *Hesperia* 75: 33–81.

Seager, R., 1967: "Thrasybulus, Conon, and Athenian Imperialism, 396–386 B.C.," *Journal of Hellenic Studies* 87: 95–115.

Sealey, R., 1955: "Dionysius of Halicarnassus and Some Demosthenic Dates," *Revue des études grecques* 68: 77–120.

Sealey, R., 1956: "Callistratus of Aphidna and His Contemporaries," *Historia* 5: 178–203.

Sealey, R., 1960: "Who Was Aristogeiton?" *Bulletin of the Institute of Classical Studies* 7: 33–43.

Sealey, R., 1967: "Pseudodemosthenes xiii and xxv," *Revue des études grecques* 80: 250–255.

Sealey, R., 1993: *Demosthenes and His Time: A Study in Defeat.* New York.

Shear, J. L., 2007: "The Oath of Demophantos and the Politics of Athenian Identity," in Sommerstein and Fletcher 2007: 148–160.

Shear, T. L., 1970: "The Monument of the Eponymous Heroes in the Athenian Agora," *Hesperia* 39: 145–222.

Shear. T. L., 1971: "The Athenian Agora: Excavations of 1970," *Hesperia* 40: 241–279.

Shear, T. L., 1975: "The Athenian Agora: Excavations of 1973–1974," *Hesperia* 44: 331–374.

Sickinger, J. P., 1999: *Public Records and Archives in Classical Athens.* Chapel Hill, NC.

Sickinger, J. P., 2008: "Indeterminacy in Greek Law: Statutory Gaps and Conflicts," in Harris and Thür 2008: 99–112.

Sickinger, J., 2013: "Greek Letters on Stone," in Yiftach-Firanko 2013: 125–140.

Siewert, P., ed., 2002: *Ostrakismos-Testimonien.* Vol. I (*Historia Einzelschriften 155*). Stuttgart.

Slater, W. J., 1994: Review of Keaney 1991. *Bryn Mawr Classical Review* 94.06.07.

Sommerstein, A. H., 2014: "The Authenticity of the Demophantus Decree," *Classical Quarterly* 64: 49–57.

Sommerstein, A. H., and J. Fletcher, eds., 2007: Horkos: *The Oath in Greek Society.* Exeter.

Sosin, J., 2016: "Death on a Road (Dem. 23.53)," *Historia* 65: 155–169.

Sprawski, S., 2006: "Alexander of Pherae: *infelix* tyrant," in Lewis 2006: 135–147.

Stengel, P., 1910: *Opferbräuche der Griechen.* Munich.

Stier, H., 1883: *De scriptore prioris adversus Aristogitonem orationis, quae Demosthenis esse fertur.* Halle.

Stroud, R. S., 1968: *Drakon's Law on Homicide.* Berkeley.

Stroud, R. S., 1998: *The Athenian Grain-Tax Law of 374/3 B.C.* (*Hesperia Supplement 29*). Princeton, NJ.

Swain, S., 2007: *Seeing the Face, Seeing the Soul: Polemon's Physiognomy from Classical Antiquity to Medieval Islam.* Oxford.

Taylor, M. W., 1991: *The Tyrant-Slayers: The Heroic Image in Fifth Century Athenian Art and Politics.* Salem, NH.

Teegarden, D. A., 2012: "The Oath of Demophantus, Revolutionary Mobilization, and the Preservation of the Athenian Democracy," *Hesperia* 81: 433–465.

Teegarden, D. A., 2014: *Death to Tyrants! Ancient Greek Democracy and the Struggle against Tyranny.* Princeton, NJ.

Themelis, P., 2002: "Contribution to the Topography of the Sanctuary at Brauron," in Gentili and Perusini 2002: 103–116.

Thür, G., 2007: "Das Prinzip der Fairness im attischen Prozess," in Cantarella 2007: 131–150.

Tiersch, C., ed., 2016: *Die Athenische Demokratie im 4. Jahrhundert—zwischen Modernisierung und Tradition.* Berlin.

Tod, M. N., 1947: *A Selection of Greek Historical Inscriptions.* Oxford.

Todd, S. C., 1990: "The Purpose of Evidence in Athenian Courts," in Cartledge, Millett, and Todd 1990: 19–39.

Todd, S. C., 1993: *The Shape of Athenian Law.* Oxford.

Treves, P., 1936: "Aprocrifi demostenici," *Athenaeum* 14: 153–174, 233–258.

Trevett, J., 2011: *Demosthenes, Speeches 1–17.* Austin, TX.

Trevett, J., 2013: Review of Kremmydas 2012. *Bryn Mawr Classical Review* 2013.04.02.

Tulin, A., 1996: *Dike Phonou: The Right of Prosecution and Attic Homicide Procedure.* Stuttgart.

Tziatzi-Papagianni, M., 1994: *Die Sprüche der sieben Weisen: Einleitung, Text, Testimonien, und Kommentar.* Stuttgart.

Usher, S., 1976: "Lysias and His Clients," *Greek, Roman and Byzantine Studies* 17: 31–40.

Vince, J. H., 1935: *Demosthenes: Against Meidias, Aristocrates, Timocrates, Aristogeiton.* Cambridge, MA.

Vlassopoulos, K., 2009: "Slavery, Freedom and Citizenship in Classical Athens: Beyond a Legalistic Approach," *European Review of History* 16.3: 347–363.

Volonaki, E., 2000: "'Apagoge' in Homicide Cases," *Dike* 3: 147–176.

Volpis, L., 1936: *Demostene: L'orazione contro Aritocrate. Introduzione e commento.* Milan.

Wagner, R., 1883: "De priore quae Demosthenis fertur adversus Aristogitonem oratione." Diss. Rostock.

Wallace, R. W., 1989: *The Areopagos Council, to 307 B.C.* Baltimore.

Wallace, R. W., 2012: "When the Athenians did not Enforce Their Laws," in Legras and Thür 2012: 115–125.

Wallace, R. W., and M. Gagarin, eds., 2005: *Symposion 2001: Akten der Gesellschaft für griechische und hellenistische Rechtsgeschichte.* Vienna.

Wallace, R. W., and E. M. Harris, eds., 1996: *Transitions to Empire: Essays in Greco-Roman History 360–146 B.C. in Honor of E. Badian.* Norman, OK.

Wayte, W., 1882: *Demosthenes:* Against Androtion *and* Against Timocrates. Cambridge.

Weil, H., 1882: Études sur Démosthène," *Revue de Philologie* 6: 1–21.

Weil, H., 1887: "L'auteur du premier discours contre Aristogiton est-il bien informé des institutions d'Athènes?" in *Mélanges Renier* (Paris 1887): 17–25.

Weiskopf, M., 1989: *The So-Called "Great Satraps' Revolt," 366–360 B.C.: Concerning Local Instability in the Achaemenid Far West (Historia Einzelschriften 63).* Stuttgart.

Welskopf, E. C., ed., 1974: *Hellenische Poleis.* 2 vols. Berlin.

Welwei, K.-W., 1974–1988: *Unfreie im antiken Kriegsdienst.* 4 vols. Wiesbaden.

Westermann, A., 1865: *Ausgewählte Reden des Demosthenes.* Berlin.

Whitby, M., 1998: "The Grain Trade of Athens in the Fourth Century BC," in Parkins and Smith 1998: 102–128.

Whitehead, D., 1977: *The Ideology of the Athenian Metic* (= *Proceedings of the Cambridge Philological Society* Suppl. vol. 4). Cambridge.

Whitehead, D., 1983: "Competitive Outlay and Community Profit: ἱλοτιμία in Democratic Athens," *Classica et Mediaevalia* 35: 55–74.

Whitehead, D., 2000: *Hypereides: The Forensic Speeches, Introduction, Translation and Commentary.* Oxford.

Wilson, D. F., 2002: *Ransom, Revenge and Heroic Identity in the Iliad.* New York.

Wohl, V., 2010: *Law's Cosmos: Juridical Discourse in Athenian Forensic Oratory.* Cambridge.

Wolff, H.-J., 1970: *Normenkontrolle und Gesetzbegriff in der attischen Demokratie.* Heidelberg.

Wooten, C., 1983: *Cicero's* Philippics *and Their Demosthenic Model.* Chapel Hill, NC.

Worthington, I., 1992: *A Historical Commentary on Dinarchus: Rhetoric and Conspiracy in Late Fourth Century Athens.* Ann Arbor, MI.

Worthington, I., ed., 2000: *Demosthenes: Statesman and Orator.* London.

Worthington, I., 2013: *Demosthenes of Athens and the Fall of Classical Greece.* Oxford.

Yiftach-Firanko, U., ed., 2013: *The Letter: Law, State, Society and the Epistolary Format in the Ancient World. Proceedings of a Colloquium held at the American Academy in Rome 28–30.9.2008.* Wiesbaden.

Yunis, H., 1988: "Law, Politics, and the *graphe paranomon* in Fourth-century Athens," *Greek, Roman and Byzantine Studies* 29: 361–382.

Zelnick-Abramovitz, R., 2005: *Not Wholly Free: The Concept of Manumission and the Status of Manumitted Slaves in the Ancient Greek World.* Leiden.

Zelnick-Abramovitz, R., 2011: "The Guardian of the Land: The Areopagos Council as a Symbol of Stability," in Herman 2011: 103–126.

# INDEX

〰〰〰〰〰〰〰〰〰〰〰〰〰〰〰〰〰〰〰〰〰〰〰〰〰〰〰〰〰〰〰〰〰〰〰〰〰〰〰